DESTROY WARSAW!

DESTROY WARSAW!

Hitler's Punishment, Stalin's Revenge

Andrew Borowiec

PRAEGER

Westport, Connecticut
London

Library of Congress Cataloging-in-Publication Data

Borowiec, Andrew.
    Destroy Warsaw! : Hitler's punishment, Stalin's revenge / Andrew Borowiec.
      p. cm.
    Includes bibliographical references and index.
    ISBN 0–275–97005–1 (alk. paper)
    1. Warsaw (Poland)—History—Uprising, 1944. I. Title.
    D765.2.W3B58 2001
    940.53'4384—dc21   2001016319

British Library Cataloguing in Publication Data is available.

Library of Congress Catalog Card Number: 2001016319
ISBN: 0–275–97005–1

First published in 2001

Praeger Publishers, 88 Post Road West, Westport, CT 06881
An imprint of Greenwood Publishing Group, Inc.
www.praeger.com

Printed in the United States of America

The paper used in this book complies with the
Permanent Paper Standard issued by the National
Information Standards Organization (Z39.48–1984).

10 9 8 7 6 5 4 3 2 1

Copyright Acknowledgments

The author and publisher gratefully acknowledge permission to use excerpts from the
following:

Zuckerman, Yitzhak, *A Surplus of Memory: Chronicle of the Warsaw Ghetto Uprising*,
translated/edited by Barbara Harshav (Berkeley, CA: University of California Press, 1993).
Copyright © 1993 The Regents of the University of California.

The History of the Polish Forces During WW II (Polskie Sily Zbrojne w II Wojnie Swiatowej),
Volume III (Armia Krajowa) (London: Historical Commission of the Polish General Staff,
1950). Courtesy of the Polish Forces Historical Commission, London.

Kumor, Emil, *Wycinek z Historii Jednego Zycia* (Warsaw: Pax Publishers, 1969). Courtesy of
Pax Publishers.

Borkiewicz, Adam, *Powstanie Warszawskie 1944* (Warsaw: Pax Publishers, 1957).

Every reasonable effort has been made to trace the owners of copyrighted materials in this
book, but in some instances this has proven impossible. The author and publisher will be
glad to receive information leading to more complete acknowledgments in subsequent
printings of the book and in the meantime extend their apologies for any omissions.

For all those who died defending Warsaw—and knew the reason why.

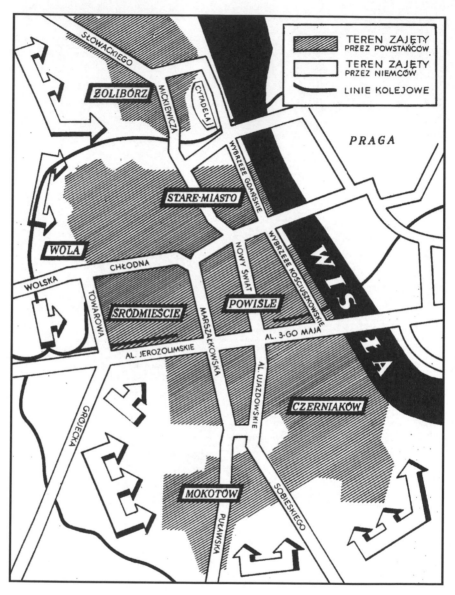

The situation in Warsaw during the first week of the fighting. (Map based on the drawing by von dem Bach at the Nuremberg trial)
Shaded areas: territory in the hands of the Polish insurgents
White areas: territory controlled by the Germans
Wide black band labeled "WISLA": the Vistula River
Thin black lines: railroad tracks
The sign **"STARE MIASTO"**: Old Town
The sign **"SRODMIESCIE"**: city center

Contents

Preface   ix

Prologue   1

1 A Tragic Heritage   7

2 The Conspiracy   19

3 "The Poles Shall Be Slaves"   27

4 The Secret Army   41

5 Death of the Warsaw Ghetto   55

6 Operation Storm   67

7 Warsaw on Fire   79

8 "Kill Anyone You Want"   93

9 A Battle for Survival   105

Contents

10 Alone in the Ruins   119

11 Condemned by Stalin   137

12 The End of Agony   157

Epilogue   175

Appendix A: Significant Dates   185

Appendix B: Military and Paramilitary Formations   189

Bibliography   193

Index   195

A photo essay follows page 117

Preface

The idea for this book was born during the gloomy autumn of 1944 in *Lazarett A, Stalag XI A*, Altengrabow, Germany. As a wounded patient in the hospital of that large camp for Allied prisoners-of-war of the dying Third Reich, I had the privilege of access to a roll of toilet paper on which I wrote my notes. (Although available at the hospital, that luxury did not exist in the camp itself, to which the patients were sent when their wounds were healed.) The notes were preserved, and, several years later, as a scholarship student in the United States, I typed them and filed them away with other memorabilia of the war and of its aftermath.

Having survived Warsaw's uprising and the city's destruction in August and September 1944, my life continued along the uncertain path of a foreign correspondent exposed to dramatic events, although few of them were as devastating as my experiences during World War II. They included coverage of the Algerian war of independence, the turmoil in Africa, and Vietnam and various Middle East conflicts. In December 1991 I was trapped in a firefight outside the Croat town of Karlovac. I was sixty-three years old and decided that it was to be my last "war experience."

While working as a full-time reporter, other books seemed more timely. Thus I have written on such subjects as the probable fate of Yugoslavia, the feud between Greece and Turkey, Tunisia's "presidential democracy," and the dilemma of divided Cyprus. In the fall of 1999, I

thought it was perhaps time for an objective look at the tragedy of Warsaw in which I had participated. The study is not a "battle journal"
although, obviously, significant or particularly dramatic events are described. Its stress is on the political and international aspects when Poland's capital was trapped between Nazi Germany and Stalinist Russia.
My prison camp "toilet paper notes" added a number of eyewitness
accounts to enhance the text. I have kept my personal feelings and views
to a minimum, leaving most dramatic descriptions to other participants
quoted in the book.

Printed sources on the Warsaw uprising and its failure are numerous
but mainly in Polish. Censorship in Poland during the forty-five years
of communist regime distorted some accounts, particularly those concerning the role of the Soviet Union. More accurate accounts appeared
in various publications by Polish emigrés, particularly in France and
Great Britain. The collapse of communism in Poland in 1989 led to more
appraisals of the uprising, generally divided into two schools: one por-
traying it as an act of unparalleled bravery and sacrifice, the other as
collective folly so typical of Poland's tortuous history. Polish historian
Jerzy Jaruzelski (no relation to Poland's last communist dictator of the
same name) feels that in the face of its traditional enemies, Germany and
Russia, Poland has always had to face solutions that "were not good or
better but were either bad or worse."[1]

Thus this book is an attempt to analyze the causes of the rising, the
political and strategic concerns involved, the international ramifications,
and the Soviet refusal to help the embattled Polish insurgents. It is basically a book about heroism and failure, the hopeless aspirations of the
Poles, the Nazi determination to punish them for their act, and Soviet
designs to subjugate the country and its defiant capital. Documents that
survived the war, transcripts of radio communications, the caution of the
Western Allies toward the uprising, and the Soviet behavior would in-
dicate that the uprising was doomed from the start. Some of those who
ordered it knew that it could only succeed with Soviet help, at the same
time resenting the very idea—an incongruous but normal Polish attitude.
Yitzhak Zuckerman, a survivor of the Warsaw ghetto and a leader of the
Jewish Fighting Organization (ZOB) aptly summed it up in his memoirs:

A great danger threatened that the liberation of Warsaw would be done by the
Red Army [*sic*]. And that meant a Red Warsaw. . . . In general, I think the Poles
were right. They didn't succeed, so they were abandoned by the Russians and
forced to pay the price.[2]

In the immediate postwar years, the Polish communist authorities attempted to denigrate the uprising. Many leading survivors were jailed
for "anti-state activities." Only later were a number of valid accounts

published, limited mainly to the Polish market. In most Western history books, the death of Warsaw is hardly more than a footnote in descriptions of Poland's fate during World War II.

In selecting the bibliography for this work, I looked for a variety of sources, including some documents from the Nuremberg trials of Nazi war criminals, a detailed history of the uprising by Adam Borkiewicz (in Polish), as well as a history of the Polish Armed Forces (*Polskie Siły Zbrojne*) commissioned by the General Staff of the Polish Forces under British Command in London in 1946.

At the beginning of this millennium, the participants of the uprising are becoming fewer and even fewer are capable of telling their stories to the Western reader. On the whole this chapter of World War II has received relatively little attention, although it involved the virtually total destruction of a major city and the death of a large portion of its population.

Throughout that war Warsaw was the scene of systematic destruction—of lives as well as of property. Although the main theme of this work is the uprising of August 1944, I felt it essential to describe other phases that preceded it: the 1939 siege by the invading German army and the 1943 ghetto uprising.

As this book deals with a resistance army in which all participants used pseudonyms and last names were not revealed until later, they are referred to in the text by their noms de guerre. Whenever possible their real names are mentioned in parentheses, as well as in the index in addition to their pseudonym. (Leading Underground commanders often used more than one pseudonym—usually one for internal contacts and one for radio communications with London.) When referring to someone by his pseudonym for the first time, I use quotation marks, indicating that it was his resistance name. The inverted commas are usually eliminated in subsequent references.

Diacritical marks such as cedillas, umlauts, and others are essential parts of the German and Polish languages. Their absence changes the pronunciation and, in some cases, the meaning of the word. Thus, because of the mark over the "o," the name of the Polish commander, General Bór, is pronounced in Polish as "boor." Equally, because of the umlaut over the "a," German General Källner is in effect "Kellner."

I would like to offer my thanks to Jerzy Jaruzelski, a specialist in Poland's recent history, for his critical remarks about several chapters of the book. Although our views differ on some aspects, we both agree that in the emotion-charged summer of 1944 it was easier—and certainly more patriotic—to contemplate a battle rather than inactivity, regardless of the cost and results.

And finally, once again I thank my wife Juliet for her helpful editing.

NOTES

1. In a letter to the author of June 17, 2000.
2. Yitzhak Zuckerman, *A Surplus of Memory: Chronicle of the Warsaw Ghetto Uprising* (Berkeley, Los Angeles, Oxford: University of California Press, 1993), p. 525.

Prologue

The Russians were advancing and reaching Warsaw. The Poles were not anxious to be liberated by the Russians and on 1 August the Warsaw Rising began, the Polish Resistance making a valiant attempt to throw out the Germans while expecting the Red Army to continue its steady advance. The Russians instead halted on the Vistula and the Poles were crushed and Hitler ordered Warsaw itself to be destroyed.

> Harry Browne in *World History—The Twentieth Century*

They streamed across Warsaw's bridges, some of the soldiers barefoot, marching slowly or stretched out on piles of straw in horse-drawn wagons. Some had abandoned their rifles. Now and then a truck filled with looted furniture would overtake these retreating Germans and their allies from various "national armies" formed from volunteer Soviet prisoners. The German Central Front appeared to be crumbling.

Warsaw rejoiced that July 1944. The terror of the five years of occupation appeared to be at an end. To the east of the city, one could hear the artillery fire of the approaching Soviet armies. To the inhabitants of Warsaw, it looked as though nothing could stop the Soviet offensive. It didn't seem to matter what would come later. The hour of revenge and liberation was approaching.

In an atmosphere of increasing tension, the headquarters of the Polish underground organization known as the Home Army (*Armia Krajowa–AK*) faced a crucial dilemma: Should it or shouldn't it order the 48,000 members of the conspiracy[1] to attack the German garrison and liberate Warsaw before the arrival of the Soviets? That certainly was the intention of its supreme authority, the Polish government-in-exile in London, which left the final decision and the timing to the Home Army's command headed by General Tadeusz Komorowski, known by the nom de guerre "Bór" inside Poland but "Lawina" in radio communications with London. An aristocratic cavalry officer who had served Austro-Hungary and Poland, an excellent rider who had participated in international horse shows, he was about to decide Warsaw's fate.

During the final days of July, Bór and his staff, as well as key members of the Warsaw regional command, met twice a day in different apartments to evaluate the situation. Records of radio reports to the General Staff of the Polish Forces under British Command in London, of which the Home Army was considered to be a component, showed constantly changing appraisals, as well as doubts of a successful cooperation with the Soviet forces. In fact there was no contact whatsoever with the advancing Soviet army of Marshal Konstantin Konstantinovich Rokossovsky, the man who was later to become a Soviet proconsul in communist Poland.

By the end of July, the stream of German army stragglers had considerably diminished and was replaced by tanks moving eastward. They included units of the SS *Panzer* divisions *Totenkopf* and *Herman Goering*[2] and the 19th Saxon *Panzer* division of General Hans Källner, all of them considerably under strength due to battle losses. (In one of war's ironies, General Källner had been among Bór's equestrian competitors and knew him in the Austro-Hungarian Army during World War I. His division was to deal a decisive blow to Polish defenses in the last stages of the Warsaw uprising. Källner wanted to renew their acquaintance after Warsaw's capitulation but the Polish commander, by then a prisoner, declined.[3])

On July 29 the 654th German Engineering (*Pionier*) Battalion mined the bridges linking Warsaw with the eastern suburb of Praga. A new military dignitary appeared in the city: Lieutenant General Reiner Stahel, appointed by Hitler himself as commander of the Warsaw garrison with instructions to defend the "Warsaw communications center with all means and weapons available" against an expected uprising of the Polish resistance (*Widerstand*) movement.[4] Including Nazi Party units such as SS (*Schützstaffel*), militarized police, and antiaircraft artillery, he commanded an estimated twenty thousand well-armed and mostly battle-hardened men. Although some Western accounts refer to the German garrison at the time as "weak," by all indications it was a powerful, disciplined and reliable military force.

The command of the Home Army believed that Warsaw was likely to become a battlefield between the German and Soviet armies. In such a case, the Underground force, which had been organized and prepared for action for several years, would become paralyzed, unable to fulfill its role as liberators of the Polish capital. And that, after all, had been the long-standing objective of the resistance and culmination of the conspiracy.

On July 25 a terse radio message to London said,

We are ready at any moment to begin a battle for Warsaw. The arrival of the parachute brigade to join the battle will have enormous political and tactical significance. We suggest that you prepare the possibility, when requested by us, of air attacks on airfields near Warsaw. Will inform you of the time of the beginning of the battle.[5]

The term "battle" (*bitwa*) rather than "uprising" (*powstanie*) was used, because in previous dispatches the latter referred mainly to plans for armed action throughout all of Poland, from which Warsaw was excluded.

The "parachute brigade" mentioned in the message had completed training in Scotland and was at the disposal of the 1st Allied Airborne Army. Between September 17 and 26, it took part—and was massacred—in Operation Market Garden around Arnhem in central Holland. The fact that the *AK* command even considered the arrival of the brigade as feasible shows a lack of understanding of such operations, particularly the enormous risk involved in transporting by air some 2,000 men and their supplies over a thousand miles of German-controlled airspace and territory. Besides, the brigade was integrated into the Allied military structure, and neither the Polish government-in-exile nor the Polish General Staff could freely decide its use.

The same considerations applied to the request "to prepare the possibility of air attacks" on targets near Warsaw. Apparently Bór and his staff had in mind the Polish components of the Royal Air Force (RAF), in the summer of 1944 consisting of fifteen squadrons (about 300 aircraft), of which five squadrons were bombers. Just as the parachute brigade, these units were integrated into the British military (in this case RAF) structure and had specific tasks as part of the Allied war effort against Germany in the west. The *AK* command should have been perfectly aware of the limitations of the use of aircraft flying from Great Britain or from Italian bases to distant Poland, particularly in view of the constant difficulties, delays, and losses connected with parachute drops of weapons and other supplies to the Polish resistance.

In a way, such expectations, which could be regarded as military aberrations, characterized the incredible optimism and lack of sense of reality of the senior cadres of the underground army, consisting almost entirely of prewar career officers.

Significantly no requests for support nor help had been made—or even suggested—to the Soviet forces which were within reach of Warsaw's eastern suburbs. The resistance army command would prefer to liberate Warsaw alone and confront the arriving Soviets with its own authority. On the other hand, it suspected that Soviet help might be needed, but on the basis of previous contacts between its units and the Soviet forces in eastern Poland, it feared the worst. In that context the reference in Bór's message to the "enormous political and tactical significance" of the arrival of a British-formed parachute brigade in British uniform (with Polish insignia) implied some hope for a change in the attitude and reaction of the approaching Soviets.

Radio and courier messages from *AK* units in territories freed by the Soviet army reported arrests of officers and the massive forceful incorporation of fighters into the Polish army being formed under Soviet command. (See Chapter 6.) In fact, on July 28 General Kazimierz Sosnkowski, commander-in-chief of the Polish Forces under British Command who was inspecting the 2nd Polish Corps fighting in Italy, radioed the *AK* headquarters via London:

In present conditions, I am categorically opposed to a general uprising. . . . Your appraisal of the situation must be sober and realistic. A mistake would be enormously expensive. It is essential to concentrate all forces, political, moral and physical, to prevent Moscow's annexation designs.[6]

According to a postuprising analysis of the situation,

The *AK* command was aware of the fact that air force aid from the West was uncertain and could only be carried out with an enormous effort by the crews under the pressure of the combat conditions in Warsaw. . . . The decision to launch a battle for Warsaw was made with the conviction that the Red Army would soon cross the Vistula and occupy Poland's capital.[7]

At the same time, Moscow and its communist allies of the "Polish National Liberation Committee," formed in the recently freed town of Lublin, were bombarding Warsaw with appeals for action. A typical such appeal on July 30 via Moscow radio said:

People of Warsaw! To arms! . . . Attack the Germans! Thwart their plans to destroy public buildings! Help the Red Army to cross the Vistula. Give it information, show the roads. May the million of Warsaw's inhabitants become a million soldiers who will throw out the German invaders and win freedom.[8]

Earlier, on July 27 at a meeting in a "safe apartment" on Chłodna street, a vote was taken by heads of various components of the *AK* general staff. The participants were dressed in a variety of civilian suits and could easily be taken for a group of merchants or office workers—except that their faces showed the strain of years of conspiracy, tension, and of incredible responsibility. Five senior officers were in favor of an uprising, and five were against. Among those against were General "Łaszcz" (Albin Skroczynski), commander of the Underground's central military district (*obszar*), and the head of the intelligence department, Colonel "Heller" (Kazimierz Iranek-Osmecki). The latter reported the arrival of new German forces to strengthen the front, including three armored divisions in the immediate vicinity of Warsaw.

Bór, who wavered between the two opposed theories, ordered a "state of readiness" of the fighting and auxiliary units. The order was issued despite an alarming report on the paltry number of weapons available, especially after recent discoveries of major caches by the Germans. According to one participant, the report "created a depressing impression."[9] The proponents of the uprising argued that the "spirit of revenge" of the underground force would compensate for the shortage of weapons, which would be captured from the Germans or supplied by air.

When the participants emerged from the meeting, the loudspeakers of the occupation authorities were broadcasting an order to men between the ages of seventeen to sixty-five to report at designated points to dig trenches along the Vistula. The Germans expected 100,000 people, but only a handful showed up the following day. In an increasingly nervous atmosphere, the *AK* command feared mass reprisals and population roundups which would paralyze its ability to concentrate for action.

The last normally planned afternoon meeting before the uprising took place on July 31. Several staff members were missing, supervising the preparations of various units scattered throughout the city. Bór addressed the only civilian present, Jan Stanisław Jankowski, deputy prime minister of the government-in-exile and its delegate in Poland, who went under the pseudonym "Soból," suggesting that an uprising in Warsaw would "change the German defeat (on the Central Front) into a total catastrophe, and cut the enemy's communication lines."[10]

Soból asked a few questions, and, apparently satisfied, said "very well, in that case begin." The cavalry general turned to Colonel "Monter" (Antoni Chruściel), a former lecturer at the Polish General Staff Academy who commanded the Underground's Warsaw area (*okręg*), consisting of the city and its immediate vicinity, and said: "Tomorrow, exactly at 17.00 hours, you will begin Operation Storm in Warsaw."

It was the signal for an uprising of sixty-three days during which the capital of Poland was turned into rubble. (Once the order was issued,

Bór apparently ignored subsequent protests by two staff members who were delayed en route to the meeting.)

A Polish military historian wrote later that "from the military point of view, the action was precipitous, marred by improvisation and violating all principles on which the resistance had been based."[11]

NOTES

1. Estimates of organized *AK* members in the Warsaw region vary from 45,300 to 49,000 men and women.

2. *SS—Schützstaffel* or "protective echelon," initially formed in 1925 as Adolf Hitler's personal bodyguard, later transformed into a Nazi elite military formation.

3. Adam Borkiewicz, *Powstanie Warszawskie 1944* (Warsaw: Pax, 1957), p. 690.

4. Instructions entered in the files of the Central Front, *AG Mitte*, under no. 65–004/1.

5. Radio message in Polish military archives in England, no. 6624/secret.

6. Polish Military Archives no. 6213/secret of July 29, 1944.

7. *Polskie Siły Zbrojne* (London: General Sikorski Historical Institute, Vol. III, 1950), p. 661. A detailed account of the activities of the Polish Armed Forces in Poland and abroad 1939–1945, commissioned by the General Staff in London, December 10, 1946.

8. Text based on a British Broadcasting Corporation (BBC) digest, July 30, 1944.

9. Borkiewicz, *Powstanie Warszawskie 1944*, p. 23.

10. Ibid., p. 27.

11. Ibid., p. 28.

CHAPTER 1

A Tragic Heritage

Amidst the deafening scream of *Stuka* dive-bombers attacking targets on the ground, the German 4th *Panzer* Division knifed through the Polish 13th infantry Division near the town of Tomaszów Mazowiecki after a two-day battle and triumphantly headed forward. The *Blitzkrieg*—or rapid war—was in its seventh day, and the astounded world was yet to comprehend the speed and power of massive armor attacks coordinated with devastating bombing raids. The objective of the 4th *Panzer* Division was Warsaw.

September 1939 was exceptionally balmy, and the Polish countryside was in its full glory of golden wheat fields, rows of sunflowers along picket fences, and apples ripening in the orchards. Storks were yet to start their migration south. The German tanks rolled across the Polish flatland, past peasant cottages and small towns with shuttered windows—as if the shutters could keep the bullets out. Flocks of noisy sparrows rose to the sky, disturbed from their perches by the roar of engines.

Having broken through the defenses of the Polish *Łódź* Army and of the partly mobilized *Prusy* Army, the 4th *Panzer* Division's commander, General Georg Hans Reinhardt, had the order to reach the Polish capital as soon as possible. As the Germans were winning on the battlefield anyway, the aim was not so much military as political and psychological. Above all, Adolf Hitler wanted Warsaw.

The strength of the 4th *Panzer* Division was bolstered by the 33rd Motorized Infantry Regiment and the elite SS *Standarte Adolf Hitler* Regiment—all told some 400 tanks, eighty artillery pieces, and seven infantry battalions. Its columns moved in clouds of dust, here and there scattering retreating Polish units and crowds of refugees. An occasional mortar barrage or machine gun fire from Polish units camping near the highways was simply ignored in order to surge ahead. (Unbeknown to General Reinhardt, less than fifty miles southwest from his armor, eight Polish infantry divisions and two cavalry brigades were preparing for the biggest counterattack of the brief and disastrous campaign. But that was not General Reinhardt's concern. Nothing was going to delay his march on the Polish capital.)

The lead tanks of General Reinhardt's "armored fist" sighted the low Warsaw skyline with the protruding sixteen-story Prudential Insurance Company building (known as Warsaw's "skyscraper") early in the afternoon of September 8. At 4:00 P.M. one column attacked the western industrial suburb of Wola, and another Ochota to the south, while, incongruously, three tanks heading toward the center found themselves within walking distance from the Klonowa Street residence of Poland's commander-in-chief, Marshal Edward Śmigły-Rydz. (The marshal and his staff had left the threatened capital the day before.)

Having encountered unexpected albeit improvised resistance, the armored assailants withdrew and harassed the Polish capital with artillery fire throughout the night. Meanwhile, however, the capital's recently mobilized defenses were strengthened by units from train transports halted at Warsaw's railway stations, as well as some retreating from the north. Thus on September 9 Warsaw was defended by seventeen infantry battalions backed by sixty-four artillery pieces and twenty-seven light tanks.[1] The night before, in his Order of the Day No. 1, Warsaw's commander, General Walerian Czuma, told his forces, "We are defending a position from which there is no retreat."[2]

In the morning of September 9, General Reinhardt's renewed assault on Warsaw met fierce resistance. His tanks were smashed by artillery and set afire by inflammatory bottles thrown from windows. One tank battalion was trapped in a minefield in open suburban terrain, and its remnants withdrew under murderous fire. Fearing that his division was faced with unsustainable losses, at 9:45 A.M. General Reinhardt ordered withdrawal to the outskirts, despite the fact that some German tanks had been close to the city center. When the command of the 16th *Wehrmacht* corps ordered another attack, General Reinhardt reported that nearly half of his tank force had been destroyed or damaged. By then other German divisions started arriving, gradually throwing a ring of steel around the city. In a few days Warsaw was under siege.

During much of its history, Warsaw appears to have been destined for tragedy. Some of its dramatic uprisings initially triumphed but eventually were drowned in blood. In 1794 the city rose against a Russian garrison "invited" by Poland's last king, Stanisław August Poniatowski. Successful at its start, the insurrection led by General Tadeusz Kościuszko (who had fought in America's War of Independence) collapsed. Its final battle was a massive Russian storm on Warsaw during which most of the population of Praga, Warsaw's eastern suburb, was slaughtered. In December 1812, Warsaw wept as the 600 Polish survivors of the 5th Corps of Napoleon's Grand Army defeated in Russia staggered into the city on frostbitten feet, nonetheless pulling their sixty cannons intact.

In November 1830, when Poland was a truncated "kingdom" established by the 1815 Congress of Vienna with allegiance to the czar of Russia, officer cadets staged an uprising against the rule of the czar's brother, Grand Duke Constantine. What was initially described by one of the reluctant Polish generals as "an act of rebellious children" turned into a full-scale war. In February 1831 a victorious battle outside Warsaw pushed back a Russian offensive and a triumphant Polish capital applauded. But in September of that year, a new Russian army arrived and stormed the city from the west. The capital fell, and Poland disappeared from the map of Europe for nearly 100 years, some of it becoming Russia's "Vistula region"; other parts were occupied by Prussia and Austria.

In 1920, barely two years after regaining independence as a result of World War I, Soviet troops approached Warsaw in a major offensive against the fledgling Polish Army, which earlier had advanced deep into Ukraine, seizing Kiev. The battle was won in what was subsequently called "the miracle of the Vistula." Warsaw's bells tolled. Describing that period in his memoirs, French General Maxime Weygand, whose military mission aided the Polish General staff, wrote:

Imagine what would have happened to Europe then if Poland had been reduced to the role of Russia's satellite. . . . The world owes an enormous debt to Poland which, once again, had become the rampart of Christian civilization.[3]

Warsaw has been Poland's capital since the seventeenth century. Before the outbreak of the war in 1939, it was Poland's geographic center and its main crossroads. The bulk of the city lies on the western (left) bank of the Vistula, rising over the riverbed, varying from 400 to 600 yards in width. North of the center is the historic Old Town, with its pastel-colored houses lining narrow streets. Farther north lies the residential suburb of Żoliborz, and south of the center also mainly residential Mokotów. The heart of the city is divided by the main east-west thoroughfare Aleje Jerozolimskie and the main south-north artery, *ulica* (street) Marszałkowska. In 1939, west and northwest of the city

center were crowded working class quarters of colorless, often depressing streets, buildings of up to six stories high with courtyards permeated
by the smell of urban poverty. A Polish poet described one such neigh-
borhood as a place where "in May children are not aware of the spring."

Before the war the center was graced by a number of eighteenth-
century palaces of the old aristocracy, the opera and the main theater,
and parks as well as historic churches, several of which survived the
turmoil of the war. The royal palace at the edge of the Old Town served
as the principal residence of the president of the Polish republic.

The western part of the capital was linked with the eastern suburb of
Praga across the Vistula by four bridges, two of them used only by rail-
ways. The city had three railway stations on the western side and two
in Praga. It had one airport with international connections. The principal
form of public transport was a tramway network. Warsaw had a well-
developed sewer system expanded at the beginning of the twentieth century. During the 1943 ghetto uprising and the subsequent 1944 uprising,
the sewers served as major routes of communication and escape.

Before the outbreak of the war, Warsaw's population was approximately 1.2 million, 819,000 of whom were Christians (mostly Roman
Catholics) and 352,000 Jews, a sizeable proportion of them Orthodox. At
that time it was probably the biggest concentration of Jewry in a European city. According to statistics published by the postwar communist
authorities, 48 percent of the population was classified as physical la-
borers and artisans and their families.

The city had a considerable and varied industry, employing about
100,000 workers. Because of the large number of relatively well-off en-
trepreneurs, members of the professional class, civil servants, and military cadres, 90,000 women worked as full-time household help. About
20,000 of Warsaw's inhabitants were unemployed.[4]

Prewar Warsaw also had a large garrison: in addition to the General
Staff, the Ministry of Defense, and vast depots of weapons and ammunition, the capital's barracks housed three infantry regiments, a cavalry
regiment, an antiaircraft artillery regiment, as well as horse artillery, armored, signal, and engineering units. An air force regiment, including
two squadrons of Poland's brand-new bombers, was stationed near the
civil airport. The city was surrounded by century-old fortifications, some
of them improved by Russians before World War I.

Throughout the first half of 1939, the international scene punctuated
by Hitler's threats and demands on Poland perturbed Warsaw's life to
a relatively minimal degree. There were few signs of tension. A chronicler of that period described the summer as being early and exceptionally
warm. There was a marked drop in cinema and theater attendance, but
beaches along the Vistula and public swimming pools were crowded.
However, tension rose following the announcement of a "nonaggression

pact" between Nazi Germany and the Soviet Union on August 24. The capital's newspapers speculated about the meaning of such a treaty between Poland's powerful neighbors and enemies. The army had already begun partial mobilization, and lines formed outside banks and savings institutions. In parks and empty lots, crowds of volunteers began digging trenches to be used as substitute air-raid shelters.

The mood was still confident and posters on the city's walls portrayed marching troops, and skies covered with aircraft with the slogan "Strong, United, Ready." Needless to say, the average *Warszawiak*—inhabitant of Warsaw—had little knowledge of the power of Germany's war machine, and the strength and readiness of the Polish Army was systematically exaggerated by official propaganda. In the increasingly nervous atmosphere, to doubt it was virtually tantamount to treason.

Nervousness rose sharply when on August 25, a radio announcement called on all civil servants to immediately return from summer vacations and report for work. Obtaining a long-distance telephone communication became virtually impossible. The beginning of the school year, normally starting early in September, was delayed. Every apartment building had been ordered to prepare a shelter in its cellars. The outdoor trenches, dug by a growing number of people, were intended for those caught by an air raid in open space. (In reality, they turned out to be useless.) Appeals were launched to prevent the hoarding of food. "There has always been enough food in Poland," repeated the newspapers.

Manfred Vasold, a German chronicler of the immediate prewar period, noted that an atmosphere of insecurity was heightened by a spate of terrorist attacks in various parts of Poland, officially blamed on members of the German minority. "But Poles were not certain who really was behind these attacks," he wrote. He also stressed the increasingly strident tone of official German and Polish statements, as well as radio broadcasts contributing to the tension.[5] According to various Polish sources, the population was convinced that a German "fifth column" was being activated to create terror as a prelude to war.

On August 30 the government announced "general mobilization" starting the following day, including older army reservists. Trenches were being dug in 230 points of the Polish capital. In his memoirs, Colonel Stefan Rowecki, who was to become the head of Poland's underground "Home Army" until his arrest by the *Gestapo* (*Geheime Staatspolizei*—State Secret Police) in 1943, noted, "I doubt that these trenches would serve any purpose. Still it was a good idea to keep the population busy rather than leaving it in the nervous expectation fueled by gossip."[6] On August 31—the last day of peace—the movement of all international trains was stopped, and traffic on suburban lines was curtailed. Trucks carrying weapons and military equipment sped through the city. Herds of requisitioned horses were led to mobilization centers.

In the fields adjacent to Warsaw, antiaircraft batteries were hauled into positions.

War came to Warsaw from the sky on a surprisingly gray autumnal morning after weeks of bright sunny weather. The first air raid was followed by three others during the day, usually by small groups of planes. The damage was relatively limited, but there were civilian victims. Rowecki observed drily in his memoirs, "Our antiaircraft artillery was firing poorly, too low and in short doses, nonetheless hitting several planes. Remnants of shells fell on rooftops and on gardens." And he added, "These groups of planes appearing throughout the day did not make much impact. Still it was amazing that they were able to travel shamelessly across Polish skies."[7] The authorities claimed that seven German planes had been shot down, some by the Polish air force fighter brigade assigned to Warsaw's defense.

Surprisingly the city took the outbreak calmly. Almost miraculously tension dropped. The inevitable had come. W. Szpilman, an observer of the events, noted in his diary: "There were no signs of panic among the population. The mood vacillated between the curiosity about what would come next and the surprise that it [war] had started in such a way." However, during the following days, Ludwik Landau, another chronicler, noted the population's "incredulity at the subsequent speed of the events."[8]

These notes illustrate the mood of Warsaw as the Polish capital faced what turned out to be the most disastrous period in its history. But as the first bombs fell on the city, neither of the two communities expected a disaster of historic dimensions: the Jews' virtually total annihilation (only an estimated 20,000 of Warsaw's Jewish population survived the war), and the Christians' heroic but doomed uprising which turned Warsaw into a heap of rubble, eventually ending up in a communist takeover.

On the third day of the war, when most of Warsaw's population had no idea about the extent of the looming disaster, France and Great Britain declared war on Germany in keeping with their pact of alliance with Poland. Crowds took to the streets to cheer the allies outside their embassies. Optimists expected a major offensive against Germany from the west.

Meanwhile, on the Polish front the situation was becoming more and more dramatic. The Polish Army had not been fully mobilized, and in any case its strength was no match for the powerful and determined assailant. Moreover the front line roughly extending along the frontiers from East Prussia in the north to the Carpathian Mountains in the south was more than 1,000 miles long, literally impossible to defend with Poland's means—thirty regular and nine reserve infantry divisions, eleven cavalry brigades, and two motorized brigades. Lack of sufficient war materiel simply precluded the formation of additional divisions from the mass of trained reservists. The German forces facing Poland consisted of sixty-two "tactical units," including six armored, four light, and four motorized divisions.[9]

The planned gradual retreat involved evacuation of industrial equipment and food and ammunition depots, most of which were located in the western areas. Soon it became clear that all carefully prepared plans were being shattered. In some areas of the wobbly front, staff officers could hardly keep up with marking the German advance on their maps. Several generals were cut off from their divisions, and retreating units had to push their way through swelling crowds of refugees, many of them on foot. The car of one general literally drove into the tail end of an armored column which had bypassed his division.

While Warsaw cheered the French and British entry into the war, German armor had already broken through Polish defenses in the southwest, and the command of the pivotal army *Kraków*, which was to protect the southern borders, asked for permission to "regroup." Massive evacuation of factories and industrial installations began from Silesia. From west to east, the country was systematically terrorized by air attacks which paralyzed administrative activity and hampered the movement of troop transports westward and evacuation trains in the opposite direction. The Polish Air Force of about 400 combat planes, some of them obsolete, was totally overwhelmed by Germany's 2,000 aircraft assigned to the eastern front. After five days of war and heavy losses, Poland's Air Force virtually ceased effective activity besides that of reconnaissance.

Marshal Śmigły-Rydz, who left Warsaw with some of his staff on September 7 for a new command post in the fortress of Brześć (Brest Litovsk) in the east, was quoted as saying he had no other choice but a general retreat east of the Vistula. He was hoping to regroup his tattered army in southeastern Poland, and counted on supplies of fresh weapons and ammunition from France through friendly Romania. All this required time that Poland didn't have. In a conversation with General Kazimierz Sosnkowski (who later led the Polish forces under British command), Smigły-Rydz insisted that he intended to "fight until the end, even at the head of three divisions."[10]

At the same time, he ordered Warsaw to defend itself as long as possible—"even in isolation." Before the city was completely sealed off by the Germans, it was bolstered by units retreating from various fronts, some demoralized by the extent of an unexpected disaster, and most of them unfamiliar with the city and untrained in urban warfare. The mass of refugees who had to be housed and fed, periodic air raids, and the increasingly intense bombardment by artillery completed the deteriorating situation of Poland's beleaguered capital.

From the military point of view, Warsaw's defense made sense as long as it tied down a number of German tactical formations, thus releasing pressure on Polish units fighting in other areas. But to the Poles as well to the rest of Europe, it was mainly a symbol of Poland's continuing and defiant resistance against impossible odds. The price was paid mainly by the civilian population.

The siege of Warsaw was the first of its kind in modern-age warfare. A city of over a million inhabitants was isolated from the rest of the country by ten German divisions supported by a mass of artillery. The fact that the civil administration functioned, orphans were taken care of, and food was distributed as long as it lasted is largely attributed to the energy of Warsaw's president, Stefan Starzyński. His daily radio appeals were considered to be a major factor in keeping up the morale of the population despite the steadily deteriorating situation. (Starzyński's authority was such that when Warsaw surrendered, the German command demanded that he countersign the capitulation agreement. He was jailed by the occupation authorities shortly afterward and sent to the Dachau concentration camp where he was executed in 1943.)

Gradually, as artillery fire increased, entire areas of the city were deprived of water, gas, and electricity. Most people spent days and nights in cellars turned into shelters. "We don't undress any more, ready to flee at the first sign of fire, our most precious belongings packed, our gas masks ready. . . . we live like cavemen or turtles in their shells," wrote one survivor.[11]

As artillery shells rained on the city, there was little significant military activity on either side. The German army wanted to wear Warsaw out; the Polish command contented itself with resisting and with an occasional foray against German positions. The defense perimeter was reduced significantly in the belief that it was easier to resist in built-up areas. Indeed, during the entire siege and despite a number of efforts, the besieging German army made no significant dent in the Polish defenses. The city was being gradually reduced to rubble, although when the damage was finally assessed, only 12 percent of Warsaw's buildings were totally destroyed.

Before the systematic siege began, the Polish high command (already from the fortress of Brześć) ordered the creation of "Army Group Warsaw," theoretically consisting of all remaining Polish armies north, northeast, and west of the capital. The largest of them were the relatively intact armies *Poznań* and *Pomorze*, which on September 9 launched a major attack in the area of Kutno, in effect forcing the Germans to reduce pressure on Warsaw. The command of "Army Group Warsaw" was given to General Juliusz Rómmel (no relation to Germany's "Desert Fox," Field Marshal Erwin Rommel), who moved into the shelter abandoned by the General Staff on Rakowiecka Street and tried to exercise some form of control despite constant breakdowns in communications. This new command had no influence on the offensive near Kutno, which, after an initial Polish success, was eventually smashed, and the remnants of Polish units tried to fight their way into Warsaw. As the senior Polish general in the capital, Rómmel found himself in charge of the city rather than of armies, and he eventually moved from the exposed Rakowiecka Street to a solid bank building in the center. By then the bulk of operational Polish units was putting up sporadic resistance east of the Vistula and San rivers. The German armies controlled most of Poland.

The Polish command's plan for defense of the southeastern areas was shattered on September 17, when Soviet troops entered Polish territory virtually along the entire frontier. The action was the secret part of the "nonaggression" pact signed in August by German Foreign Minister Joachim von Ribbentrop with his Soviet counterpart, Vyacheslav Molotov. The Soviet armies were moving to the line of the Bug and San rivers, also known as the Curzon Line when Poland's eastern frontiers were discussed in the aftermath of World War I. In Polish terminology the demarcation line became known as "the Molotov-Ribbentrop Line." Once again Poland was divided between its enemies. The government and the high command fled to Romania just as the Soviet troops were advancing, encountering only sporadic and halfhearted resistance from disoriented Polish units. Encircled, abandoned, and without hope, the Polish capital was to last another ten days to "safeguard Poland's honor."

Continuing to obey the order to defend the city "even in isolation," General Rómmel could do little but listen to the deafening salvoes of German artillery and pore over reports of diminishing food and ammunition stocks of the Polish defenders. At 6:00 A.M. on September 25, some 1,500 German guns of various calibers simultaneously opened fire on the city, continuing until 8:00 P.M. The following day German infantry supported by tanks attacked from the west, east, and southeast. When the attackers threatened Warsaw's western railway station (*Dworzec Zachodni*), the Polish command ordered into action its last reserves, the remnants of the 25th infantry division. The soldiers "marched in small groups along burning streets littered with decaying corpses for what was to be their last battle of the campaign."[12] As night fell on the city, most positions were held. But much of Warsaw was burning, and there was no water with which to fight the fires.

In such an atmosphere, key generals and members of the recently formed "citizens' committee" met in the underground command shelter to assess the sense of further resistance. Three crucial questions were asked: "Do we have ammunition for antiaircraft guns and do we still have any planes? Is there anywhere in Poland an army capable of rescuing Warsaw? Is there any prospect of restoring the water supply?"[13]

The answers were categorically negative. The decision to negotiate "honorable surrender" was made without a vote. At a similar meeting of unit commanders, a proposal was made to take the army out of the city and continue the war. This was outvoted as making no sense. Those present agreed that Warsaw had done all it could.

General Tadeusz Kutrzeba (who began his military career before World War I in the Austro-Hungarian army) was designated to negotiate surrender with General Johannes Blaskowitz, commander of the 8th German army, on September 27 while fighting continued in several areas. The German side accepted most Polish conditions, and fighting stopped on the following day. The German army agreed to provide one million rations for the starving population and medical supplies for the wounded, whose number was estimated at 36,000. Officers were to be taken to prisoner-of-war camps; noncommissioned officers and privates were to be grouped in transit camps before being formally demobilized and released. At that point the garrison consisted of 5,031 officers and 97,425 other ranks. Losses throughout the siege were estimated at 2,000 military personnel killed and 16,000 wounded; the civilian population suffered 25,000 dead and 20,000 wounded.[14]

The first German units began entering the city's suburbs on September 29. In the morning of October 1, a long column of Polish officers led by generals marched out of the shattered capital in accordance with the capitulation agreement. At 3:00 P.M. a company of *Wehrmacht* infantry, their boots freshly polished, goose-stepped across the dust of war into the heart of Warsaw and posted sentries outside the empty garrison command building. Warsaw was to be their prisoner for five bitter years.

NOTES

1. *Polskie Siły Zbrojne (Polish Armed Forces)*, Vol. III, Part 2 (London: General Sikorski Institute, 1950), p. 606.

2. Warsaw's socialist daily *Robotnik*, September 9, 1939.

3. Maxime Weygand, *Memoires: Mirages et Realité* (Paris: Flammarion, 1957), pp. 159–60.

4. Marian Drozdowski, *Alarm dla Warszawy* (Warsaw: Wiedza Powszechna, 1964), p. 18.

5. Manfred Vasold, *August 1939* (Munich: Kindler Verlag, 1999), p. 207.

6. Stefan Rowecki, *Wspomnienia i Notatki Autobiograficzne* (Warsaw: Czytelnik, 1988), p. 154.

7. Ibid., p. 157.

8. Drozdowski, *Alarm dla Warszawy*, pp. 70–71.

9. Friedrich Stahl, *Heereseinteilung 1939* (Bad Nauheim: Wehr Kund, 1954), pp. 170, 182.

10. *Polskie Siły Zbrojne*, Vol. I, p. 384.

11. Drozdowski, *Alarm dla Warszawy*, p. 192.

12. Juliusz Rómmel, *Za Honor i Ojczyznę* (Warsaw: Wiedza Powrzechna, 1959) p. 197.

13. *Drozdowski, Alarm dla Warszawy*, p. 197.

14. Ibid., p. 217.

CHAPTER 2

The Conspiracy

The beginning was modest: seven dispirited career army officers shattered by Warsaw's capitulation swore "before Almighty God" to "defend Poland's honor, conscientiously carry out all orders, and guard secrets regardless of what may happen to me." Their organization was to be called the "Polish Victory Service" (*Służba Zwycięstwu Polski—SZP*). During the following four years, through several transformations and changes of names, this embryonic group was to become an underground army of some 350,000 men and women.[1]

At the time of that first oath in a Warsaw apartment building damaged by artillery shells, the shock of the capitulation was all-pervasive and devastating. Logically, there could have been no other way out. Warsaw had neither food nor water, and the artillery of the besieged city had ammunition only for one more day. Yet some of the defenders, particularly career officers, could not mentally adjust to the act of surrender, no matter how inevitable it was that disastrous September. Their main hope was that, sooner or later, a massive offensive of Poland's allies in the west would give Germany a mortal blow and thus lead to liberation.

The Poles were not the only ones who believed in the prospect of a major offensive in the west. Contemporary accounts as well as postwar documents show that the German High Command (*Oberkommando der Wehrmacht*) was seriously concerned about such a possibility, particularly as France had already completed the mobilization of its large armed forces. Thus, within days after the end of the Polish campaign, long columns of troops were rushed from Poland toward Germany and then farther westward over the famous *Autobahn* network (a novelty in Europe) to be quickly available on the French borders, until then protected by a thin screen of reserve divisions. They were to spend what has become known as "the phony war" in boredom—until the victorious German attack in the west in the spring.

Some of Warsaw's buildings still smouldered, and the tense city awaited the arrival of the occupation forces when the conspirators went to work. Their plans were still vague, but their immediate objective was to stash away arms and explosives before all were handed over to the conquerors. Above all they needed blank identity papers with all the correct stamps and signatures. Stefan Starzyński, president of the Warsaw city council, provided them with 500 such documents which later proved to be invaluable. Starzyński himself declined an invitation by General Michał Tokarzewski (pseudonym Karaszewicz) to join the conspiracy by invoking the need to remain at his official post. "As long as the Germans allow it, I will remain with the people of Warsaw," he was quoted as saying.[2] Tokarzewski himself was informally released from the obligation to go to the prisoner-of-war camp. In fact several hundred officers simply abandoned their units and disappeared, ignoring the conditions of surrender under which they should have become prisoners. (Many of them were hunted down and arrested when the *Gestapo* machinery moved into the city.)

During the last days of September 1939, Warsaw was like a man woken up from as nightmare realizing that another is about to begin. When the firing stopped,

thousands of people emerged from their shelters, cellars, literally from under the ruins, searching for their relatives, friends, anxious to see if their places of work were still intact. Crowds moved like waves in different directions. There were no loud conversations. Here and there groups of people stood reading the announcement of the capitulation posted on walls.[3]

Among the officer cadres of the army that defended the city, the state of depression reached alarming proportions, leading to the mass suicide of a group of officers in the so-called Luxembourg Gallery (*Galeria Luksemburga*). The speed and magnitude of the defeat, the failure of the Polish defense in the face of a superior enemy, the flight of the government and of the general staff created a feeling of helplessness, apathy, and resignation among many. To some, going to a prisoner-of-war camp seemed the easiest solution. It required no difficult decisions, dangers, or risks. Yet there were others who felt that the fight had to go on, albeit in a different form.

One of those was General Tokarzewski, who, after the battle of Kutno, had made his way to besieged Warsaw on foot across the heavily wooded area northwest of the city known as the Kampinos forest. The day of the capitulation he told his aide, Captain Emil Kumor: "I have two choices: one is that of those of the *Galeria Luksemburga*, which I consider to be cowardly, and the other is to continue the struggle against the occupying power. I have chosen to fight."[4]

According to one version, he took a piece of paper, and wrote by hand, "I hereby authorize Brigadier General Michał Karaszewicz-Tokarzewski to remain in Poland and create an underground army for further struggle against the Hitlerite occupant." He then submitted the text to General Rómmel, whom he considered at that time to be the senior military authority in Poland. "Rómmel signed the paper without comment and wished good luck to Tokarzewski as well as those who were willing to follow him."[5] Some reports claim that Rómmel also authorized payment of 750,000 Polish *złotys* (at the time equivalent to $150,000) to finance the beginning of the conspiracy.

It was interesting that the authorization to continue the struggle spoke of the "Hitlerite occupant," and did not mention the Soviet Union which at that time controlled one-third of Poland's prewar territory.

However, another version of the beginning of the conspiracy claims that an order to form an underground army came from Marshal Smigły-Rydz who had fled to Romania, and that it was brought to Warsaw on September 26 by a courier who landed his plane despite intense German artillery fire. The order, according to this version, left the name of the designated commander of this "army" blank and Rómmel put down "Tokarzewski" at his own request.[6] Regardless of these differing accounts, the fact remains that Tokarzewski became the first commander of the Polish resistance, which throughout its existence considered itself to be a continuation of the Polish Armed Forces. And although thousands of its members perished in Nazi concentration camps, Soviet gulags, or were simply shot when captured, in the final stages of the resistance, particularly in Warsaw, the Germans treated them as prisoners-of-war according to the Geneva conventions.

Almost immediately after "legalizing" his appointment, Tokarzewski ordered his aide, Captain Kumor, to contact various officers to recruit them for his budding conspiracy before they marched off to captivity. Kumor returned shortly afterward, dejected. "All answers were negative," he reported. "They claimed to be psychologically exhausted, unable to cope or make decisions."[7]

Nonetheless, the following day he succeeded in finding seven willing officers and brought them to Tokarzewski, who told them: "Gentlemen, you have half an hour to decide. Your choice is a prison camp or the continuation of the struggle. I am not trying to convince or pressure you." When all those present agreed to join the movement, General To-karzewski swore them in, stressing "I consider you to be the embryo and cadres of the Underground Army." A few hours later, five women were sworn in as auxiliaries.[8]

The version that the creation of an "underground army" was ordered by Marshal Śmigły-Rydz appears to be based on the ultrasecret prewar plans of the Polish General Staff to conduct resistance in areas expected to be occupied by Germany in the event of war. Apparently a "Major Galinat" was in charge of forming such a network in parts of western and central Poland. The plans were so secret that very few officers were familiar with them—certainly not Rómmel and Tokarzewski. According to some accounts, "Major Galinat" was aboard a plane from Romania, which landed in besieged Warsaw on September 26. Tokarzewski sub-sequently saw Galinat and, as commander-in-chief of the new secret army, ordered him to inspect his network, which had been set up before the war, and report by October 15 to an address in Warsaw. The mys-terious major claimed that he could not find any of his contacts and proposed to make his way back to Romania to collect a large amount of money deposited there for the conspiracy.[9]

The first formal meeting of the "general staff" of the Service for Po-land's Victory took place on or about October 14, 1939, at Chmielna ulica (street) no. 62, apartment no. 12, owned by Stefan Weinzieher. It was attended by Tokarzewski, who at that time used the nom de guerre "Doktor," Colonel Stefan Rowecki ("Stefan"), and Captain Emil Kumor ("Emil"). Rowecki, whose motorized brigade was destroyed around Sep-tember 17, had made his way to Warsaw with his driver. After the ca-pitulation he contacted the conspirators. Of utmost concern to this miniature staff was the question of the "legalization" of identity cards and the availability of printing presses and equipment needed for for-gery.

According to the official history of the Polish Armed Forces in World War II published in London, Tokarzewski named Rowecki as chief of staff and second in command.[10] By then other appointments had already been made, particularly of area commanders in parts of German-occupied Poland. All members of the conspiracy were career officers who had either managed to avoid going to prisoner-of-war camps or fled en route and made their way to Warsaw. One of their major problems was how to cope with increasing identity controls which required iron-clad documents, including periodically renewable "work cards" (Arbeitskarte) proving their gainful employment.

Terror came to Warsaw gradually, by stages. At the beginning of the occupation, it was limited to announcements of draconian decrees such as the death penalty for possession of weapons or radios or for helping escaped prisoners. All private cars had to be handed over to the German authorities. The local administration tried to function as before under German supervision; Starzyński was still in his office in the City Hall but his role became more and more constrained. The occupation army was ubiquitous, but the repressive apparatus was not yet in place. German military police (*Feldgendarmerie*) directed the sparse traffic, but eventually the occupation authorities started recruiting former Polish policemen. They retained their prewar uniforms and ranks, except for removing the Polish eagle (national symbol) from their round caps. They were generally referred to as *granatowa policja* because of the navy-blue color of their uniforms. Initially their functions were limited to traffic control and nonpolitical criminal investigations.

One by one tramway lines were being reestablished. Warsaw's 4,000 taxis were paralyzed by a lack of gasoline, but horsecabs were functioning. Shops in the buildings that survived undamaged were reopened, but the only demand was for food and clothing for the winter. According to the instructions from the occupation authorities, ration cards of three types were being issued: for ethnic Germans (*Volksdeutsche*), Polish Christians, and Jews. The last category had rations that were barely sufficient for survival. People who could find a German among their ancestors or had German names—as a number of Poles did—were encouraged to sign the *Volksliste*, or the claim to the "ethnic German" status. This included special rations and access to well-stocked shops *nur für Deutsche* (for Germans only). Those who did were usually scorned and avoided by their friends and neighbors. A number of new rules of conduct were placarded on the city's walls. A daily Polish language newspaper, *Nowy Kurier Warszawski* (*New Warsaw Courier*), started publication, edited by a group of collaborators and filled with decrees and official German propaganda. It also carried small ads placed by people trying to locate missing family members or in need of accommodations. Gradually the streets were cleaned of war debris but the skeletons of burned out and smashed houses reminded all of the terror of the siege.

Telephones began to function again, but it was impossible to obtain long-distance connections. On the other hand, postal and telegraph services were reestablished relatively fast. Suburban trains began to function, and owners of small businesses and factories were ordered to register. The objectives were to determine the number of Jewish-owned enterprises, which were later seized and given German administrators, and to establish which enterprises could be useful to the German war effort.

From the beginning a clear official distinction was made among the population of the occupied country: the Christians were referred to as Poles or "Aryans," the Jewish Poles simply as "Jews." Late in 1939 Jews were ordered to wear white armbands with the blue Star of David on their right arm. (When most of Europe fell under Nazi rule, Jews in several occupied countries wore a yellow star on their chest.) It took a year for more drastic measures, including the establishment of the ghetto. All Jewish schools—and there were quite a number in Warsaw— were shut. Only elementary and trade schools were allowed for Poles, and the teaching of history and geography was banned.

The western part of occupied Poland was annexed to the German *Reich* (state), and the rest was given the official name of *Generalgouvernement*, consisting of four "districts" with the capital in Cracow (Krakau in German) in southern Poland. The Germans apparently felt more secure to place the highest occupation authority in a smaller city undamaged by war which had no record of Warsaw's resistance to invasions or foreign presence. Soon new banknotes of occupation currency were distributed, at the rate of two Polish *złotys* to one *Reichsmark*, wiping out most bank and savings accounts. (The gold reserves of the Polish government had been shipped to Romania during the September campaign and then to Great Britain.)

The placing of virtually all central occupation authorities in Cracow made Warsaw much more convenient for conspiracy and its growth. The city was large and traditionally defiant, and the number of ethnic Germans was small. The conspirators could count on increasing support and complicity. The very size of the population did not facilitate immediate and all-pervasive police control.

Such was the atmosphere in which "Doktor" (Tokarzewski) began expanding the activities of his organization. He soon realized that a number of prewar political figures, including some leading members of various parties, were still in Warsaw and that some had started forming informal circles which were hardly more than discussion groups, analyzing the causes of the defeat, as well as weighing prospects for the future. Although Doktor's aim was principally to create an underground army, he felt that such an organization could be effective only with the support of Polish society and cooperation with political activists.

He proposed the creation of a "political council" which would work closely with the command of his *SZP*, including representatives of three major parties—Polish Socialist Party, the Peasant Party (*Stronnictwo Ludowe*), and the arch-conservative National Party (*Stronnictwo Narodowe*).[11] Although this "political council" eventually grew into a full-fledged organ in liaison with the Polish government-in-exile (see Chapter 5), their ideological differences were to plague the "political underground" virtually until the end of its existence.

Doktor also discovered that during the first months of the occupation there was a proliferation throughout Poland of secret resistance organizations planning armed action. Most acted in total isolation, and some considered themselves as "militias" of various political parties. The commander of *SZP* embarked on the difficult tasks of contacting these groupings—some of them considerable—to incorporate them into his organization, giving them "legal status" in the underground force. It required a considerable degree of diplomacy and persuasion.

The Polish government-in-exile, formed in France and headed at that time, as prime minister, by General Władysław Sikorski, was the legal basis of the *SZP*. As the organization expanded and eventually became *Armia Krajowa* or Home Army, its contact with the government-in-exile became permanent via radio and special couriers, particularly after the fall of France when the exiled Polish authority moved to Great Britain.

Thus, in December 1939 the *SZP* reported to Angers in France, where the exiled government was billeted, details of the plans, statutes, and the extent of the organization under the German occupation. (The conspirators had no easy access to the territories controlled by the Soviet Union, where underground activity was complicated by the presence of large national minorities, mainly Ukrainian and Byelorussian.)

The overall objectives were described as "a decided and unswerving struggle against the invader in every field of activity until Poland's liberation with its pre-war frontiers."[12] The plan also proposed working to raise the morale of the cadres of the underground army and to increase its cooperation with civil underground authorities which were being organized. It outlined the state of the organization to date (headquarters and five regional commands), the creation of special armed groups for the protection of the command centers, and the degree of contacts with members of political parties.

For its part, the government-in-exile—which regarded itself as the constitutionally legal continuation of Poland's prewar authorities—had already created a "ministerial committee" to deal with the situation in Poland. It also appointed General Kazimierz Sosnkowski, who had made his way to France, to be commander-in-chief of the resistance army, although it wasn't quite clear how this appointment affected the role of the commander who functioned "underground" in Poland. Sosnkowski never reached occupied Poland, and his function was abolished as impractical.[13] Later he became commander-in-chief of the Polish Forces under British Command in Europe and the Middle East.

The political aspects of the conspiracy in Poland and its links with the exiles illustrate the conditions in which resistance began to function. It is unquestionable that the conspiracy was intended as a military operation, instigated and sanctioned by the military authorities on the eve of Warsaw's surrender. During the next five years, the organization was directed by career officers, organized along military lines, awarded its members military ranks, and was interested mainly in armed action. Nonetheless the political aspects of the underground had considerable impact on the functioning of the "underground army." The unending political debate frequently reflected prewar squabbles and was marred by the settling of old accounts and some uncompromising ideological statements which were often detrimental to the process of creating national unity in the face of the enemy.

The first arrests and executions of suspected conspirators took place as one of coldest winters of the century shrouded Poland. Coal was lacking and Warsaw shivered in unheated apartments. From Cracow, the capital of the *Generalgouvernement*, increasingly restrictive decrees were regularly showered on the conquered country.

NOTES

1. *Polskie Siły Zbrojne* (Polish Armed Forces) Vol. III (London: General Sikorski Historical Institute, 1950), p. 119.

2. Emil Kumor, *Wycinek z Historii Jednego Życia* (Warsaw: Pax, 1969), p. 38.

3. Stanisław Ordon, *Łuna nad Warszawą* (London: Thomas Nelson and Sons, 1941), p. 79.

4. Kumor, *Wycinek z Historii Jednego Życia*, p. 35.

5. Ibid., p. 34.

6. Statement by Colonel L. Głowacki to the Polish Historical Commission in Warsaw of September 30, 1963.

7. Kumor, *Wycinek z Historii Jednego Życia*, p. 36.

8. Ibid., p. 37.

9. Ibid., pp. 34–35.

10. *Polskie Siły Zbrojne*, p. 99.

11. Ibid.

12. General Tokarzewski's report of December 14, 1939.

13. Jerzy Kirchmayer, *Powstanie Warszawskie* (Warsaw: Czytelnik, 1959) pp. 13–14.

CHAPTER 3

"The Poles Shall Be Slaves"

Although Soviet intentions concerning the eastern Polish territories—ceded to Moscow as part of its agreement with Germany—remained vague at the beginning of the occupation, Germany did not take long to spell out its plans for the conquered areas and their inhabitants. Almost immediately after the Polish campaign, Hitler made semiconciliatory statements, mainly to confuse Poland's Western allies, Great Britain and France, hoping that they would take his words at face value and start negotiations. The *Blitzkrieg* against Poland was a blunt and awesome example of modern German power and a warning to the rest of Europe. The Nazi dictator believed that with Poland "out of the way," prostrate and again divided between its two ancient enemies, the West would be more tempted by the possibility of talks rather than of war. Just before Warsaw fell after a three-week siege, the German press and radio launched a major propaganda campaign with the theme "there is nothing to fight about, Germany wants nothing in the West."

At a special session of the *Reichstag*, Nazi Germany's rubber-stamp parliament, on October 6, 1939, Hitler "explained" his reasons for attacking Poland, insisted on Germany's "peaceful intentions," and spoke of guarantees for British and French interests in Europe—and even of disarmament. He dwelled on the need to create a "living space" (*Lebensraum*) for the German people in central and eastern Europe, as well as on the prospect of a "new Polish state." Such a state, he said, would have to guarantee that it would not be part of "any conflict against Germany or center of intrigue against the *Reich* and the Soviet Union." Britain's Prime Minister Neville Chamberlain described the statements as "vague and uncertain." Edouard Daladier, prime minister of France, said in a radio address that Germany "had unmasked itself" in its desire to dominate Europe.

Such reactions by Poland's allies—at that stage inactive and settling down to "phony war" or what the Germans called *Sitzkrieg* (sitting war)—convinced Hitler that the conflict would not end with the conquest of Poland and that it had to be carried further. From then on Hitler and the leading Nazi officials never mentioned the idea of "a Polish state" again. On the contrary they reiterated periodically that "the Polish state has ceased to exist and will never exist again." The decrees issued during the following months showed clearly that Germany intended to be totally uncompromising in dealing with the conquered Poles.

The alliance between Nazi Germany and Communist Russia stunned the world, although its full extent became known only after the entry of Soviet troops into Polish territory on September 17, 1939. Long after the war, secret documents of the German Foreign Affairs Ministry revealed that Germany had been seeking agreement on Poland with the Soviet Union in April and then in June 1939. When the first shots were fired at dawn on September 1 by the battleship *Schleswig-Holstein* on the Polish outpost of Westerplatte near Danzig (Gdańsk), Europe thought that diplomacy still had a role to play. But within forty-eight hours, while German armies poured into Poland, the exchange of cables, diplomatic notes, and mild threats became visibly pointless. Germany was bent on conquest. During the preceding four years, it had marched into demilitarized Rhineland, annexed enthusiastic Austria, Czech Sudetenland, and then the rest of peaceful and highly antimilitaristic Czechoslovakia. Poland, with its tradition of frequently hopeless wars, was going to be another matter although no one had expected German *Panzers* to reach Warsaw in eight days. (With considerable foresight, such a dramatic armored thrust had been feared and discussed by the Polish General Staff in the spring of 1939. Most senior officers preferred not to think about it. Equally daunting for Polish strategy was the possibility of Soviet participation in the war, with a general conclusion that "Poland could not fight on two fronts.")[1]

Under treaties with Great Britain and France, Poland had guarantees that inspired optimism. But while the British guarantee was general, the French was specific—or at least it was interpreted as such by the Poles. It was signed on May 19, 1939, as the Franco-Polish Military Convention, which was viewed in Warsaw as assuring French help in case of conflict. According to an American historian, it was agreed that the French would "progressively launch offensive operations against limited objectives toward the third day after General Mobilization Day."[2] Poland also received French credits and arms contracts.

Neither France nor Britain was ready for war—and certainly not war of the rapid kind that Germany had demonstrated on the battlefield of Poland. Nonetheless, Poland's two allies duly declared war on Germany on September 3, convinced that "the Poles might be quickly beaten but they would not surrender."[3] Despite the general chaos and despair during the Polish retreat, the Polish General Staff seriously envisaged the possibility of holding out in southeastern Poland pending an offensive in the west. The massive entry of Soviet forces dashed all such hopes.

The "unholy alliance" between Germany and the Soviet Union—historically most unnatural partners—was born on August 23, 1939 in a "nonaggression treaty" between Berlin and Moscow, signed by the foreign ministers of the two countries, Joachim von Ribbentrop for Germany and Vyacheslav Molotov for the Soviet Union. Although alarm bells were ringing in chanceries across the world, the most important secret protocol had not been published. In it Nazi Germany and Communist Russia clearly spelled out their vision of how influence should be divided between the Baltic and the Black Sea, and Poland's elimination from the map of Europe—including Soviet annexation of its eastern territories. On September 28, 1939, another secret clause was added, stipulating the line of Poland's partition along the rivers San and Bug.

As German troops advanced mercilessly across the Polish flatlands during the first half of September, German diplomacy intensified pressures on Moscow to fulfill its side of the "bargain," that is, military entry into the part of Poland assigned to it by the secret clause of the nonaggression treaty. For an unexplained reason, the Soviet side was procrastinating, claiming it needed time to mobilize before moving a large army into Poland. In several diplomatic notes showing impatience, Germany stressed the necessity "to help the German Army" and "occupy the areas intended for the Soviet Union." At the same time, representatives of the Foreign Affairs ministries of the two countries had difficulties in the wording of a joint communiqué explaining their new "cooperation."

The Germans opposed the original Soviet intention to claim the need to help the Ukrainian and Byelorussian minorities in eastern Poland, "threatened by Germany." Eventually a compromise was reached and on September 18 the world learned from a joint German-Soviet statement that Soviet and German troops were conducting operations on Polish territory "in line with the Soviet-German non-aggression pact" to "restore in Poland peace and order destroyed by Poland's collapse." The two invading countries also claimed their intention was to help "the Polish population to determine conditions of its political existence."[4]

The Polish government—which had left Warsaw and changed lodgings several times as the German offensive advanced—learned of the

Soviet decision from a radio message sent by the embassy in Moscow and transmitted through the facilities of the Polish river fleet in the Pripet marshes. The Polish ambassador, Wacław Grzybowski, was informed of the forthcoming invasion of his country at 3:00 A.M. of September 17—or one hour before the planned action took place. Summoned to the Soviet Ministry of Foreign Affairs in Moscow, he was not given the document; it was merely read to him by an official. The text referred to "the collapse of the Polish state," "the non-existence of Warsaw as Poland's capital," and "the necessity to protect brotherly Ukrainians and Byelo-russians." The stunned diplomat refused to accept the note that was then proffered, verbally rejected its contents, and returned to his embassy where he sent his dramatic message. The Polish government—this time in the town of Krzemieniec near the Romanian border—wired back its approval of the ambassador's rejection and advised him to obtain the necessary documents to leave Moscow. There was little doubt that a new partition of Poland was now a fait accompli.

In his analysis of that event, the American historian William L. Shirer wrote:

This time Adolf Hitler was aided and abetted in his obliteration of a country by the Union of Soviet Socialist Republics, which had posed for so long as the champion of the oppressed peoples. This was the fourth partition of Poland by Germany and Russia. . . . Hitler fought and won the war in Poland, but the greater winner was Stalin, whose troops scarcely fired a shot. The Soviet Union got nearly half of Poland and a stranglehold on the Baltic States. It blocked Germany more solidly than ever from two of its long-term objectives: Ukrainian wheat and Romanian oil.[5]

Although Germany tried to minimize its losses in the Polish campaign, according to official German figures 10,572 of its soldiers were killed, 30,322 wounded, and 3,400 were missing. Neither Germany nor the Soviet Union believed that their alliance was permanent or that they could live in peace for a long time. But with the "Polish question" solved—at least for the time being—Hitler could devote his entire attention to the situation in the west. Meanwhile, Poland was going to pay another steep price for its geographic position.

The original German plan was to annex Poland's western regions corresponding to Germany's "historic, economic and ethnographic realities" and turn a truncated central Poland into a vassal state. In a somewhat revised version, the plans were announced in Hitler's decrees of October 8 and 12, 1939, effectively dividing German-controlled Poland into two areas: the "annexed" territories and the "occupied" part. The occupied part became known as *"Generalgouvernement"* (General Government) with Hans Frank as governor general.

Historians have few kind words for Frank, a long-standing member of the Nazi party deeply committed to its objectives and its Führer. Dark-haired, dapper, and energetic, he combined an unquestionable intelligence with political fanaticism. At the same time, he was said to have been a devoted husband and father to his five children. He left behind a forty-two-volume journal of his activities, particularly in occupied Poland, used during the Nuremberg trials and described as "one of the most terrifying documents to come out of the dark Nazi world."

Even before Frank's appointment, Hitler's top generals knew exactly what fate had been reserved for Poland. According to various diaries and records of conversations involving Admiral Wilhelm Canaris, head of the Intelligence Bureau of the German High Command (*Oberkommado der Wehrmacht*), General Franz Halder, chief of the General Staff, and General Edouard Wagner, quartermaster general, Poland was to undergo a complete "housecleaning," affecting particularly "Jews, intelligentsia, clergy and the nobility." The occupied part was to become a *Nebenland*, or Germany's adjunct country. According to Frank's statement upon his arrival in Cracow, "The Poles shall be slaves of the German *Reich*."

The gradual liquidation of Poland's Jews (nearly 4 million before the outbreak of the war) was overseen personally by Heinrich Himmler, the powerful head of the *Schutzstaffel* (SS), Hitler's praetorian guard, and later minister of the interior. Frank's main job was to supply Germany with Polish slave labor, with whatever raw materials and produce were available, and eliminate the intelligentsia. The last task was "legalized" as the "Extraordinary Pacification Act." According to Frank's diaries introduced at the Nuremberg trials, Hitler's wish was to "liquidate the men capable of leadership in Poland. Those following them . . . must be eliminated in their turn. There is no need to burden the *Reich* . . . no need to send these elements to *Reich* concentration camps."[6]

After a meeting with his top police officials on May 30, 1940, Frank noted in his diary that about 2,000 men and several hundred women had been arrested and that most of them had been "summarily sentenced," meaning executed. Frank had expected their number to rise to 3,500 before too long. As governor of occupied Poland, Frank was also concerned with the Jewish question. A year after his appointment, he actually apologized to an assembly of Nazi functionaries for the delay in carrying out Hitler's orders by saying "I could not eliminate all lice and Jews in only one year. But in the course of time . . . this end will be attained."

Two months later he told his police officers, "As far as the Jews are concerned, I want to tell you quite frankly that they must be done away with in one way or another. Gentlemen, I must ask you to rid yourselves of all feeling of pity. We must annihilate the Jews."[7]

Frank's scrupulously kept diaries were not the only indication of "the dark Nazi world." Among many statements of which he was apparently proud was his conversation with a German journalist who mentioned that the occupation authorities in Czechoslovakia had recently put up posters announcing the execution of seven Czech students. Frank laughed and told his visitor "If I wished to order posters for every seven Poles shot, there would not be enough forests in Poland with which to make the paper for these posters."

The winter of 1939 shrouded occupied Poland with plunging temperatures and misery. Warsaw's hospitals were still filled with wounded civilians and soldiers. Demobilized soldiers, many on crutches, begged at street corners, playing mouth harmonicas or singing a haunting song about church bells tolling as colleagues carried the bloodstained body of a lancer. At crossing points of the newly established frontier between the Soviet Union and Germany, hundreds of thousands of refugees who had fled the German advance clamored to get back to their homes. No one suspected what plans Germany held in store for Poland, and home seemed better than temporary shelters in monasteries or makeshift camps. Special German commissions were set up to study each application, and people waited for days in freezing temperatures outside their offices. At the Przemysl railway station on the Soviet-controlled side of the San River, the wounded of the *Nowogrodzka* Cavalry Brigade lived in unheated boxcars waiting for the Soviet authorities to decide their fate. Their officers had already been arrested and deported. While the *Gestapo* began to rule the German side of the occupied territory, in the Soviet part the notorious *NKVD* (National Committee for Internal Affairs) was gradually establishing its all-pervasive presence.

The September 28 secret protocol on the "exchange of nationals and suppression of dissent" set the stage for close cooperation between the secret police forces of the two occupying powers. According to the intelligence service of the Polish army-in-exile, which at that time was being organized in France,

German and Soviet secret police met several times in Cracow, Lwów and Zakopane. These sessions had a twofold purpose: first to coordinate so-called resettlement policies in the German and Soviet spheres, as well as other plans to eliminate the Polish intelligentsia; and second to devise effective policies for combatting the Polish underground. . . . These gatherings represented a fraternity of miscreants who shared similar goals but used different methods.[8]

While in Cracow, Hans Frank was proceeding with his plan to turn the Poles into slaves of the Third Reich, in the western areas which were now considered part of Germany, Hitler's special proconsul, Wolfgang Foerster, declared an uncompromising war against everything Polish.

The military campaign was barely over when Foerster announced his intentions in clear, blunt language:

I was appointed by the *Führer* as the trustee (*Treuhänder*) of the German cause in this land, with specific orders to make it German again.... During the next few years everything Polish, regardless of its nature, will be removed and those who belong to the Polish nation will have to leave.[9]

Considering that 90 percent of the population in the annexed territories was Polish and that during their occupation by Prussia for 127 years (until 1918) efforts to turn the Poles into Germans generally failed, Foerster's task was not going to be easy. His initial idea was to remove all Poles and replace them with ethnic Germans (*Volksdeutsche*) from other parts of eastern Europe, including the Baltic states. The program was to be supervised by the newly created Commissariat for the Strengthening of German Nationhood with Himmler at its head. In addition to mass expulsions, this "ethnic cleansing" was to include arrests, executions, and deportation for slave labor inside Germany proper. Yet those carrying out the plan soon realized that stripping the area quickly of most of its population would inevitably paralyze the economy and, above all, the agricultural production, particularly as most Poles were farmers.

The first to be shipped in cattle trains to the areas east of the Vistula River were Jews, together with Polish Christians considered to be "unfit for assimilation." All told within one year over 300,000 Polish Jews and 1.2 million Christians were ousted from their homes, but Foerster only managed to find 497,000 *Volksdeutsche* to replace them. Thus the tactics had to be adjusted to the reality, at the expense of the speed of the "Germanization."

The "resettlement plan" was carried out in three main phases, at first affecting all owners of agricultural or other commercial property, as well as all members of the intelligentsia (educated class). The property of those expelled was confiscated, and they were allowed to take between forty to 100 pounds per person of personal belongings, as well as a small sum of money. The process, including informing those affected and the time to allow them to pack their belongings and report to the assigned railway station, varied from one to three hours—sometimes less.

The majority of the expelled was transported during the exceptionally severe winter of 1939/1940, in unheated trains, frequently in open flatcars; the trip lasted from several days to several weeks, without food supplies, drinking water or medical care. Consequently, each transport suffered victims among children and elderly or exhausted people.[10]

Those spared from the expulsion and allowed to stay—temporarily—in the annexed areas were stripped of their civil rights, including property ownership and professional activity other than that of "hired hands."

Subsequently four categories of "German nationality" were introduced in the annexed areas: "nationally conscious and active" Germans; Germans "aware of their nationality but passive"; persons of mixed marriages or with regional ethnic roots; and, finally, "persons of German origin but under Polish influence." The three "lower" categories were nonetheless pressured to sign the so-called "German national list" (*Volksliste*), an act that would dramatically change the constraints of their existence in the newly acquired part of the German *Reich*.

Eventually however, the invasion of the Soviet Union in June 1941, as well as the extension of Germany's military involvement in other areas of Europe (including Yugoslavia and Greece), induced changes in the "nationality policy." Germany needed cannon fodder, and the national categories were adjusted, allowing conscription even among those who had declined to sign the *Volksliste*. Thus the Poles who were permitted to remain in the annexed areas—mainly Christians—were classified as *Schutzangehörige des Deutschen Reiches* (subjects of the German state). They could only work at the lowest wages, had no rights of defense in courts, and those accused of anti-German activities were liable for the death penalty. The teaching of the Polish language was banned, as well as its use in religious ceremonies. (The Roman Catholic Mass at the time was said in Latin.)

The stringency of such laws varied from area to area, but was more relaxed in Silesia. Eventually all Jews were deported, either to the ghettoes established in all major cities of *Generalgouvernement* or to extermination camps. The non-Jewish population of the annexed areas became subject to conscription which provided the German army with some 300,000 reluctant soldiers, most of them used on the eastern front, where the traditionally anti-Russian Poles were less likely to desert to the enemy.

During the first two years of the occupation, Poland's morale and capability to resist were exposed to severe strains. The expected Allied offensive in the spring of 1940 turned into disaster with another German blitz across Norway, the Netherlands, Belgium, and France. The triumphant entry into Paris by the German army was a particular blow to francophile Poles, who had expected a miraculous victory of their French allies. Church bells throughout occupied Poland were ordered to toll for ten minutes while euphoric occupation troops fired their guns into the air. During the following year, other nations fell before the German onslaught. Perhaps the only consolation to the Poles was that Poland was not the only country flattened by the German war machine.

Frank's activities to turn occupied central Poland into a colony of Germany suffered a minor and basically meaningless temporary pause when Germany attacked the Soviet Union in 1941. There were some feeble efforts to convince the Poles of the "justice of the German cause" and even hints of a possible joint "anti-Bolshevik front." Basically all such moves were intended to secure peace in the areas adjacent to the front. After the lightninglike German successes which took the German armies to the gates of Moscow, all efforts at luring the Poles stopped. In any case the occupation authorities were unable to find a Polish quisling.

The continuation of the previously outlined German parameters for Poland was further underlined by Frank in a speech at Berlin University in November 1943, in which he said,

Generalgouvernement and Germany's activities on its territory are part of the centuries-old effort to take back the areas long ago settled by Germans. The Vistula territories belong to Germany and will remain German. The Polish problem does not exist any more.[11]

Frank continued to repeat this theme until the very end, even when German cities crumbled under Allied bombs and the front approached occupied Poland. According to his diary submitted at the trial of Nazi war criminals at Nuremberg, he envisaged several phases in Poland's transformation. During the first phase, the territory of the *Generalgouvernement* was to be "a reservation for the conquered Polish nation," subsequently becoming "a place of residence of the Polish population under the German administration," and finally "the first colonial territory of the German nation." Eventually the term "Poland" disappeared from all official correspondence and documents, replaced by *Generalgouvernement*, or *GG*. A series of postage stamps published by the occupation authorities displayed the portraits of various Germans—and Poles with Germanic names—describing them as *Kulturträger in Weichselraum*—the bearers of culture in the land of the Vistula.

Cracow, Poland's capital before the seventeenth century, was now Frank's capital. With its old royal castle perching on a hill, massive medieval bastions, ancient streets, and ninety churches, Cracow soon swarmed with Germans in a variety of uniforms. Many streets were given German names (with Polish names underneath but crossed out). The forward part of the city's blue-and-white streetcars bore signs *Nur für Deutsche* (for Germans only). Jews were ordered to take their hats off before every uniformed German. The best apartments inhabited by Jews were seized for an army of German civil servants. Cracow's Jews were gradually being "resettled" in a shabby part of the city across the Vistula, where a ghetto was soon established, surrounded by barbed wire and guarded mainly by blue-uniformed Jewish police with truncheons. Deportations to death camps started two years later.

But already in February 1940, SS *Oberführer* Richard Gluecks, head of the Concentration Camp Inspectorate, reported to Himmler that he had found a "suitable site" for a new "quarantine camp" a short distance from Cracow.[12] Work started immediately, and by June the camp was opened for Polish political prisoners, including members of the Catholic clergy. The nearest town near the camp was Oświęcim—called by the Germans Auschwitz, soon known as one of the most notorious extermination camps of the Nazi era and the graveyard for several million Jews from all countries of occupied Europe.

Terror on a massive scale in occupied Poland started December 26, 1939, when 107 innocent people were executed at Wawer for the wounding of a German soldier by a common criminal. From then on, in each town the occupation authorities held a number of hostages, who were to be shot at the average ratio of twenty Poles for one German. In the bureaucratic terminology, the system became known as "collective responsibility." The terror by the occupying power intensified in the latter stage of the war, when it became obvious that the Polish resistance was becoming increasingly active. In all police and administrative units of the GG, special teams were organized for tracking down and fighting the resistance movement. Periodically entire streets were blocked off as the men from the *Sonderdienst* (Special Service) conducted searches and arrests, rounding up suspects or even innocent people for deportation. Frequently mass executions were carried out in public places, particularly in Warsaw, with police and SS units rounding up passersby or streetcar passengers to watch them. In 1943 some 6,000 Poles were executed in this manner in Warsaw alone. Hans Frank clearly believed that terror was his best weapon against the Poles.

In February 1943 Germany suffered its worst defeat of the war—the surrender of Marshal Friedrich Paulus at Stalingrad after a long battle in which 60,000 Germans died and 91,000 marched into captivity on frostbitten feet. Only a few thousand survived that ordeal—no accurate figures are available. During the entire siege of the encircled troops by Russian armies, little was said by the German propaganda machine. The final German communiqué on February 3 was filled with Nazi pomposity:

True to its oath of allegiance, the Sixth Army under the exemplary leadership of Field Marshal Paulus has been annihilated by the overwhelming superiority of enemy numbers. . . . The sacrifice of the Sixth Army was not in vain. As the bulwark of our historic mission, it has held out against the onslaught of six Soviet armies. . . . They died so that Germany might live.[13]

A three-day period of mourning was declared throughout the Reich and occupied territories, with solemn music played on the radio but no flags flown at half mast. Occupied Poland celebrated with an exceptionally high consumption of alcohol (duly recorded by the police). In the German restaurant *Haus Krakau* in the center of Cracow, the few normally subdued and silent Polish clients who had illegally obtained coupons for the *Eintopfgericht* (a thick soup with potatoes and chunks of meat) exchanged knowing grins. The adjacent room was filled with young German soldiers en route home on leave from the *Ostfront*, who obviously ignored instructions about the mourning. They downed glasses of *schnapps* and then shuffled across the room sitting astride their chairs and bouncing like on horseback. They celebrated not being in Stalingrad.[14]

The campaign to recruit labor for Germany intensified toward the middle of 1940, with quotas assigned to regional administrations, towns, and villages. The introduction of work cards (*Arbeitskarten*) facilitated the issuing of individual summonses. Failure to report usually resulted in the arrest and deportation of entire families and even seizure of their property. That, too, was part of the policy of "collective responsibility." Needless to say many Poles found ways of avoiding slave labor, usually by obtaining fictitious *Arbeitskarten*. The fact that in August 1944 thousands of healthy young people turned up to fight in the Warsaw uprising proves that the occupation laws could be circumvented.

The conditions of those who were unable to avoid forced labor varied according to the place of work and, above all, of the employer. Poles assigned to work on farms were often adequately fed and treated without cruelty. The fate of those employed in factories was different. According to official instructions issued in 1942, "all workers should be fed and treated in a manner allowing their maximum exploitation at a minimum cost." There were also Poles who volunteered for work in Germany, lured by the promise of higher wages than those paid in Poland.

Inside the GG everything was being done to turn the area into a workshop for the German war industry. Reserves of raw materials, machinery, and other equipment were seized. Enterprises judged unnecessary were to be transported to Germany. The territory and frontiers of the GG were purposely designed to prevent any form of economic self-sufficiency. All major prewar industrial areas such as Silesia were annexed by the *Reich*. In addition to efforts to destroy whatever was left of Poland's economy, the occupation authorities fought a permanent battle against national tradition in all its forms. Thus the GG

was gradually becoming a giant camp of 16 million, governed by most rules applying to concentration camps, except for living in barracks. Terror, humiliation, destruction of cultural life and freedom dominated all Polish life in the *Generalgouvernement* until the last days of the occupation.[15]

The Soviet Union's plan for the territories seized by the Red Army was also intended to stifle Polish nationalism and identity but was handled differently. Unlike their German partners, the Russians did not present themselves as a "master race" and did not proclaim any intention of turning the Poles into slaves simply because all inhabitants of the Soviet Union were slaves. The initial activity of the repressive apparatus was aimed at stamping out the significant components of the prewar system: army officers, policemen, the clergy, judges, prominent members of political parties, the "bourgeoisie," and more prosperous farmers. With time other "enemies of the people" were added to the list. At the same time, the new authorities tried to exploit the already existing friction between the Poles and Ukrainians and to a lesser degree Byelorussians.

Already toward the end of September 1939, leaflets distributed by the Red Army called on workers and peasants to attack "land owners and capitalists responsible for the outbreak of an imperialist war." In October the first deportations took place. At the same time, the seized territory was divided into a Ukrainian part in the south and Byelorussian in the north and incorporated into the two neighboring Soviet republics.

From an economic point of view, the Soviet ruble was made equivalent to the Polish *złoty*, although the latter was worth four times more before the collapse of the Polish state. Such an exchange rate allowed Soviet military and civilian personnel to buy up most goods from well-stocked shops in major cities and towns. (Women's underwear was much in demand, bought in large quantities regardless of size and quality by Soviet officers.) All significant property was seized without compensation and all bank accounts over the paltry sum of 300 *złotys* were frozen.

After the eastern territories were annexed by the Soviet Union, all men became subject to military service. The first draft took place in 1940, and within a year some 150,000 Poles were shipped to army posts throughout the Soviet Union. Mass deportations of entire families followed. During 1940 and the first half of 1941, four waves of "resettlement" affected 1.2 million people, mostly Poles and some Ukrainians. Most transports were sent to the southern portions of Soviet Asian republics, particularly Kazakhstan. Depending on the origin or social status of those deported, they were either sent for "free resettlement" or to "reeducation labor camps." A different fate awaited army officers. More than 4,000 bodies in Polish army uniforms were subsequently discovered by the invading Germans in a mass grave near the Katyn forest west of Smolensk; the Nazi propaganda apparatus triumphantly gloated about the gruesome discovery.

Most Poles—in occupied Poland and in exile—believed the killers were Russians, especially as some 20,000 Polish officers captured by the Germans in 1939 continued to be held in prison camps in Germany and corresponded with their families. The mass graves of Katyn marred relations between Moscow and the Polish government-in-exile, with Western allies generally accepting the Soviet version that the atrocity was committed by the Nazis. British and American newspapers accused the Poles of acting as a Nazi propaganda tool and harming the war effort. At that time—spring of 1943—Poland's contribution to the war paled compared with the burden and losses of the Red Army. It wasn't until the collapse of communism in the early 1990s that Moscow admitted its responsibility for the massacres. (See Chapter 11.)

Unlike the Germans, the Soviets rarely published their intentions concerning the occupied country or its population. There were few official statements comparable to those of Hans Frank and other Nazi officials in charge of conquered Poland. But by the time Nazi Germany invaded the Soviet Union in June 1941, it was quite obvious that Moscow had planned to transplant most of the Polish population of what had become Soviet Ukraine and Byelorussia to the far regions of the Soviet Union. To Soviet dictator Joseph Stalin, it was mainly the question "of the availability of cattle wagons."

Some historians believe the Soviet system was more ruthless and more devastating than the Nazi one, with more than 16 million people perishing in gulags between 1929 and 1936. According to one authoritative view, the German police apparatus was not pervasive, and the *Gestapo's* efforts were not as effective as those of the *NKVD*, its Soviet counterpart. It is significant to note that the Polish Underground and its army eventually became the largest and perhaps most effective resistance organization in occupied Europe—but only in the area controlled by Germany. Despite efforts in 1940 and the beginning of 1941, the Poles appeared unable to organize an effective resistance group east of the San and Bug rivers. The *NKVD* worked in depth and methodically, building networks and recruiting informers in factories, schools, and offices. The *Gestapo* tracked down suspects, often liquidating them immediately, thus cutting off leads to other members of the organization. More significantly, "Soviet rhetoric did not assault Polish culture and was much less offensive generally. Goals fully as imperialistic as the German ones were camouflaged by high-sounding slogans and ideals."[16]

NOTES

1. Stanisław Kopański, *Moja Służba w Wojsku Polskim* (London: Veritas, 1965), pp. 266–306.

2. William L. Shirer, *The Rise and Fall of the Third Reich* (New York: Simon & Schuster, 1960), p. 839.

3. Ibid., p. 796.

4. *Polskie Siły Zbrojne* (London: General Sikorski Historical Institute, 1950), Vol. III p. 3.

5. Shirer, *The Rise and Fall of the Third Reich*, p. 836.

6. Ibid., p. 875.

7. Nuremberg Trials records, Volume VII, pp. 468–469.

8. Allen Paul, *Katyn, The Untold Story of Stalin's Polish Massacre* (New York: Charles Scribner's Sons, 1991), pp. 65–66.

9. *Polskie Siły Zbrojne*, Vol. III, p. 11.

10. Ibid., p. 12.

11. Author's translation.

12. Shirer, *The Rise and Fall of the Third Reich*, p. 878.

13. Antony Beevor, *Stalingrad* (London: Penguin Books, 1999), p. 399.

14. Author watched the scene.

15. *Polskie Siły Zbrojne*, Vol. III, p. 28.

16. Paul, *Katyn, The Untold Story of Stalin's Polish Massacre*, pp. 66–67.

CHAPTER 4

The Secret Army

Poland's partition between Nazi Germany and the Soviet Union was solidified by the creation of a strongly manned demarcation line. "Population transfers" between the two zones, authorized by the occupation authorities, were firmly controlled. Refugees who found themselves in eastern, Soviet-ruled Poland could thus apply for return to their original homes, a process mired in red tape and myriad difficulties which required time and a lot of patience. There were also cases—rare—of Polish Jews from the German-held areas being authorized to go east, ostensibly to "rejoin their families."

Crossing the daunting barrier of two rivers, the San and the Bug, which were patrolled day and night, turned out to be a difficult and highly dangerous task for the Polish conspirators, particularly in view of the gradual expansion of the underground movement and increasing controls on both sides. It soon became difficult to coordinate the activities of two underground networks in two separate territories from Warsaw. A round trip between Warsaw and Lwów (today's Ukrainian Lvov) often took a courier up to twelve days. Trains worked sporadically, and at least part of the trip was by horse-drawn peasant cart, bicycle, or even on foot. During the first phase of the conspiracy, there were no radio communication facilities. The Polish government-in-exile, at that time in France, tried to stay in touch with the Lwów command via networks set up in Hungary and Romania, both countries sympathetic to Poland.

Eventually it was decided to establish a separate command in Lwów and General Tokarzewski (Doktor), the official founder of the resistance, was dispatched to take over the eastern operation in March 1940. Shortly after crossing the border, he was arrested by the ubiquitous *NKVD* and shipped to Moscow's Lubyanka prison, where he survived until the signing of a Polish-Soviet military cooperation agreement which followed the German invasion of the Soviet Union in 1941. His quick interception and arrest confirmed the pervasive efficiency of the Soviet security apparatus, which in a number of cases turned out to be more efficient than that of the Germans.

The exiled government appointed Colonel Stefan Rowecki (subsequently promoted to general's rank) as temporary commander-in-chief of the growing organization in the German-controlled territories. Until his arrest by the *Gestapo* in 1943, Rowecki used a number of pseudonyms as part of the conspiracy's tactics. He had been known as "Kalina," "Rakon," "Jan," "Tur," and finally "Grot." It was under the last nom de guerre that he became best known to the rank-and-file of the underground. (For the sake of simplicity, he is referred to as Grot in the remainder of this book.)

At the same time, the "Service for Poland's Victory" became "Union for Armed Struggle" (*Związek Walki Zbrojnej–ZWZ*), maintaining all the principles and military aspects of the original organization. In formal directives to the resistance, the government in Angers, France, underlined that the ZWZ

is a component of the Armed Forces of the Polish Republic. All officers and other ranks of the Polish Army participating in the action of the ZWZ are regarded as continuing their front line military service. . . . All members of the ZWZ who have not previously served in the Polish Armed Forces can be promoted to officer's rank at the suggestion of the commander-in-chief.[1]

The text thus clearly confirmed the conspiracy as a purely military organization with military objectives—in line with the intentions of its founders.

At the age of forty-five, Grot was not new to conspiracy. As a youth, prior to World War I, he belonged to the clandestine Polish scout movement in the Russian-held part of Poland, and several times he crossed illegally to the Austrian area for quasi-military training in Józef Piłsudski's "Legions." In those days Russia was Poland's sworn enemy, and it was under the banner of war against Russia that Piłsudski took his *Legiony* to fight at the side of the Austro-German coalition in 1914.

In 1918, when Poland emerged again as a state, members of Piłsudski's Legions found themselves in a privileged position. The cadres of the new, "reborn" Polish Army consisted of officers who had started their careers in the armies of the former occupying powers: Russia, Austria, and Prussia, as well as from an army formed in France toward the end of the war. Following Piłsudski's seizure of power in 1926, the former members of his *Legiony* became virtually a ruling class and held an inordinate number of senior military posts. Grot advanced quickly, and by 1938, as a full colonel with a Higher Military Academy (*Wyższa Szkoła Wojenna*) diploma, he was deputy commander of an infantry division. He was the author of numerous articles in military publications—including one on urban warfare. War found him at the head of a newly organized motorized brigade, destroyed on September 17—the day Soviet forces crossed the Polish border. Having made his way to Warsaw, still smouldering after the siege, Grot became one of the few initial members of the underground military organization. Several months later he was its commander-in-chief—at a time when many Poles rightly or wrongly blamed Poland's quick collapse in 1939 on "Piłsudski's clan."

In May and June 1940, Poland's hopes for an Allied offensive in the west lay in tatters as France succumbed to the German military might. The Polish government-in-exile, still intent on continuing its struggle against Germany, was evacuated to Great Britain.

For the expanding underground movement, the implications of another disaster were obvious: although most Poles still believed in the final victory of their cause, no one expected a quick or easy end to the conflict. German power triumphed. Apathy began to set in and the number of volunteers for the ZWZ dwindled.

During its dispirited evacuation to yet another exile in Britain, the government succeeded in sending Grot hasty directives that were to govern his conduct in the immediate future.

You have full ZWZ powers in the whole country with the right of decision in the event of loss of contact with the government. . . . In view of the catastrophe of France, the government, loyal to its commitment and obligations and confident in the future, will continue the struggle in close cooperation with the British government. Until further orders, you are to avoid armed action except in cases necessary for the security of the organization. Work for long-term objectives, reduce the organization stressing its nature as that of cadres, strengthen selectivity and conspiracy in order to survive the bad period with a minimum of losses.[2]

The directives were signed in Libourne, France, on June 18, 1940, by Gen. Władysław Sikorski as commander-in-chief of Poland's Armed Forces. (He was also the prime minister.) Along with the government, evacuated to Britain by various means and often in chaotic conditions, were Polish units which had fought in France and in the Franco-British expedition to Narvik in Norway. In July 1940 the Polish forces on British territory consisted of 27,614 men, including 6,429 air force personnel and 1,505 sailors.[3]

The next message to Grot came from Britain, appointing him commander-in-chief of ZWZ forces in Poland and ordering the creation of a "ZWZ General Headquarters."

The morale of the Polish conspirators improved somewhat when it became clear that Great Britain would fight on and that there was no question of surrender. Of considerable comfort to the Poles was the news of the participation of Polish pilots in the Battle of Britain during the summer of 1940. (During the second half of 1940, Polish pilots flying either in purely Polish or mixed squadrons were credited with shooting down 203 German planes and damaging 36, or 11.7 percent of the *Luftwaffe*'s losses.[4])

While Britain was left alone to continue the war, the Polish underground was preoccupied with plans for its potential expansion, as well as with winning support from various political groupings and their militias. The ultimate objective was a general uprising against the occupying powers, but obviously the situation that followed the fall of France eliminated such a possibility in the then foreseeable future. Thus, while waiting for the "bad period" to be over, armed action was insignificant.

Meanwhile the headquarters of the ZWZ was considerably expanded, becoming a large apparatus, in effect combining the general staff and defense ministry of the embryonic underground army. It consisted of no fewer than thirty-one different departments and cells dealing with problems that included propaganda, training, supplies, coordination with clandestine political parties, and even projects concerning Poland's future air force and navy! On the basis of charts and documents giving details of the organization and revealed after the war, the command of the ZWZ was in the process of becoming a vast bureaucratic machine. With the benefit of hindsight, much of its work and preoccupation seems superfluous if not pointless. The whole intricate setup was also complicated by the necessary secrecy, changing codes and changing pseudonyms of its members.

One of the most essential branches of the expanded underground headquarters was known as the "Legalization Department." In its hands lay the production of documents for members of the conspiracy, ranging from identity cards (*Kennkarten*) to special passes for after-curfew hours or travel to the annexed zones. The department had its own printing presses and elaborate photography equipment, as well samples of such essential documents as birth, death, or marriage certificates. One of the early conspirators noted that

[o]ur men could thus move freely throughout the *Generalgouvernement* as well the *Reich*. We had a number of premises at our disposal where various documents

were prepared. Security was, on the whole, guaranteed. In case of raid and arrests, only a handful of people would be affected.[5]

The purely military side of the ZWZ was worked out pragmatically, with a maximum of simplicity. Given the nature of the underground army, the vigilance of the occupying powers, the degree of repression, and the permanent threat of arrest, the units had to be small, and contacts among the conspirators had to be limited. A platoon was designated as the basic tactical unit, consisting of between fifty and fifty-five men. Some platoons were "skeletal," to be expanded when necessary. In addition to such platoons regarded as the "infantry," there were special units dealing with signals and explosives, as well as women's auxiliary formations. From the beginning of 1943, larger units began functioning, mainly in the heavily wooded areas of the countryside. Later on a number of partisan "divisions" operated in several areas of Poland. According to one chronicler,

Normally, when the term "division" is used, it implies a mass of men with all necessary support units. During the period of conspiracy and subsequent transition to open struggle, the situation looked different. The strength of a division averaged three thousand men, in exceptional cases reached six thousand. Battalions, companies and platoons were usually far below numbers prescribed by regulations.[6]

Some partisan units had prewar Polish uniforms or uniforms fashioned by local tailors in towns and villages where the unit operated. Parts of German uniforms and particularly helmets were often used. Many partisans wore civilian clothes with a red-and-white armband as the only identifying sign. Shoes were the main problem, and in some cases, after a successful clash with the occupation troops, partisans removed German jackboots from corpses. Medical equipment was always in short supply.

Weapons remained a serious problem. The initial source was weapons buried or hidden by Polish units after the 1939 campaign. Another source was arms seized from the Germans, either in combat or in raids on storage depots. The big advantage of such weaponry was that ammunition could easily be found. In 1942 parachute drops from England to specific "reception zones" intensified. All told an estimated 600 tons of British weapons and equipment were dropped on occupied Poland, particularly in central areas.

Finally there were also weapons produced locally in underground workshops. Throughout the war such workshops produced 800 copies of the British Sten submachine gun, 800 of its Polish version known as

Błyskawica (lightning), 900 flame throwers, and about 150,000 pounds of explosives.[7]

The ZWZ became *Armia Krajowa* (*AK*) or Home Army in February 1942, and step by step various parallel paramilitary organizations were absorbed. They included the so-called "Peasant Battalions" (*Bataliony Chłopskie–BCH*) and several socialist militias, as well as the vast youth movement based on scout ideology known as the "Grey Ranks" (*Szare Szeregi*). The latter included boys and girls from age thirteen, as well as elite sabotage units known as "Assault Groups" (*Grupy Szturmowe–GS*), responsible for some of the most daring actions against Nazi targets and high officials.

There was open hostility between the *AK* and the communist "People's Army" (*Armia Ludowa–AL*) which *AK* command bluntly described as "clearly a foreign agency under Moscow's command under a mask of patriotism."[8] In areas where partisan units were in action, there were occasional clashes between *AK* and *AL* groups. The *AK* had an uneasy relationship with the extreme right-wing National Armed Forces (*Narodowe Siły Zbrojne–NSZ*), whose leadership opposed all those connected with Poland's prewar regime. Its members were recruited from among middle-class youths, particularly in Warsaw, and were known for their quasi-fascist views and anti-Semitism. However, by 1944, in areas where military activity took place, most *NSZ* partisan units operated either jointly with *AK* or under *AK* command. This was also the case during the Warsaw uprising.

The underground army loyal to the government-in-exile made a particular effort to influence the young, not only to "keep them off the streets" but also to keep up the spirit of patriotism and hostility against the enemy. Those aged between sixteen and eighteen formed the "Battle Schools" (*Bojowe Szkoły–BS*), and besides the usual scout and paramilitary training, their activities included distribution of the underground press, painting slogans on the walls to remind the population that "Poland fights on," delivering warnings to people about to be conscripted for compulsory work in Germany, and similar other activities labeled as "small sabotage." Several *BS* platoons took part as fighting units during the Warsaw uprising. At the beginning of 1944, the youth movement under the auspices of the *AK* had approximately 8,000 members. It frequently worked in conjunction with a vast system of "underground education," consisting of maintaining secondary and higher education, banned under the Nazi occupation. Such secret courses were usually held in groups of between six and ten pupils, and were known as *komplety*. In the Soviet-controlled zone, schools were open, but their curriculum was adjusted to the communist model.

To a great extent, all underground activities were simplified after the

German invasion of the Soviet Union in June 1941 and the lightninglike Nazi advance across the formerly eastern Polish territory. By the fall of 1941, Germany controlled all of eastern Poland, generally referred to as the *Ost* (east). The previously impregnable frontier cutting through Poland disappeared, but there were internal cordons between various regions requiring special passes. Still the *AK* command had easier access to the network in the eastern regions and, above all, had only one enemy to worry about—Nazi Germany. Difficulties with the Soviet Union were to emerge later. (See Chapter 11.)

The state of the underground army—that is, of the units loyal to the government-in-exile—generally reflected the political situation affecting the country's morale. Thus, following the fall of France, the number of platoons dropped from 2,190 to 1,466. The German invasion of the Soviet Union and the subsequent entry of the United States into the war saw a growth of between 500 to 900 platoons every six months. By the beginning of 1944, the *AK* was at the peak of its strength, particularly after the incorporation of several other underground "armies." According to official *AK* figures, its ranks consisted of some 350,000 sworn members, including 10,756 officers and 87,886 noncommissioned officers.[9]

A vast majority of conspirators lived at home and met regularly for training, awaiting action. Only partisan "divisions" waged a permanent full-scale war, usually causing reprisals by the occupying army in the towns and villages which served as their bases. There were also special "subversion" units credited with a number of attacks on carefully selected targets. These included the bombing of a German gambling casino in Warsaw, the blowing up of railway lines, the burning of two hangars filled with recently completed propellers for the *Luftwaffe*, the burning of fuel depots, and attacks on cafés reserved for German military personnel. Among senior Nazi officials "executed" by *AK* assault groups was Franz Kutschera, SS and police commander for the Warsaw district and organizer of public executions. He was shot down on a sunny spring morning in a quiet Warsaw street adjacent to the "police quarter" as he walked along with his wife who was wheeling a pram with a newborn baby. All such actions—including executions of Polish collaborators, police informers, or postal workers who stole packages destined for concentration camp prisoners—were usually sanctioned by formal verdicts in underground courts.

Prior to June 22, 1941, the *AK* command considered the Soviet regime to be another occupying power. However, there are few records indicating how the underground intended to cope with a Soviet presence in approximately one-third of Polish territory. The official view, sanctioned by the government-in-exile and automatically approved by the *AK* leadership, was that

By signing a non-aggression treaty with Germany in August 1939, Soviet Russia willingly helped Germany to start the war. The Russians entered the territory of the [Polish] Republic and annexed half [sic] of Poland under a false political pretext. As far as the war fought between the Allies and Germany was concerned, Soviet Russia opted for a form of neutrality favoring Germany, facilitating its [Germany's] spreading of the war across all of Europe. Russia scrupulously carried out its obligations toward Germany, supplying it with raw materials and agricultural products and, above all, with oil. From the beginning of the war, Soviet Russia's policy toward Poland was that of conquest in total harmony and agreement with Germany.... After the German attack, which forced Russia to enter into the war earlier than expected, Russia found itself on the same side as Poland. Such a situation led Russia to the establishment of diplomatic relations with a country which she helped erase from the map of Europe. Nonetheless the basic attitude of Russia toward Poland remained unchanged. Annexation was still the objective.[10]

In evaluating the feeble prospects of a major uprising against Germany involved in a war on the eastern front, the leadership of the *AK* (at the time still ZWZ) appeared to have been impressed by the outcome of the Soviet Union's disastrous war against Finland. It analyzed the situation in the following terms:

The possibility that the Bolsheviks will be successful in the war against Germany should not be excluded, although it seems unlikely. If they [Russians] succeed in pushing the Germans out of Poland, it would be sheer folly to oppose an adversary capable of defeating the German army. In such a case our role should be to maintain the whole apparatus in conspiracy, to await a moment when the Soviet state and system, in turn, start crumbling.[11]

All plans drafted for an insurrection against the German occupation forces stressed the necessity of outside help, mainly in the form of the participation of the Polish Air Force units from Britain and, subsequently, of their parachute brigade and other combat units. The reports to London bluntly spelled out that, considering the state of its weaponry, the underground army alone would be incapable of capturing the most important German military objectives. The *AK* command made various suggestions about seizing major airfields and establishing bases to which supplies and reinforcements could be flown from Britain. The rapid advance of the German forces deep into the Soviet Union made all such plans irrelevant.

Despite the traditional animosity between Poland and Russia, one day after the German invasion General Sikorski, prime minister of the government-in-exile and commander-in-chief of the Polish Armed Forces, made a radio address from London aimed at Poland. The gist of it was that Russia should be welcomed to the common struggle against

Nazi Germany and that the Poles were willing to put aside the past. He also appealed to Moscow to release Polish prisoners and deportees and renounce the treaties with Germany which had resulted in Poland's partition.

After a prolonged exchange of messages and considerable British pressure, an agreement was signed on July 30, 1941, despite the fact that Moscow ignored some key Polish demands. Three of Sikorski's ministers resigned in protest. In another radio appeal to Poland, Sikorski said the agreement "enables us to form Polish military units from prisoners of war now languishing somewhere in Russia and longing to fight for Poland." It became ominously clear to the Poles in exile as well as in Poland that the war which started in September 1939 was no longer a fight to keep Poland's integrity but to defeat Hitler. And Russia, Poland's historic enemy, was going to play a major role in it. (See Chapter 11.)

The agreement with the Soviet Union and the beginning of the gradual release of Polish prisoners in Russia elicited a series of messages between the Polish General Staff in London and the *AK* headquarters. A typical example was a message from General Tadeusz Klimecki, Polish chief of staff, to Grot, in which he wrote,

Despite the treaty [with the Soviet Union], in the event of Germany's defeat it is impossible to be certain of Russia's attitude toward Poland. There is a possibility that, when the country [Poland] begins armed action against Germany, the Red Army entering Polish territory without agreement by the Polish government will create a *fait accompli*. The commander in-chief [Sikorski] feels that in such a case the entry of the Red Army must be considered as a hostile act and meet with armed resistance on our part. . . . In the event of a lack of further instructions, your actions should depend on the attitude of Soviet troops toward the [Underground] civilian and military authorities existing in the country.[12]

Thus the Polish government-in-exile, which regarded itself as the legal successor of the prewar regime, anticipated the worst from the new Soviet allies. Although the subsequent events proved it to be correct, at the time such an attitude created myriad difficulties. (See Chapter 11.) In any case it was hard to imagine how anyone could possibly consider a situation in which the winning Red Army would be adequately opposed by ill-equipped Polish resistance units, formed to fight the Germans. The very idea that the Soviet Union should seek the "agreement" of Polish exiles for its offensive against a crumbling Germany is simply unbelievable, particularly as Moscow considered the territories east of the so-called Curzon Line (the San and the Bug rivers) as its own.

The Soviet victory in the battle of Stalingrad in February 1943 turned the tide of the war, with a mass of men and materiel gradually pushing the German armies westward—toward Poland. At the same time, the

Polish underground continued to expand and organize partisan units in the territories that the Soviet Union had annexed as a result of its treaty with Germany. While continuing resistance against Nazi rule and waiting to be liberated, the Poles looked to the future with considerable foreboding. Many hoped that the two enemies would "bleed each other to death"—with Poland as the beneficiary.

Meanwhile, however, other events turned 1943 into a year of death and political disaster for Poland and the Poles.

On April 13 Berlin radio announced the gruesome discovery by the Germans of "thousands of officers of the former Polish Army, interned in the USSR and bestially murdered by the Bolsheviks." The massacre at Katyn, west of Smolensk, and Polish suspicions that for once the Nazi propaganda machine was right led to the break off of diplomatic relations between Moscow and the London-based government-in-exile. It caused unprecedented tension within the Allied coalition and a debate filled with fear, bitterness, and recrimination which continued until 1990, when Soviet President Mikhail S. Gorbachev admitted Moscow's guilt. (See Chapter 11.)

On April 19, when SS *Brigadeführer* and Police General Juergen Stroop decided to "finish" the dying remnants of the Warsaw ghetto, units of the Jewish Fighting Organization (*Żydowska Organizacja Bojowa–ŻOB*) attacked the unsuspecting Germans in what turned out to be a monthlong suicidal uprising. There was no other choice. According to William L. Shirer, who minutely recorded Nazi misdeeds, it was "the first time and the last in the history of the Third Reich that the Jews resisted their Nazi oppressors with arms."[13] (It should be noted, however, that in the subsequent Warsaw uprising in 1944, there were at least two *ŻOB* units fighting alongside the *AK* under its command.) The help offered the Jewish fighters by the *AK* in 1943 was minimal. Because the Russian front was still far away, the *AK* command saw no prospects for the ghetto's survival and did not want to prematurely compromise its network. Some 150 members of the *ŻOB* were led to safety through the sewers by special resistance units. No one suspected that sixteen months later the rest of Warsaw would meet a similar fate. (See Chapter 5.)

Although the city was terrorized by large-scale roundups of the civilian population for slave labor in Germany and public executions, General Grot continued directing the stubborn—and growing—underground army. He had "ironclad" documents masterfully prepared by the "Legalization Department" of his headquarters and several "safe" apartments at his disposal. The most elaborate, prepared virtually for every eventuality, was in a drab building at Twarda Street 36, where *AK* carpenters and electricians linked three apartments into a veritable fortress with several exits in different directions. Its center was a fortified room overlooking an intersection, its entrances camouflaged by electrically controlled, book-lined artificial walls. It contained a fourteen-day stock of food for six persons and an arsenal consisting of two heavy machine guns, ten Sten submachine guns, two antitank Piat launchers, and 100 hand grenades.[14]

On June 30, 1943, prior to a scheduled conference of the *AK* leadership, Grot stopped to pick up some documents at Spiska Street 14 in the city center where the *AK* had a special "mailbox" in the apartment no. 10. He still had half an hour before the meeting which was to take place in a location that was a five-minute walk from there. In order to reduce the risk (he never used bodyguards), Grot decided to wait at the Spiska street address before starting to walk.

But shortly before leaving he heard the noise of automobile engines and, peering through a window, he saw helmeted German troops disembark from trucks and run in all directions. At the same time, several uniformed *Gestapo* men, accompanied by a civilian, entered the building. Minutes later the building's caretaker rushed from apartment to apartment, repeating the *Gestapo* order that all men, women, and children, regardless whether old or sick, had to come down to the courtyard and line up in two rows.

Grot's documents carried the name of Jan Sokołowski, an employee of the city hall, and had been stamped by the German security authorities. This false identity had successfully passed the test of a number of random inspections by street patrols.

In the courtyard, the *Gestapo* separated men from women and children and then headed straight for Grot. Speaking in Polish, one of them said, "You are the commander-in-chief of the *Armia Krajowa*. Your pseudonym is Grot. Your name is Stefan Rowecki and you have the rank of general. Your identity card is of no interest to us. It is false." The *Gestapo* official then showed Grot his prewar photograph in a colonel's uniform. Those who assisted at the scene say Grot merely nodded. He was handcuffed and led to a car waiting outside where an estimated one hundred *SS* troops had deployed at both ends of the street. Machine guns were in position on adjacent roofs. The occupation authorities had scored their most important victory against the Polish Underground. They had the man who knew all the secrets of the "underground state" and of its army.[15]

The arrested general was taken to the *Gestapo* heaquarters and shortly afterward to Okęcie airport where he was put on a special plane that took him straight to Berlin. The Germans did not want to risk any attempt by the Underground to rescue its commander.

According to some accounts, in Berlin Grot was approached by the Germans to cooperate in forming a joint Polish-German "anti-Bolshevik front." They apparently thought that a man of his authority could rally the Poles against the Soviet Union, particularly after the discovery of the

Katyn graves. Nothing is known about the nature of the interrogation to which he was submitted. From Berlin he was sent to the nearby Sachsenhausen concentration camp, where he was treated as a "special prisoner." He wrote several letters to his family—delivered by the *Gestapo* and obviously censored. He complained of poor health and asked for the liver deficiency medicine he had used before his arrest. The last indication that he was alive was a letter in the spring of 1944. (See Chapter 8.)

In Warsaw, the *Gestapo*, the police, and the SS triumphed, celebrating their victory with a massive consumption of alcohol. For the first time inebriated SS men and police officers were seen in the streets. Medals were showered on members of the security apparatus. The degree of self-satisfaction was such that the *Gestapo* neglected to search the "safe apartment" where Grot waited before his arrest. Profiting from such an unprecedented mistake, the resistance quickly withdrew all documents held there in a safe camouflaged in a sculptured Christ's head and never returned to the Spiska Street address again. Although the underground was prepared for a series of arrests following Grot's interrogation and took the necessary precautions, nothing of the sort happened. (Postwar revelations in then communist-ruled Poland blamed Grot's arrest on three traitors—two men and a woman.)

Within days of the arrest, *Biuletyn Informacyjny*, the official organ of the *AK*, printed on clandestine presses, in a small format on wafer-thin paper, the announcement of the appointment of "General Bór" as Grot's successor. The announcement was accompanied by a brief "order of the day" in which Bór pledged to continue the struggle "until final victory."[16]

During his activity in the resistance, Tadeusz Komorowski (Bór) also used the pseudonyms "Znicz" and "Lawina," the latter in radio communications with London. Born in 1895, he was a career officer in the Austro-Hungarian cavalry between 1913 and 1918, when he joined the newly reestablished Polish Army. Winner of numerous Polish equestrian competitions, in 1924 he took part in the Paris Olympics, and in 1936 he became director of the Polish saddle-horse team at the Berlin Olympics. Before World War II, he commanded the 9th Lancer Regiment and in 1938 the Cavalry Training Center. During the 1939 campaign, he was in charge of a reserve cavalry group. He managed to avoid captivity and joined the conspiracy in 1940, becoming the regional commander in Cracow and deputy commander-in-chief of the *AK* in 1941. Poland, and almost all those under Bór's command, learned his real name when the capitulation act of Warsaw's city center, the last bastion of the 1944 uprising, was announced on October 3, 1944. The German command already had that information. (A wounded *AK* lieutenant, lying next to the author in a gutted building in Mokotów on September 28 pending transport to a prisoner-of-war camp, said that during his interrogation by the Germans he had been told Bór's name with the quip, "Congratulations, you were commanded by a count and Olympic champion.")

Bór took over the *AK*'s command at a particularly difficult time, when the organization debated what attitude to take toward the approaching Red Army and the difficult relationship between the government-in-exile and Moscow. Several senior *AK* officers, including Colonel Stanisław Tatar and Lieutenant Colonel Jerzy Kirchmayer, recommended establishing contacts with the Soviets and a "more pragmatic attitude," even at the cost of Polish concessions. According to a postwar analysis published in London, such views were not shared by many members of headquarters.[17]

On July 4 1943, four days after Grot's arrest, Poland suffered another shock: the plane carrying General Władysław Sikorski, prime minister of the government-in-exile and commander-in-chief of all Polish forces abroad and in Poland, crashed on takeoff at Gibraltar, killing Sikorski and the other passengers. Only the Czech pilot, Edward Prchal, survived. Although official investigation established the crash to be an accident, all kinds of suppositions followed for years. Sikorski had been opposed by a number of Polish officers in the Middle East who felt that he was too conciliatory toward the Soviet Union. The Allies were annoyed with him for pressing for an international investigation of the Katyn massacre; it was more convenient to blame the massacre on the Nazis. Nazi propaganda claimed that the Royal Air Force had orders to shoot the plane down and called Sikorski "the last victim of Katyn." Yet British Prime Minister Winston Churchill told Sikorski's successor, Stanisław Mikołajczyk, "I loved that man. He was truly one of the great statesmen of this war."[18]

One thing was certain after Sikorski's untimely death: the stature of the Polish government-in-exile was virtually doomed and so were hopes for any form of agreement between the exiles and the Soviet Union. (See Chapter 11.) As far as the *AK* headquarters was concerned, resistance to the Nazi occupation would continue and plans were made to intensify it.

NOTES

1. Author's translation of the official text.
2. Ibid.
3. Zygmunt Bielecki, *Wojsko Polskie 1939–1945* (Warsaw: Interpress, 1984), p. 33.
4. Ibid., p. 35.
5. Emil Kumor, *Wycinek z Historii Jednego Życia* (Warsaw: Pax, 1969), p. 77.
6. T. Kryska-Karski, *Piechota 1939–1945* (London: Polish Institute, 1974), p. 23.

7. Figures cited in a Radio Free Europe broadcast, October 14, 1965.

8. *Polskie Siły Zbrojne* (London: General Sikorski Historical Institute, 1950), Vol. III, p. 119.

9. Organizational Report by *AK* command, no. 6874/44.

10. *AK* records at the Sikorski Institute, London. Author's translation.

11. Ibid.

12. Author's translation of message no. 3853 of November 20, 1941.

13. William L. Shirer, *The Rise and Fall of the Third Reich* (New York: Simon & Schuster, 1960), p. 1270.

14. Kumor, *Wycinek z Historii Jednego Życia*, p. 90.

15. The account of Grot's arrest is based on a number of reports published in Polish, by the Underground during the occupation, and after the war.

16. The author, then fourteen, helped distribute the *AK*'s underground publications.

17. *Polskie Siły Zbrojne*, Vol. III, p. 551.

18. Allen Paul, *KATYN: The Untold Story of Stalin's Polish Massacre* (New York: Charles Scribner's Sons, 1991), p. 238.

CHAPTER 5

Death of the Warsaw Ghetto

The flames leaped high above the twelve-foot wall covered with broken glass, and firemen in gleaming helmets were called to the scene. But when they aimed their hoses at the burning buildings across the wall, an SS officer waving a pistol shouted at them to stop wasting water. They were there not to extinguish the burning Jewish part of city but to prevent the flames from spreading to the "Aryan" side of Warsaw. Nearby factories produced uniforms and spare parts for German army vehicles. The firemen stood there, useless and helpless, together with a crowd of silent Polish onlookers, numb with horror and fear. Several women wept. Then Lithuanian police in black uniforms arrived and told the crowd to move on.[1]

The Warsaw ghetto was burning, covered with black smoke like a funereal shroud. Somewhere in the middle of houses ignited by German flamethrowers, the last survivors of Warsaw's Jewry desperately fired their remaining bullets and threw their last hand grenades "to save as much honor as they could."[2] There was no help from anyone, and the only hope was escape through the sewers. Only a handful succeeded.

April 1943 was unseasonably sunny and bright. But it was not because of the weather that SS *Brigadeführer* and Police General Juergen Stroop decided to "complete the resettlement" of the last inhabitants of the ghetto. Three months earlier, in January 1943, his boss, Heinrich Himmler, visited Warsaw and was surprised that so many "subhumans" were still alive. He ordered Stroop to act by February 15—not necessarily by burning the ghetto, created on November 15, 1940, but by shipping its remaining population, estimated at 60,000, straight to extermination camps. The German defeat at Stalingrad (see Chapter 3) and the need for trains and other means of transport by the command of the Eastern Front, under heavy Soviet pressure, had delayed Stroop's plans. Stroop's task was further complicated by an armed attack by Jewish fighters on a German column inside the ghetto toward the end of January. It signaled a new dimension of the problem, until then based on the premise that "Jews don't fight."

Because of the possibility of "some obstruction" in the "resettlement action," Stroop had had enough authority given to him by Himmler to decide on the ghetto's total destruction. In a way his decision was a prelude to what happened to the rest of the Polish capital sixteen months later.

Stroop assembled a force of some 2,000 men, about half of them either *Waffen SS* or *Wehrmacht*, the rest consisting of paramilitary police and a unit of Lithuanian auxiliaries. The Polish police were ordered to watch all points through which the besieged were likely to flee.

The small extermination army entered the ghetto at dawn of April 19, expecting to round up the people for the *Umschlagplatz* (distribution center) and then for further transport. Instead the army was unexpectedly showered by hand grenades, incendiary bottles, and gunfire. The German reaction was of incredulity. In Stroop's mind it was inconceivable that the Jews would oppose his "resettlement action," initially planned to last three days. The fighting was to last for four weeks.

On April 20 a brief message from the Polish underground radio station *Świt* (dawn) informed the government-in-exile in London that the ghetto was fighting. "We can hear shots and explosions of grenades. The Germans are using tanks and armored cars. They have suffered losses." The Polish exiles immediately informed the British authorities. But according to Zofia Korbońska, the woman who handled *Świt*'s traffic and encoded its messages, "the British didn't believe us. They thought that it was exaggerated anti-German propaganda, presumably to get the Western allies more interested in Poland."[3] The report on the ghetto fighting coincided with the discovery of the mass grave of Polish officers at Katyn which the Germans blamed on the Russians. Polish demands for international investigation of the massacre had annoyed the Western Allies, who at that time had had enough of Poland's problems.

Eventually, however, London became convinced that the ghetto was indeed burning, and that the last of Warsaw's Jews had been condemned to death. "We suggested ways of helping or at least delaying this mass execution," Mrs. Korbońska said. "We proposed that the Allies bomb railway lines over which Jews were transported to death camps, that they

attack the barracks of troops used to liquidate the ghetto. All this I encoded myself."

The answer came as the smoke of the burning ghetto was spreading
over the rest of Warsaw. "They [London] told us they had other priorities
and that their main job was to win the war," Mrs. Korbońska said.[4]

The ghetto under attack on April 19 was all that remained after suc-
cessive deportations of most of its inhabitants to extermination camps.
After two massive forced expulsions known as *aktsias*, mainly to the Treblinka death camp, the area initially allotted to the ghetto had shrunk,
measuring about 1,000 by 300 or so yards. Initially, when Warsaw's Jews
and others brought from various occupied countries were put in the
walled-in area, the ghetto stretched from the edge of the Old Town (*Stare
Miasto*) to the western suburb where the Jewish and Christian cemeteries
lay side by side. According to one chronicler, "The ghetto was established in stages. They took Jews out of the streets where they lived in
Warsaw and moved them to special streets; the liquidation was carried
out afterwards."[5] In 1940,

Jewish Warsaw was swollen by many uprooted people who were simply dying,
even before Treblinka. . . . Families lived by selling their goods in the market until
they ran out of things. Then they died. . . . There were about half a million Jews
in Warsaw at that time. Many died of typhus and other diseases, and from hunger.[6]

The decision on the "final solution"—or the elimination of European
Jewry—was made by Hitler himself and relayed to the lower echelons
via such trusted lieutenants as Himmler, Hermann Goering, and Reinhard Heydrich. The latter, in charge of an organization known as
the *Reich* Security Main Office, was assassinated in Czechoslovakia in
May 1942 as the Czech Underground's punishment for the destruction
of the town of Lidice. The mass deportation of Jews to death camps,
which started in 1942, was codenamed "Operation Reinhard" in his
honor.

Tormented by the loss of morale after the fall of France in 1940 and
then by a sudden upsurge of hope after the German attack on Russia
which soon evaporated, most Jews in Poland simply did not believe that
they were under a death sentence. According to Yitzhak Zuckerman, one
of the founders of the Jewish Fighting Organization (*Żydowska Organizacja Bojowa–ŻOB*) in Warsaw, "We read in *Mein Kampf* that Hitler would
destroy the Jews. But we didn't take it seriously. We saw it as rhetoric,
not as expression of something he would carry out."[7]

The official history of the Polish underground *Armia Krajowa (AK)*,
prepared in London after the war, describes the attitude of Jews at the
beginning of the war as that of caution. In Poland, Jews "adjusted their

behavior to the actions of the occupant. In the areas occupied by Germany, cut off from the outside world by the walls of ghettoes, they began organizing self-defense only when the terror took its most drastic form."[8]

The center of the ghetto was the old Jewish quarter, inhabited mainly by the working class. According to a Polish writer,

It was the most vibrant of all of Warsaw's quarters, an area of small trade and cottage industry of countless Jewish families. . . . What movement, what driving force, what contrasts! Each house literally covered by signboards, every courtyard surrounded by annexes filled with people working from dawn to dusk. Next to firms dealing in millions, there are miserable shops selling goods worth pennies.[9]

According to prewar Polish statistics, Warsaw's Jewish population was 352,200.

Arnold Zable, a writer who nurtured the memories of those days, describes

a maze of courtyards and neighborhoods, of self-contained kingdoms of stone-clad tenements teeming with feverish activity. . . . The cries of newborn babies mingled with the relentless clatter and chatter of commerce." In another area, near the Vistula, "Pedestrians chewed bagels on the run. Bearded Hasidim hurried to and from prayer averting their eyes from the temptations of modernity; and the sons and daughters of wealthy bankers and financiers flocked to the Bar Central nightclub to hear Rosenbaum's jazz band play music of the New World.[10]

The first Jews arrived in Poland in the fifteenth century, at the invitation of King Kazimierz III or Kazimierz Wielki (Casimir the Great in Western texts). The king left behind him a legacy of improved administration and codification of the law, as well as better relations with Lithuania, Hesse, Silesia, Brandenburg, and the Holy Roman Empire. He also fought successfully against Russia, the Teutonic Knights, and the Bohemians. The Jews were fleeing Spain's Holy Inquisition, and Kazimierz saw in them a valued factor in expanding the country's commerce, trade, and cottage industry.

Gradually Jews from other countries flocked to Poland where they lived apart but were able to freely practice their religion. Throughout the following centuries, large Jewish communities were established in most towns of central and eastern Poland. They were generally Orthodox, were considered "Jews" rather then Poles. There was no assimilation nor intermarriage with Catholics, until late in the nineteenth century. The dominant Roman Catholic Church generally looked askance at the growing Jewish community and frequently urged their conversion. Historians trace Polish anti-Semitism to the difference in the religion, dress, and mores of the Jews who were considered a nation apart. Unlike czarist Russia, where Jews were banned from certain areas, there were no regions of Poland where they could not settle. There was open hostility toward Jews in Poland's Ukrainian regions, where the favorite slogan of Ukrainian nationalists was "Death to Poles and Jews."

The assimilation of some Jews began in the latter part of the nineteenth century, with Jewish intelligentsia increasingly speaking Polish rather then Yiddish. The rebirth of Poland in 1918 after more than a hundred years of partitions by Russia, Germany, and Austria accentuated this trend. The independent and predominantly Roman Catholic Poland guaranteed Jews freedom of religion and equal status, but there was frequent discrimination, particularly on the level of regional and municipal administration. In Warsaw, where out of every 100 professionally active people fifty-four were Jewish and where Jews constituted 29 percent of the population, the Jewish parties in the elected advisory body of the city council (samorząd) had nineteen out of 100 seats. (Out of the 305,000 votes cast in the last election in 1938, 44,000 voted for *BUND*, or General Jewish Workers' Union, which received sixteen seats, and 28,000 for the Jewish "middle class party," alotted three seats.[11])

The number of conversions to Catholicism increased, particularly among educated and "assimilated" Jews, who apparently felt that a change of religion would help their professional or social advancement. Like all Polish citizens, Jews were subject to compulsory military service. Men with secondary education certificates had the right to enter training courses for reserve officers, thus shortening the usual two-year period of service. Jews with medical degrees were in particular demand by the army.

The growth of Zionism found many adherents among Polish Jews and was exploited by the extreme right wing with demonstrations and slogans such as "Jews to Palestine." The threat posed to Jews by Nazi Germany brought a number of German Jews to Poland, but, at the same time, Nazi propaganda helped fuel the anti-Semitism of the Polish extreme right. (The government tried to combat it with such slogans as "We are all of the same blood.") In official Polish statistics, Jews were listed as a minority, along with Ukrainians and Byelorussians. In popular parlance, they were always referred to as Jews or "Polish Jews," rarely as Poles. Although there were many Jews among Polish writers, poets, and artists, few Jews participated in Polish political life, turning to their own, specifically Jewish parties with varying ideologies.

Between the two world wars Poland was pulsating with Jewish cultural, intellectual, and political life, and Warsaw was its center. It was in the Polish capital that intense debate on the future of Judaism and the degree of its assimilation went on, confronting various political and religious tendencies. In passionate discussions, proponents of Zionism and emigration of Palestine argued against "assimilationists" who believed that their future was in Poland.

Theater groups played to full houses every night; provincial circuses pitched their tents in vacant lots; and news vendors sold Yiddish dailies, Hebrew periodicals, Polish tabloids and cheap paperback romances. Circles of aspiring artists and writers gathered in cafes. . . . Warsaw was the vortex that absorbed the creative energies of a people who had honed their survival skills on the piercing edges of wildly fluctuating fortunes and centuries of impending disaster. And in the final years of [the] 1930s it stood poised, a community of 350,000 Jews, teetering on the brink of annihilation.[12]

The ghetto created by the German occupation authorities was never hermetically sealed. There were always ways to get in and out: through the sewers; with special passes for the few who worked outside the ghetto; contacts with the Polish underground; or by bribing the guards. There were breaches in the wall—unknown to the Germans—either through houses that abutted it or through cellars under the wall. According to Zuckerman, after the first mass deportations, "Jews started leaving in every possible way; they looked for Polish friends or for apartments. . . . Some had money, others had friends. . . . But there was danger from Polish blackmailers lurking on the other side."[13] Zuckerman, who survived the war and the slaughter of the Jews largely due to what he described as his "Aryan looks," writes,

Some Poles are humanitarians, with a special nobility and those are the ones who saved Jews during the war. I should point out that even some of the *Endeks* [Polish fascists] saved Jews. Even though they wanted to see the Jews out of Poland, they could not tolerate the horrors of the German solution.[14]

Offering any form of succor to a Jew was punished by death. Zuckerman estimates that there were 20,000 Jews hiding outside the ghetto in Warsaw until the 1944 uprising and that at least 40,000 Poles were involved in saving them. "And this stood out against a strong and deep-rooted anti-Semitism in the Polish people."[15] In October 1942 Jan Karski, a member of the *AK*, was given a tour of the ghetto from which he emerged shattered. His report to the government-in-exile in London was ignored by the Allies.

Although almost until the end the telephone between the ghetto and the rest of the city functioned, the Jewish conspirators decided to use it rarely. They generally relied on couriers, mostly women, because men were more vulnerable. (When arrested or even stopped for identification outside the ghetto walls, men were often asked to lower their pants to see if they were circumcised.) Having "Aryan looks," as one of the survivors pointed out, was "worth a fortune." When placing agents outside the wall to prepare apartments, arrange for shipments of weapons, and false documents, the organization always looked for preferably blond men and women.

The Jewish Fighting Organization (ŻOB) was founded on July 28, 1942, by Zionists but served as an umbrella for all Jews who wanted to resist. Thus, in the end it included members of seven main Jewish parties, often ideologically opposed, active in Poland. Its commander was twenty-four-year-old Mordechai Anielewicz, with Yitzhak Zuckerman, at the time twenty-seven, as his deputy. The organization had to cope with the *Judenrat* (Jewish Council), the German-sanctioned administration of the ghetto which always urged caution, and with the population which opposed armed attacks on Germans, fearing reprisals. The role of the *Judenrat* was hard to imagine: among its tasks was supplying people for deportation to death camps. The pressure was such that Adam Czerniaków, president of the *Judenrat*, committed suicide on July 23, 1942, shortly after the first mass deportations started. To many inhabitants of the ghetto, his death was a clear signal that there was no hope left.

The newly created ŻOB also had to confront the Jewish police, a force of some 3,000 men armed only with batons created by the occupation authorities. "There were different kinds of policemen, more brutal ones and less brutal ones. . . . In general, this was a period of human degradation and moral decline. . . . It was the Jewish policemen who caught and took out the masses of Jews."[16]

Nearly sixty years after the ghetto's destruction, it is hard to imagine the feelings of its last defenders, initially some 500 men and women who were members of twenty-two combat groups formed under the umbrella of the ŻOB. Flamethrowers were used, grenades were thrown by the Germans into sewer manholes, and men, women, and children were shot as they were dragged out from house after house. Couriers still traveled between the doomed quarter and the "Aryan" part of the city. The fighters were influenced and inflamed by their first action against the Germans in January. Referring to the period which followed, but before the uprising, Yitzhak Zuckerman writes,

The January Uprising gave us wings, elevated us in the eyes of the Jews, and enhanced our image as fighters, giving us a good name. . . . So many legends were going around that the Polish press, not only in the ghetto, told of our tanks. The January events had extraordinary repercussions even in the *Armia Krajowa* *(AK)*, which had always eschewed us and now agreed to give us 50 pistols immediately (in reality we got 49). They also supplied us with grenades and the explosives we needed.[17]

The official *AK* version of that period is that

Armia Krajowa stayed in contact with the ŻOB and, at the time of its armed action, offered help, delivering to the ghetto a certain amount of weapons and ammunition. At the same time *AK* units attempted to break from outside the German ring surrounding the ghetto to facilitate a breakthrough. Despite the horror of the fate of the Jews, the country's general situation did not allow a premature uprising in their defense.[18]

The command of the ŻOB learned of Stroop's plan to exterminate the ghetto's remaining population on the eve of the planned operation. Zuckerman, the deputy commander, happened to be outside the ghetto's walls on one of his missions to solidify contacts with the Polish Underground and obtain more weapons. He talked with both the mainstream *AK* and the small communist *Armia Ludowa (AL)*. (In his memoirs he admits sympathy for the communists.) His contacts with the communists were criticized by some aides to General Grot, the *AK's* commander-in-chief. The *AK* was also critical of the executions of Jewish policemen and traitors by the ŻOB, claiming that it supplied costly weapons to "fight the Germans and not Jews." The main *AK* organization dealing with the ghetto was the Polish Council for Aid to the Jews, codenamed ŻEGOTA, established late in 1942. ŻEGOTA was also in charge of rescuing those who could leave the ghetto and of finding hiding places. Its surviving members received Israeli decorations.

From the beginning, the *AK* headquarters did not believe in the success of the Jewish uprising. The best the *AK* could offer was to take the fighters out of the ghetto and somehow transport them to nearby forests where they could form guerrilla units. And that, according to the *AK*, required time. Apparently the Polish Underground had no information about Stroop's plan and was surprised when gunfire swept the ghetto on April 19, and the Jewish fighters hoisted a Polish flag on the infamous wall near Krasinski Square.

It was obvious that the *AK* did not want to part with its arsenal, which the 1944 uprising demonstrated to be pathetically paltry. The *AK* had enthusiastic members but weapons were always in short supply. (Beginning in 1943 purchases from German soldiers increased considerably. A Polish historian notes that during that year the organization purchased in this manner 881 pistols, 18 submachine guns, 424 rifles, 13 light machine guns, and 9 heavy machine guns.[19] A rifle cost the equivalent of $20 but the average price of a pistol, a weapon easier to handle in conspiratorial conditions, was $35.)

Zuckerman, who watched the ghetto burn from the outside, writes that he appealed to the *AK* for help several times but was unable to meet its commander, General Grot. Instead he received a letter signed "Konar" which started "The Polish Army salutes the Jewish fighters!" but said that "now is not the time for this meeting; this is the time to act."

("Konar" was one of the psuedonyms used by the Warsaw area commander, Colonel Antoni Chruściel.) Embittered, Zuckerman concluded that "They [AK] weren't an aid society but a military organization. As a military organization, we were superfluous for them, both in the fighting ghetto, and as fighting groups on the Aryan side of Warsaw."[20]

It was clear that as one bunker after another fell in the ghetto, Grot and the career officers who were in charge of the underground organization had no interest in joining what they saw as a losing cause. To them the ŻOB was a small group of people with no experience, no proper planning, and no future. Even rescuing a handful of people from the burning ghetto was virtually a miracle. The AK, with its radio stations, parachute drops from England, and a large mass of Poles willing to back it and shelter its members, simply waited for a better opportunity to confront the Germans. As it turned out, its own future was almost equally grim.

Throughout the ghetto uprising, *Biuletyn Informacyjny* (The AK's official organ) printed several ŻOB communiqués from the command bunker at Miła Street 18, usually with delays of one to two days. The *Biuletyn* also printed constant appeals to the population to help all those who managed to flee the ghetto.

In his memoirs Zuckerman refers to the sympathy of the Poles "who were as miserable as we were—they wanted to help but couldn't. They saw who had influence in the AK, since the AK had the means and probably could have done something. Their behavior was deliberate and conscious." He adds, however, that the AK's reasoning was that "If our uprising spread beyond the wall, Polish Warsaw would be prematurely inflamed by an uprising doomed to failure because the Germans would easily put it down."[21]

Suggestions have been made that Grot's decision to avoid a major confrontation over the ghetto or even more effective help was partly due to his mistrust of Jews, particularly as soldiers. In his memoirs covering the period up to September 17, 1939, he complained that Jews had not contributed enough to Poland's defense spending and made critical remarks about several senior officers to whom he referred as "Jews." He described General Bernard Mond, commander of the 6th infantry division, as "a courageous Jew, but lacking qualifications to lead a division."[22] (General Mond's superiors had different views. In their evaluation reports on Mond were such phrases as "First class combat officer and excellent in dealing with the officer corps. Full of initiative and energy," and "Capable of gaining confidence of those serving under him. Exceptional ability to cope in difficult situations."[23] Mond was captured by the Germans in 1939 and spent the rest of the war in a prisoner-of-war camp, unmolested. After the war he returned to Poland.)

Four days after the outbreak of the ghetto fighting, Anielewicz succeeded in sending a letter to Zuckerman, his deputy, in which he wrote,

We are switching to a system of guerrilla action. At night, three of our units go out on two missions: an armed reconnaissance patrol and the acquisition of weapons. Know that the pistol has no value. We need grenades, rifles, machine guns, and explosives. I can't describe to you the conditions in which the Jews are living. Only a few individuals will hold out. All the rest will be killed, sooner or later. . . . There are many fires in the ghetto. Yesterday the hospital (at Gęsia street 6) burned. Blocks of buildings are in flames. . . . The main thing is that the dream of my life has come true. I've lived to see a Jewish defense in the ghetto in all its greatness and glory.[24]

Anielewicz was killed on May 8 in his command bunker at Miła 18, together with his fighting team.

When Himmler realized that German shock troops and flamethrower units had to fight literally for every doorstep, and that the defenders of the ghetto showed no signs of surrendering, he ordered Stroop to act "with the greatest severity and relentless tenacity." Stroop recorded his activities daily and submitted the reports in a bound, seventy-five-page book entitled *The Warsaw Ghetto Is No More*, later used in the Nuremberg trials. A typical example of his prose describes how

The Jews stayed in the burning buildings until, because of the fear of being burned alive, they jumped down from the upper stories. . . . With their bones broken, they still tried to crawl across the street into buildings which had not yet been set on fire. . . . Despite the danger of being burned alive, the Jews and bandits often preferred to return to the flames rather than risk being caught by us.

Stroop obviously kept detailed statistics of his "action." He summed it up on May 16:

Of the total of 56,065 caught, about 7000 were destroyed in the former ghetto during a large scale operation, 6,929 Jews were destroyed by transporting them to Treblinka; the sum total of Jews destroyed is therefore 13,929. Beyond that, from five to six thousand Jews were destroyed by being blown up or by perishing in the flames.[25]

The remaining 36,000 who were in the ghetto at the time of the operation were most likely gassed, but Stroop's report does not mention it. He claimed German losses were sixteen killed and ninety wounded, although the figure appears too low for four weeks of fierce fighting for virtually every house. The ŻOB had no time or possibility to keep its own statistics. Although some documents found their way to the other side of the wall, most were burned during the following year's uprising.

No one knows how many fighters were able to reach safety because, beside the *AK*, the communist *AL* was also involved in the rescue operation, and the two did not communicate. The ghetto was turned into a vast ruin except for a workshop in Gęsiówka where several hundred Jews from various European countries, including Poland, worked in concentration camp conditions, mainly repairing German army vehicles. The camp was liberated in the first days of the 1944 uprising by Scout battalion *Zośka*. Four of the prisoners identified themselves as doctors and joined one of the AK's hospitals. A number of Polish Jews joined the battalion, and some were subsequently killed in action. (I saw two of them in the suburb of Mokotów three days before I was taken prisoner on September 27, 1944.)

Zuckerman estimates that "thousands" of Jews fought in the 1944 uprising, but the *AK* did not keep such statistics. Zuckerman himself headed a small unit of *ŻOB* members who manned one the barricades defending the Old Town. When the area fell, he and his men made their way through the sewers to the northern suburb of Żoliborz, where they stayed until the end. Zuckerman emigrated to Palestine in 1947, where he was among the founders of the Ghetto Fighters' Kibbutz. Another prominent surviving leader of the *ŻOB*, Marek Edelman, remained in Poland where he finished medical school and became a well-known cardiologist in Łódz.

There was another victim of the ghetto a thousand miles away, in London. Szmul Artur Zygielbojm, a representative of the *BUND* (General Jewish Workers' Union) in the Polish government-in-exile, committed suicide on May 11, 1943. He had failed to convince the British media and government that European Jewry was on the brink of annihilation. His pleas to the British Foreign Office had proved futile. His efforts to convince American diplomats also had been to no avail.

Bomb Auschwitz, he had pleaded. Save the remnants, he had begged. But the tale he told seemed too incredible. And those who believed him claimed that little could be done; their aircraft and personnel were required elsewhere. As a last resort, Zygielbojm had taken his own life and left a note with his grim tidings. Perhaps with his death, he concluded, he would be able to arouse the "conscience of humanity."[26]

In a tribute to the ghetto fighters dedicated to "the memory of Szmul Zygielbojm," Polish Poet Władysław Broniewski wrote:

They fell in combat formation
Defenders of the Warsaw ghetto.

I dip my pen in blood
And my heart is drenched with tears
For you, Polish Jews.[27]

NOTES

1. The author was at the scene.

2. Yitzhak Zuckerman, *A Surplus of Memory: Chronicle of the Warsaw Ghetto Uprising* (Berkeley, Los Angeles, Oxford: University of California Press, 1993), p. 214.

3. Mrs. Korbońska in conversation with the author in 1993.

4. Ibid.

5. Zuckerman, *A Surplus of Memory*, p. 94.

6. Ibid., pp. 66–67.

7. Ibid., p. 69.

8. *Polskie Siły Zbrojne* (London: General Sikorski Historical Institute, 1950), Vol. III, p. 47.

9. Marian Drozdowski, *Alarm dla Warszawy* (Warsaw: Wiedza Powszechna, 1964), p. 14.

10. Arnold Zable, *Jewels and Ashes* (New York, San Diego, London: Harcourt Brace & Company, 1991), pp 40–41.

11. Drozdowski, *Alarm dla Warszawy*, p. 39.

12. Zable, *Jewels and Ashes*, p. 41.

13. Zuckerman, *A Surplus of Memory*, p. 276.

14. Ibid., p. 437.

15. Ibid., p. 492.

16. Ibid., pp. 207–208.

17. Ibid., p. 317.

18. *Polskie Siły Zbrojne*, Vol. III, p. 47.

19. Adam Borkiewicz, *Powstanie Warszawskie 1944* (Warsaw: Pax, 1957), p. 34.

20. Zuckerman, *A Surplus of Memory*, p. 363.

21. Ibid., p. 374.

22. Stefan Rowecki, *Wspomnienia i Notatki Autobiograficzne* (Warsaw: Czytelnik, 1988), p. 100.

23. Jozef Kuropieska, *Wspomnienia Oficera Sztabu* (Kraków: Krajowa Agencja Wydawnicza, 1984), pp. 354–356.

24. Zuckerman, *A Surplus of Memory*, p. 357.

25. Excerpts of the report from various Nuremberg trial documents.

26. Zable, *Jewels and Ashes*, p. 152.

27. Author's translation.

CHAPTER 6

Operation Storm

In the gloom of the Polish autumn of 1943, punctuated by mass executions of hostages in the ruins of the Warsaw ghetto, the headquarters of the underground *Armia Krajowa* was informed that it should not count on substantial help from the Western Allies. The gist of the message received from London by Bór, who replaced Grot as the *AK*'s commander-in-chief, was that a general uprising could not be backed by Western air cover, bombing raids, nor by airborne troops. Poland was simply too far away, and the Western Allies were busy preparing their landing in France. It was also fairly obvious that the West already considered Poland to be in the Soviet sphere of influence and left it up to the Poles to sort out their relationship with the advancing Red Army.

To the Polish leadership in London and inside Poland, the Western attitude was the result of

Stalin's political victory, based on military power, confirmed later by the decisions of the Tehran and Yalta conferences. Poland was thus placed in a desperate situation. It was faced with a powerful Soviet Union which not only demanded Poland's eastern territories but also wanted a friendly postwar government which in practice would mean a communist government and total obedience to Moscow.[1]

On October 27, 1943, the government-in-exile instructed the Underground that, if an uprising nonetheless took place, military and civilian authorities should not "reveal themselves" to the Red Army entering the country. The *AK* command thought the directive was impossible to carry out and that the existing underground institutions should instead "act as hosts" to the entering Soviet armies. Such an attitude "contained a strong element of risk but was the only way of underlining Poland's right to the liberated territories."[2]

Although deprived of support for the idea of a general uprising and forced to deal alone with the advancing Soviet armies, the *AK* command intended to carry out intensified operations against the Germans. Thus was born "Operation Storm," which would activate some 50,000 to 60,000 partisan units, mostly in eastern Poland, mainly to underline Poland's commitment to a relentless war with Germany—and to stake a formal claim to the contested territory. While scoring a number of local successes against the German occupation troops, the operation also exposed the population of towns and villages to reprisals. Above all, as the Soviet troops advanced westward, it gradually revealed the grim reality of Soviet intentions vis-à-vis Poland.

As far as the officers in the *AK* command were concerned, solving that crucial problem was beyond their capability. Like the government-in-exile in London, they stood on the principle that the eastern Polish territories that lay in the path of the advancing Red Army were sacrosanct—and Polish.

The news of reduced Western support dampened the spirit of the men at the top of the AK's structure. Nonetheless the usual underground activity continued, and the number of new volunteers grew. Obviously the rank-and-file *AK* membership had no idea about high-level plans or intentions. Men and women were joining, mainly to take revenge on the Germans who were clearly losing the war. Despite the vicissitudes patriotic spirits were high.

Rescue actions increased, particularly to free arrested members of the organization as they were transported from one prison to another. So did the executions of suspected *Gestapo* agents and other spies. According to *AK* statistics, during 1943 a total of 1,246 agents were "liquidated." (No statistics for the month of April are available.)[3]

Regardless of political complications resulting from Poland's attitude toward the Soviet Union, the *AK*'s operational contact with Great Britain continued. Thus, during the duration of "Operation Riposta," from August 1943 to July 1944, Royal Air Force planes dropped on Poland a total of 4,069 containers filled with weapons, explosives, medicine, and uniforms. (British crews carried out seventy-four flights and Polish crews 131). The number of specialists and officers of the Polish Armed Forces under British Command parachuted into Poland during that period was estimated at 146 (including ten couriers from the Interior Ministry). Funds delivered to the *AK* consisted of $16 million in banknotes and gold plus smaller sums in German marks and in occupation Polish *złotys*. Sixteen aircraft and four parachuted agents were lost.[4]

The initial plan for a general uprising was prepared in the summer of 1942 under the direction of General Grot. It was based on instructions from General Sikorski, premier of the government-in-exile, and carried by Lieutenant Colonel "Heller" (Kazimierz Iranek-Osmecki) who was parachuted into Poland. (Later Heller became the *AK*'s chief of intelligence.) The plan expected relatively easy success in attacks on German installations in smaller towns but anticipated serious difficulties in Warsaw. The action in Warsaw was to be carried out at night with attacks on all major German installations, railway stations, bridges on the Vistula, the three telephone exchanges, and two nearby airfields (Okęcie and Bielany). Units formed of conspirators in the vicinity of Warsaw were to protect the city in the event of attacks by German units retreating from the east.

Contrary to expectations the German retreat westward was being carried out in order and with stubborn resistance. In November 1943 the idea of an insurrection throughout Poland was definitely scrapped, replaced by "limited action phase" or "Storm" (Polish *Burza*). Plans for Storm were drafted by General "Erazm" (Stanisław Tatar), one of the few *AK* senior officers recommending a search for a political accommodation with the advancing Soviet army.

The main objectives of Storm were to "demonstrate our will to fight the Germans," protect the civilian population during the German retreat, and particularly "destroy the German army, facilitate the advance of the Soviet armies and, subsequently, concentrate [the fighters] and create [regular] Polish army units to continue the war together with the Red Army."[5]

It was clear from the beginning that in order to be completely successful, to a great extent Storm depended on the plans and advance of the Soviet army which the *AK* headquarters did not know. Conscious of the potential difficulties, Bór periodically urged London to establish high-level rapport with the Soviet command via Moscow. There is no record of the result of these demarches.

Thus, in December 1943 and during the first six months of 1944, the *AK*'s efforts concentrated on harassment and major attacks involving units of several thousand men on German targets, mainly east of the "Molotov-Ribbentrop" line which had split Poland into two parts in 1939. As the front rolled westward, Warsaw was also due to take part— but not on the scale outlined in the initial plans. However, in March 1944 the *AK* command decided to exclude the Polish capital from *Burza*—"to avoid destruction and spare the population." Instead the *AK*'s Warsaw district received orders to "protect the population" in the event of forced

resettlement as the front approached, and the Germans made plans to
resist in the city.

As a result of this decision, large quantities of weapons produced in
Warsaw's underground workshops as well as those received in parachute drops and stored in the capital were sent eastward to partisan
units. It was only when Bór ordered a general alert on July 27 in anticipation of the uprising—contrary to earlier plans which excluded the
capital—that the *AK* command realized the extent of the loss caused to
the city's arsenal. In short, by supplying the partisan units, Warsaw was
stripped of the weapons needed for its own action—decided virtually at
the last minute.

Details of Operation Storm were completed by November 26, 1943,
but because at that time the entire *AK* radio network was threatened by
German monitors, they could only be communicated to London early in
January 1944. In addition, a lengthy radiogram (about 1,500 words) addressed to General Kazimierz Sosnkowski, the new commander-in-chief,
showed preoccupation with the reaction and attitude toward the Soviet
troops entering the territories east of the Bug and San rivers. Thus Bór
wrote,

In the event of a second Russian occupation I am preparing, in deepest secrecy,
a skeleton command of a new underground organization at your disposal. I will
inform you about the details when the preparations are completed. In any case,
it will be a separate network, not connected with the organization of the *Armia
Krajowa*, which to a great extent is already known to elements in Soviet service.

Instructions to the commanders of the units scheduled to participate
in Operation Storm stressed that

All our war preparations are intended to intensify armed action against the Germans. Under no circumstance armed action should be undertaken against Russians entering our territories in pursuit of the Germans, except, of course, in self-
defense. . . . [Your] task will consist of determined harassment of retreating
German units, of acts of sabotage throughout the entire territory, particularly
aiming at communication lines.

Concerning the attitude toward Soviet partisan units, usually consisting of escaped prisoners-of-war with officers parachuted from the Soviet
Union, the instructions specified that their operations should be facilitated and "all friction should be avoided." It stressed that *AK* units which
had already been involved in clashes with the Soviets "should be transferred to other areas."[6]

Toward the Red Army arriving in the area, the *AK* formations should
play "the role of hosts. The local commanders, accompanied by a rep-

resentative of the civilian (Underground) authorities, should report to the commanders of Soviet units and comply with their wishes." However, the instruction stressed that all efforts to incorporate *AK* units into the Soviet Army or the Polish Army being formed by the Russians "should be considered as an act of force and thus opposed."[7]

In London, General Sosnkowski, an officer well known for his fear of Soviet intentions, acknowledged the instructions with considerable foreboding. In an answer to Bór dated January 11, 1944, he reiterated his view that the Soviet Union regarded the eastern Polish regions as its own territory where "the Russians don't intend to respect our role as hosts or any existence of Polish authorities. Finally, attempts to incorporate your units are more than likely."

Sosnkowski obviously referred to the incorporation into the Polish army being formed under Soviet command and led by General Zygmunt Berling, a colonel in the prewar Polish army. He concluded his ominous message:

It is not excluded that there will be Allied pressure on the [Polish] government to accept Soviet territorial demands. Personally, I consider all efforts at territorial compromise as pointless. In my view, the final aim of the Soviet Union is to transform Poland into a vassal communist republic or simply into the 17th Soviet republic.[8]

It was hardly cheerful news for the command of a guerrilla army as it prepared to crown its existence by what it considered to be a major offensive against the German enemy. And the events that followed proved the words of the general in London to be prophetic.

It is not clear to what extent the *AK* command was aware of details concerning the future of Poland discussed by the Anglo-American allies with the Soviet Union. Little if anything was known about what happened at the Tehran conference in November 1943, where Stalin, Churchill, and President Franklin D. Roosevelt basically settled the future of Poland by agreeing to the Molotov-Ribbentrop Line as Poland's eastern frontier. (That border was also referred to as the "Curzon Line," after Lord George Curzon, the British foreign secretary, who first mooted it in 1919.) Poland's frontiers, considerably expanded eastward, were subsequently agreed upon in 1921 after its victorious war with the Soviet Union. At Tehran, Churchill suggested to Stalin that the Allies compensate Poland by giving it the eastern part of Germany, thus moving the Polish nation 150 miles westward. The move, Churchill said, was "like soldiers taking two steps left close."[9]

The Anglo-American allies had little sympathy with the emotional aspects of the problem, involving not only ceding the territories the Poles considered as theirs but also particularly two major cities, Lwów (today's

Ukrainian Lvov) and Wilno (Lithuanian Vilnius). Throughout Polish history, the two cities were closely linked with Poland's vicissitudes and its struggle against Russia. But the allies, particularly Churchill, thought the Poles were unreasonable in making this a major issue at a particularly sensitive period. Above all, they wanted to avoid a clash with Stalin, a crucial ally. Although World War II began over Poland, the Polish problem was no longer dominant—except, perhaps, as an irritant. (See Chapter 11.)

In any case, at that stage whether or not the Poles were right made no difference. What did matter was the fact that although the Soviet Army was advancing relentlessly into Poland, the Polish government-in-exile and staunchly anti-Soviet emigré Poles were incapable of facing that brutal reality.

Their impetuous position, predictable to those familiar with Poland's history, galvanized that conservative Polish emigré community the year following General Sikorski's death. The result was "a paralysis that gripped the government-in-exile at a time when flexibility alone might have saved it."[10]

As far as the government-in-exile was concerned, only two of its members were ready to agree to a compromise, including Prime Minister Stanisław Mikołajczyk. His pragmatism led to an open feud with General Sosnkowski, the commander-in-chief in London, and "long periods passed in which the two men refused to speak to each other."[11] It was highly unlikely that, given the official nature of his communications with London, Bór and his staff were aware of the feud. Bór was certainly aware of the grim predictions of Soviet intentions by Sosnkowski, and his radiograms to London reflected it. After all, it was Bór who reported organizing "a skeleton command of a new underground organization" to cope with Soviet intentions, which left little doubt in his mind. Although the political aspects of the problem were not part of Bór's mandate, he was obviously preoccupied about the future of the units he ordered to take part in Storm.

On January 11, 1944, the Soviet government announced that it considered the question of annexation of the eastern territories to the "Soviet republics of Ukraine and Byelorussia" as definitely solved. Three days later (January 14), the Polish government in London responded by avoiding the territorial question and asking for a resumption of diplomatic relations (broken off the previous year by Moscow) which would allow official contacts to solve the frontier problem and other issues. On January 17 Moscow rejected the Polish note—including the proposal to resume relations.

Unaware of the exchange of diplomatic notes and the growing isolation of the government-in-exile, the AK command pursued its planned offensive. One of the first targets were German units in the area of

Kowel, approximately 100 miles from the prewar border with the Soviet Union. In the spring of 1943, intense hostility between the Polish and Ukrainian populations of the region caused massacres of entire villages. Ukrainian units consisted of those armed and equipped by the Germans as well as of the anti-German—but also anti-Soviet—*Ukrainian Partisan Army (UPA)*. The slaughter of civilians diminished before the winter, but the regional *AK* commander felt he had to face three enemies: the Germans, the pro-German Ukrainians, and the Soviet partisan units formed by agents of the *NKVD* who were generally hostile to Poles.

During the night of January 15–16, a group of *AK* officers left Kowel and headed for the wooded countryside, wearing local sheepskin coats and traveling in one-horse peasant carriages. They were to direct the concentration and operations of the *AK*'s 27th division. (*AK* field units were generally identified by the same numbers as divisions and regiments stationed in their areas before the war.) The man in charge of the 27th division was Major "Oliwa" (Wojciech Kiwerski), recently dispatched from Warsaw. The division consisted of eight battalions, two squadrons of cavalry; and units of signals, engineers, and military police, as well as two field hospitals, the total numbering close to 6,000 men. It was armed with 4,500 rifles, 700 pistols, 140 submachine guns, about 100 machine guns and three antitank guns.[12] Most of the weapons had been preserved from the 1939 campaign. It was by far one of the best armed of *AK* partisan formations, and it had a solid support in the area's Polish villages where various workshops, bakeries, and slaughterhouses were set up. The state of uniforms was poor, and there were shortages of medical supplies.

After a series of skirmishes with German and pro-German Ukrainian units, the division's command established contact with the approaching Red Army. Major Oliwa reported by radio that he had met twice with Soviet commanders, who, according to him, accepted the fact that his unit was receiving orders from the West. In response to Oliwa's report, the RAF carried out a parachute drop by two aircraft, consisting of weapons ammunition, a radio station, and some uniforms.[13] It was the only RAF flight to supply a Polish partisan unit east of the Curzon Line.

Until the end of March, the division carried out a number of operations, some of them jointly with Soviet forces. It reported a number of successes—as well as the text of a message from an SS general in the area, saying,

I know that there are Polish bands numbering several thousand south of Kowel. In view of the approaching common danger from the east, I propose joint action, supplying you with weapons according to your wishes and leaving you a free hand as far as the Ukrainian matter is concerned.[14]

The proposition was ignored by the Polish unit.

Further messages from Major Oliwa were much more alarming. They reported the shooting of two Polish unit commanders by Soviet partisans and efforts to disarm one battalion. Subsequent news from the area prompted the *AK* commander-in-chief to inform London that a Polish outpost had been disarmed and its commander executed, that in another area twenty members of the 27th Division had been captured and deported while three were hanged, and that in villages and towns freed by the Soviets young men were being inducted into the Red Army.

On March 26, Oliwa reported that he had met the commander of the Soviet forces operating against Kowel, whom he identified as "General Sergyeev," who asked for the division's total submission to Soviet command, at the same time promising free contact with the *AK* headquarters. He proposed to supply the necessary weapons to transform the division from a partisan to a regular unit. The following day Oliwa received from the *AK* headquarters in occupied Warsaw agreement to the Soviet proposal provided that "the division maintains a character of a reconstructed unit of the Polish Army and will carry out military operations assigned by the Polish authorities. It cannot be deported to Russia and all its (new) members must be sworn in according to the standard *AK* military oath."

Within weeks the Polish division became involved in heavy fighting against four German divisions, including SS *Panzer* Division Viking. Apparently there was no support from the Red Army. Several hundred men, including Oliwa, were killed as the division fought its way out of the cauldron, heading north. After a two-day march in two columns toward the Pripet Marshes, one unit of the division known as *Garda* was surrounded by Soviet troops and incorporated into the Berling Army. The rest, under a new commander, marched westward, continuing to harass or destroy German units, according to the directives of Operation Storm. At the beginning of August, as the division attempted to march to Warsaw to help the uprising, it was surrounded by Soviet troops and disarmed.

A similar fate met the 30th *AK* division which carried out Operation Storm in an area known as Polesie. The division consisted of some 3,000 men armed with rifles and machine guns, and was commanded by Lieutenant Colonel "Trzaska" (Henryk Krajewski), who was parachuted in from England. After a number of clashes with German units in the area mainly in June and July, Trzaska established contact with the advancing Soviet Army in order to coordinate operations. According to a Polish account, "such repeated efforts failed, there were no joint operations whatsoever but there were increasing pressures to put (the division) under General Berling's orders."[15]

When he received orders from Bór in August to march with his unit to help embattled Warsaw, Trzaska dismissed some of his men and led the rest westward. After contacting the Soviet command, the diminished division obtained permission to march toward Warsaw but was surrounded and disarmed on August 15. The soldiers were incorporated into the Polish Army under Soviet command, and the officers were deported to Kiev and, later, farther east.

AK units in the northeastern area of the prewar Polish territories around Wilno (today's Vilnius) conducted a series of operations attacking Germans and also clashed with Lithuanian SS units active in the region. As before in the case of the 27th Division near Kowel, various German commanders tried to persuade the Poles to join forces against the Russians and promised to supply them with arms. In several cases such offers included threats of "total pacification" in the event of refusal. Again the Polish side ignored all such efforts.[16]

Early in July 1944, Lieutenant Colonel "Wilk" (Aleksander Krzyżanowski) assembled some 10,000 men in the region of Wilno and attacked the German garrison of the city from four directions. Almost from the beginning, all attacking AK units cooperated with the Red Army which backed them with tanks, artillery, and air strikes. The city was liberated, and its Polish inhabitants decorated their homes with red-and-white Polish flags. The Soviet command allowed the AK to control Wilno for two days while General Ivan Tchernyakhovski, commander of the Third Byelorussian Front, discussed with Wilk the prospect of forming an infantry division and a cavalry brigade from the Polish partisan forces.

On July 17 Wilk and his officers were asked to report to the Soviet command "for a conference" while their men were designated a specific area outside the city in which they were to concentrate. Wilk and about seventy officers were immediately arrested and deported to the Soviet Union. Their units, estimated at 6,000 men, were surrounded by Red Army troops who proceeded to disarm them while the Poles chanted rhythmically "We want Wilk, we want Wilk."[17] Most men as well as some officers were then loaded onto trains and deported to Kaluga in the Soviet Union. Several hundred managed to break through the Soviet ring but were later surrounded and massacred. Only a few survived.

Another major action of Operation Storm in the territories claimed by the Soviet Union took place in Lwów (Lvov), at that time a predominantly Polish city of some 300,000, where the German garrison consisted of four depleted infantry divisions and auxiliary units. The commander of the AK 5th Division, Colonel "Janka" (Władysław Filipkowski), assembled some 3,000 men, poorly armed and equipped, and launched an attack on the city while Soviet units were already fighting in its eastern suburbs. (Among Janka's units was one commanded by "Draza," a Yugoslav officer by the name of Dragan Sotirovic, who had escaped from a prisoner-of-war camp.) After three days of fighting, Lwów was captured, and Janka set up his headquarters in a building on Kochanowski Street in the city center. On July 25 he was summoned for talks with officers of the First Ukrainian Front who praised the performance of *AK* troops. But on July 27, Janka reported by radio to the *AK* headquarters that he had been told by an *NKVD* general that "finally Lwów is Soviet and Ukrainian but this does not exclude later modifications between the governments."[18]

In subsequent radiograms Janka reported that he had been ordered by the Soviets to disband his troops, who would have a choice of joining the Red Army or the Polish Army under Soviet Command. On July 31 the Soviet authorities summoned senior *AK* officers to a conference. All those who attended—about thirty—were jailed in Lwów as "criminals and Polish fascists." The area's *AK* command reported that "arrests of *AK* members continue as well as searches of apartments used by them." It asked for intervention and protest.[19] At the same time, the civilian underground administration—known as *delegatura*—of the Lwów area asked, in another radio message, for "an Allied commission" to investigate the situation and pleaded for intervention "on behalf of imprisoned *AK* members as well as of mistreated officials of the *delegatura*." There was little the *AK* command in Warsaw, by then inflamed by the uprising, or the government-in-exile, could do. Instead the *AK* instructed its units behind the Curzon Line "to accept the offer of joining the Berling Army." The message in effect ended Operation Storm in areas which the Polish government-in-exile stubbornly refused to cede to the Soviet Union, increasingly victorious on the battlefield.

Partisan activities continued elsewhere in Poland, but the outbreak of the Warsaw uprising forced the organization to concentrate on efforts to come to the city's rescue rather than to fight locally. (See Chapter 10.) But to the *AK* command and Poland's exiled leaders in London, the Soviet message was eminently clear: The Soviet Union had its own plans for Poland, and no compromise was envisaged. Yet the London emigrés stubbornly insisted on their legitimacy as Poland's only authority, and the *AK* followed them—perhaps not so much out of loyalty but out of conviction that they were more qualified to represent Poland than the men collaborating with Moscow.

And as the Soviet armies advanced deep into the heart of Poland, Moscow relentlessly pursued its plan for the country's takeover. On July 22, in the newly liberated town of Lublin where *AK* troops were also in action, a Soviet-backed "Committee of National Liberation" was formed with "legal and provisional executive authority" over all liberated Polish territory. "Most of its self-proclaimed leaders were Moscow-trained professional communists whose names were completely unfamiliar to their countrymen."[20] On July 26 the Soviet government officially recognized the Lublin committee as the supreme sovereign body in all liberated areas. At the same time, the Red Army was granted broad powers in these areas for the "establishment of public safety and order."

The development deepened the gloom of the government-in-exile which feared recognition of the Lublin regime by the Western Allies. Meanwhile the advancing Red Army was

arresting and executing underground leaders; thousands of rank-and-file members of the Home Army were being shipped to Siberia. Soviet propaganda was spewing out blatant falsehoods designed to erode Home Army strength: The Underground, according to the Soviets, refused to fight the *Wehrmacht*. Soviet propaganda still alleged that the Home Army was collaborating with the Germans.[21]

Operation Storm unquestionably demonstrated the *AK*'s ability to concentrate large combat units and successfully confront the occupation forces in many parts of Poland. Towns were liberated—only to be turned over to the arriving Russians. Politically it was a major disaster. Intended to show the world that "Poland fights on," it did not get international publicity, much of which was devoted to the Soviet Union's victorious march westward. Jan Karski, a member of the underground who in 1942 visited the Warsaw ghetto, felt that

As a result of the continuous and unrestrained propaganda on behalf of the Soviet policies, and the inability of the Poles in London to present their case, the public opinion in the West increasingly considered the "Polish exiles" obstinate, reactionary or unrealistic.[22]

During and after Storm, officers who could have constituted cadres of a new Polish Army were sent to gulags, swelling the ranks of Stalin's Polish victims. Most officers of the Berling Army, increased by forcibly incorporated members of the *AK*, were Russian. "More and more it was clear that the absence of an agreement between Moscow and the exile government could cost the Poles their country."[23] But in July 1944, after the recognition of the Lublin committee by Moscow, it was already too late.

General Bór drew no lessons from Operation Storm, with which he was more familiar than anyone else. He and his aides thought that a rising in Warsaw would definitely attract the West's attention to Poland's plight and change its relations with the Soviet Union. Besides, Warsaw's Underground army wanted to fight. Thus Bór's orders to Monter to "begin Operation Storm in Warsaw" on August 1 represented continuation of a failed policy of shattered hopes.

NOTES

1. Tadeusz Kryska-Karski, *Piechota 1939–1945* (London: Polish Institute, 1974), p. 25.

2. *Polskie Siły Zbrojne*, Vol. III (London: General Sikorski Historical Institute, 1950), p. 473.

3. Ibid.

4. Ibid., p. 404–405.

5. Instructions on "the application of Plan B" received by the commander of the *AK*'s 9th division.

6. Author's translation of official texts.

7. Ibid.

8. Ibid.

9. Allen Paul, *Katyn: The Untold Story of Stalin's Polish Massacre* (New York: Charles Scribner's Sons, 1991), p. 246.

10. Ibid., p. 281.

11. Ibid.

12. *Polskie Siły Zbrojne*, Vol. III, p. 589.

13. Kryska-Karski, *Piechota 1939–1945*, p. 27.

14. *Polskie Siły Zbrojne*, Vol. III, p. 589.

15. Kryska-Karski, *Piechota 1939–1945*, p. 28.

16. *Polskie Siły Zbrojne*, Vol. III, p. 603.

17. As told to the author by a survivor in a prisoner-of-war camp in Germany late in 1944.

18. Janka's dispatch recorded by the *AK* under number Ldz/7013/tjn 44.

19. Dispatch recorded as Ldz 6725/tjn 44.

20. Paul, *Katyn: The Untold Story of Stalin's Polish Massacre*, p. 288.

21. Ibid., p. 289.

22. Karski quoted in Paul's *Katyn: The Untold Story of Stalin's Polish Massacre*, p. 286.

23. Ibid., p. 284.

CHAPTER 7

Warsaw on Fire

The first clash of the "battle for Warsaw" took place in the northern suburb of Żoliborz between a *Luftwaffe* patrol and a resistance unit transporting weapons. No one has determined who, and for what reason, fired first, but the shooting eventually spread throughout the suburban apartment blocks, villas, and gardens where groups of young conspirators had begun to gather for action that was due to begin on August 1, 1944, at 5:00 P.M. The timing of the "W Hour" ("W" stood for Polish *walka*—combat) had been changed the day before, causing innumerable mobilization and concentration problems.

In that first incident of the uprising, the German patrol was apparently completely surprised. The airmen, unused to street fighting, appeared to be trapped. But soon several truckloads of helmeted militarized German police arrived at the scene. Amid bursts of machine gunfire and grenade explosions, the insurgents continued their unexpected action. A bystander recalled seeing three tanks with the SS *Totenkopf* (death's head) emblem race at high speed toward the sound of the battle. At the viaduct near the *Gdańsk* railway station, the tanks deployed for combat and opened fire.

It was just before 2:00 P.M.—three hours before the designated time of the uprising.

At 3.30 P.M., not far from the site of the first clash, platoons 218 and 221 of the *Żyrafa* (giraffe) group became involved in the fighting just as their members were being issued weapons from an underground cache. After a brief but violent exchange of gunfire, the unlucky unit was massacred by tanks.

The sound of intense firing—as well as radio calls by the tank crews—brought more German reinforcements to the area. By sheer chance the arriving Germans stumbled into several small trucks transporting weapons for the insurgents in other parts of the city. They included submachine guns for the unit assigned to protect General Bór and his staff.

As one participant noted, "For our side, the outcome of this premature firing was disastrous."[1] It was becoming ominously clear that sporadic fire exchanges were erupting throughout the city and that the element of surprise on which the *AK* command had counted was quickly evaporating.

In the heart of the city, uncoordinated firing broke out in several points, mostly for unexplained reasons. Historians later attributed the outbreaks to the nervousness of the young, frequently untrained insurgents.

At Dąbrowski Square several trucks filled with German police, alerted by the spreading clashes and the intensity of shooting, screeched to a halt outside the block numbered 2/4. While the Germans hastily deployed in an open area, insurgents who were inside the soup kitchen of the three-story building (platoons 101 and 116 led by Lieutenant "Bohun") rushed to the windows, firing with pistols and submachine guns. For most of them, these were their first shots against living targets. Several Germans fell, killed or wounded. (Two corpses remained, unclaimed and unburied, for days in front of the Polish positions.) Lieutenant Colonel "Radwan" (Edward Pfeiffer), who had been designated as *AK* sector commander, was trapped by the shooting for several hours, and members of his staff trying to reach the large block of apartment buildings were delayed.

At 4.20 P.M. shooting swept nearby Napoleon Square (*Plac Napoleona*) near the fortified main post office and the sixteen-story Prudential Insurance Company building. Believing that the time of the battle had been moved up, Lieutenant "Kosa," commander of the well-armed *Kolegium B* unit which had assembled in the area, stormed and captured the Hotel Victoria on Jasna Street, according to plan, albeit ahead of schedule. Thus the command of the Warsaw region had obtained its planned headquarters—literally in the center of the capital. At that time its commander, Colonel "Monter" (Antoni Chruściel), had no idea about what was happening elsewhere. With him were several teams equipped with short-distance radio transmitters destined for other parts of Warsaw, which could not be delivered because of the intensity of the fighting. At least temporarily the region's command had no contact with its subordinate units. The telephone worked, but, in the well-established conspiratorial tradition, no one wanted to use it. In any case the three main telephone exchanges were in German hands, and all calls were monitored.

In the western industrial suburb of Wola, Bór and his staff, as well as "Soból," the deputy premier of the government-in-exile, arrived well ahead of the "W Hour" at their temporary quarters in Kamler's furniture factory on Dzielna Street. Their defense consisted of a platoon of thirty-three men, mostly workers employed by the factory, armed with fifteen rifles and thirty hand grenades.[2] (The weapons sent from a depot in Żoliborz were by then in German hands.) Nearby was a heavily fortified tobacco factory, protected by some fifty German soldiers.

Firing began when a truckload of Germans arrived at Kamler's factory, apparently to collect uniforms which had been stored there. Other German units billeted in the vicinity to protect various industrial installations joined in the fighting, in effect cutting off the *AK*'s commander-in-chief and his staff.

When finally "W Hour" struck, all of Warsaw reverberated with the sound of gunfire and grenade explosions. The long-awaited uprising had spread throughout the city although rarely according to carefully prepared plans. For the time being, Bór was unable to inform London—his radio team could not reach the besieged factory which turned out to be a precarious billet under attack rather then a functioning command post.

Bór was not the only one in Warsaw who had problems with radio communications. Unbeknown to the *AK* general staff, a member of the Soviet intelligence service, Captain Konstantin Kalugin, was hiding in Warsaw to report on the situation in the Polish capital to Marshal Rokossovsky, the front commander. When the uprising swept the city, Kalugin was cut off from his operator who had been hiding elsewhere—with his radio and the latest codes. The missing radioman was never found.

One of the main factors responsible for chaos, loss of weapons shipments, and tardy—or premature—concentrations of various units was the change in the timing of the uprising. Initially, considering the weak weaponry of the insurgents and the unquestionable advantage of fighting under cover of darkness, a night action was planned. With that in mind, some units belonging to the central area of the city (*Śródmieście*) had been mobilized on July 28—only to be sent home again after a tense, sleepless night. Such a change had a negative impact on the cohesion of units and the morale of the insurgents, particularly as the alert revealed the dramatic paucity of weapons.

Mobilizing some 40,000 men and women in a large city was not an easy or quick task, especially because most orders were delivered by runners who traveled on bicycles or simply in crowded streetcars. The telephone was used only in emergency. Thus time was dramatically short when, on Monday, July 31, Monter received Bór's order to "begin Operation Storm in Warsaw" the following day at 5:00 P.M. It was the height of Warsaw's rush hour, and the command believed that a concentration by groups of highly visible young people carrying heavy packs—and frequently clumsily wrapped weapons—would have a better chance of success and was likely to cause chaos and problems for the German garrison. As it turned out, there was more chaos for the insurrection. The bodies of poorly armed and overenthusiastic attackers soon littered the streets outside well-protected German positions.

Warsaw's "Underground army" (just as all of the *AK*) was based on a system of platoons, to be formed into companies, battalions, and larger groupings at the time of action. Each platoon had an assigned "identity number," and larger groups were named after city regions or used the names of their commanders. All told there were 701 platoons (some estimates put the number at 594), varying in strength from thirty to sixty people. The training, enthusiastic but limited by the constraints of conspiracy, was in small groups, mostly in apartments or during outings in surrounding forests. Some units based in Warsaw had had partisan combat experience, but a majority of the volunteers, whose age generally ranged from sixteen to twenty-five years, had never fired a shot in anger. The underground had its officer cadet schools, but most officers were of prewar vintage, men who managed to survive a disastrous war, roundups, deportation, and other vicissitudes of the ruthless occupation. The fact that so many had survived until the Warsaw uprising was virtually a miracle.

To some degree this untested resistance army operated on a class system stemming mainly from the method of recruitment. Usually members already sworn in would contact friends to enroll them in their unit. Thus entire platoons grouped sons of middle-class families (generally referred to as intelligentsia), whereas other units consisted mainly of factory workers, butchers, and shopkeepers recruited by friends in their own social milieu. When concentrated, it often happened that one company had an *inteligencja* platoon of teenagers and two others consisting of older members of the working class, some with prewar military service. Eventually, because of losses, reorganization, or amalgamation of units, social differences disappeared.

Immediately after receiving Bór's order on July 31 to begin action in the afternoon of the following day, Monter went to the "safe apartment" of his staff at Filtrowa Street 68 and issued the following coded message to area commanders:

Alert. I am ordering "W" August 1st, 17 hours. Address of my headquarters: Jasna (street) 22 effective with W hour. Confirm immediately receipt of this order.[3]

The most dramatic flaw of the plan was in the timing. Monter's staff encoded the message at 7:00 P.M., but, under the emergency situation imposed by the occupation authorities, curfew in Warsaw started at 8:00 P.M. Public transport and all other forms of civilian traffic usually started coming to a halt earlier. Consequently the order to begin the uprising could not be delivered until the following morning.

The sudden and unexpected call to action stunned most area and unit commanders, some of whom did not receive it until later in the day. They needed time to send the required instructions to "mailboxes"— apartments each subunit visited twice a day during the period of "anticipation" which had existed since July 27. Each unit also needed time to collect weapons from hiding places, and in some cases those in charge of such caches claimed they could not issue anything without written orders! (Several major underground depots were not located until after the war.)

A typical Underground unit, recruited through friendships or contacts in the place of work, had members scattered throughout the city. The unit's "location" was considered to be that of the "mailbox," and that's where the action orders were sent. Each unit, in turn, had to inform subunits and individual members. It was estimated that during the morning hours of August 1, some 6,000 runners were crisscrossing Warsaw, carrying instructions for concentration and targets of the planned attack—some of which had been changed following the previous mobilization. Area commanders received the general order between 7:00 and 11:00 A.M., individual units mostly in the early afternoon. All this created an atmosphere of extreme tension, subsequently blamed for premature or uncoordinated action, as well as for delays in the arrival of weapons.

In the early afternoon hours of that fateful August day, Warsaw's streets swarmed with young people carrying rucksacks, frequently wrapped in easily available brown paper. Despite balmy August weather, some wore raincoats to hide their weapons. Most members of conspiracy had instructions to keep in readiness a rucksack containing two changes of underwear, a sweater, a flashlight, soap, towel, and at least one day's supply of canned food. The insurgents also received armbands which were to serve as their "uniform"—white and red (Poland's national colors) with the Polish eagle, letters WP (*Wojsko Polskie*—Polish Army), and the platoon number stamped on. (Some armbands were stamped with the letters *AK* instead of WP.) Most resistance members reported for action in their everyday civilian jackets, windcheaters, sweaters, or simply in shirtsleeves.

Watching the streets of the capital hours before the uprising, many senior officers feared a German alert at the sight of thousands of young people rushing to their concentration points. The city was heavily patrolled by *Wehrmacht* and various militarized police units, each patrol varying from five to ten men. In addition armored cars and open trucks with mounted heavy machine guns cruised along the main streets. According to subsequent German accounts, the patrols did not report anything unusual—at least not before the outbreak of the first clashes. Here and there patroling soldiers tried to joke with passing girls (some of whom carried five-liter containers filled with petrol for "Molotov cocktails").

The reactions of various senior officers of the insurgency to this spectacle differed considerably. While Colonel "Prezes" (Jan Rzepecki) of the headquarters staff saw "no sign of nervousness or excitement" in the crowded streets, Lieutenant Colonel "Radosław" (Jan Mazurkiewicz), commander of an elite attack group, felt that conspiratorial discipline had given way to "excitement, feverish expectation and growing tension."[4]

On Jerozolimskie Aleje (boulevard) facing the Central Railroad Station (*Dworzec Główny*), the *Soldatenheim*—"soldier's home"—was filled with German servicemen of all formations. Many sat outside within the barbed-wire enclosure on the sidewalk, sipping beer and looking at the traffic which seemed perfectly normal. Groups of young men and women passing by with their packages did not arouse any suspicion. Now and then tanks of *Panzer* reinforcements clattered by, heading east toward the bridges on the Vistula. A German command car halted at a pastry shop near Zbawiciela Square, and the officers inside it asked for ice cream which the Polish waiter brought on a tray to their vehicle while members of the Underground (including the author) walked by en route to assembly points. Groups of people still clustered around wall posters—the German ones pledging to turn Warsaw into an "anti-Bolshevik fortress" and those of the resistance appealing for calm and discipline pending further instructions.

The Underground's training was based on a manual called *Walka* (combat), which took into account the expected paucity of weapons and specific conditions of urban fighting. Thus it was assumed that a squad of between fifteen and eighteen insurgents would fight mainly at close quarters with hand grenades, supported by one or two submachine guns—until more weapons were captured from the enemy or were dropped by parachute from England. According to postwar accounts, Warsaw's resistance units on August 1 had about 44,000 hand grenades (some made in the Underground's workshops), 3,846 pistols, 657 submachine guns, 30 flamethrowers, 29 antitank rifles, 2,600 rifles, 200 light and heavy machine guns, and 16 mortars.[5] Rifles were not a favored weapon in conspiratorial conditions, being too difficult to hide or transport for training. In some units barely 10 percent of insurgents were armed; the others carried hand grenades or incendiary bottles. Because

Warsaw had not been included in Operation Storm in the initial plans, virtually on the eve of the uprising the region's command shipped some 600 submachine guns to resistance units operating in the nearby countryside. In 1947—two years after the war—a cache containing 678 British Sten submachine guns was declared to the authorities by its guardian who claimed that no one had ever asked for the weapons.

Only elite units, to be used as a tactical reserve of the *AK* command, such as *Baszta* and *Radosław*, were relatively well armed. In many others the grenade and inflammatory bottle were the prevailing weapons. Although perhaps there was reason to believe that, given the state of weaponry, a surprise night attack might succeed against some objectives, ordering poorly armed and mostly inexperienced fighters against heavily fortified German positions in broad daylight smacked of criminal irresponsibility. Yet those in charge of the planning were officers who, during the 1939 German *Blitz* against Poland, watched Polish divisions "melt like candles" in clashes with German armor. However, fighting without weapons appears to be in the Polish tradition. In 1794 peasants from the Cracow region wielding scythes (the so-called *kosynierzy*) stormed and captured twelve Russian guns in the battle of Racławice, and members of the 1863 rising against Russia went to battle with hunting rifles or scythes. Even at the start of the 1944 uprising, some officers spoke of arming their units with pickaxes!

Bór's own analysis of the situation, according to his radio dispatch of July 14 to the commander-in-chief of the Polish Armed Forces under British Command, was pragmatic. Given the strength of the German forces and their defensive preparations, "an insurrection has no chances of success. It could only succeed in the event of Germany's collapse and the disintegration of its army. . . . In view of the present situation, even with strong support of the air force, parachute forces and supplies of new weapons, an insurrection would cause heavy losses." At the same time, however, he pointed out that "inactivity of the *AK* at the time of Soviet entry on our territory would be tantamount to passivity," opening the door to communist influence and domination. "The guiding thought of our final struggle is to demonstrate to the world our unswerving attitude toward Germany and of our inflexible will to fight."[6]

A week later Bór's report to London was decidedly optimistic. The *AK*'s commander-in-chief informed his superiors that the armies on the German "Central Front" in the east were virtually collapsing, that there was no sign of reinforcements, and that after the abortive attempt to assassinate Hitler in July, the morale of German troops was crumbling. The Soviet armies, Bór believed, could easily continue their advance and cross the Vistula—and thus Warsaw.[7] Although not all members of his staff agreed with the general, from that day on he started believing in the feasibility of the uprising.

At "W Hour," the delays and hasty mobilization caused by the sudden change in the time of the uprising found thousands of insurgents en route to their assembly points. As the fighting spread, many were unable to reach their units and often joined the first group they encountered wearing red-and-white armbands. It is estimated that at the start of the uprising only some 20,000 members of Warsaw's *AK* district—or approximately half of its strength—were at their designated posts or already engaged in fire fights. Like the "rebellious children" dismissed haughtily by one of Napoleon's Polish generals 114 years before, Warsaw's new generation had been launched into something that could not be stopped.

To many inhabitants of the capital, the proverbial Rubicon had been crossed. A woman living in the city center recalled how "an insurgent (*powstaniec*) appeared in the middle of the pavement and unfurled a large red-and-white flag. He looked to us like a magician. Applause thundered from the windows. And, suddenly, everything became clear and simple."

The spreading fighting found many Germans—military or civilian members of the occupation administration—walking in the streets or looking for bargains in shops. Amidst growing confusion many of them sought shelter in doorways or in courtyards. According to one *AK* officer trying to reach his assigned post in the city center,

from time to time single shots were heard from all directions. It was a hunt for weapons. Soon the firing became intense. Every German in uniform with a gun was a target. It did not matter whether he was good or bad. Every German was a good target and if he was armed—a very good target.[8]

Although the German command in Warsaw had been prepared for some form of action by what was referred to in official correspondence as the Polish *Widerstand Bewegung* (resistance movement), the time of the uprising and its extent was a complete surprise, at least until the first clashes. The Germans had a well-rehearsed defense plan, and all billets and public buildings had been equipped with bunkers and other fortifications, including coils of barbed wire. The initial clashes were considered by the German command as limited, but, as the fighting developed, the strength and armaments of the insurgents were often exaggerated in reports. (See Chapter 8.) According to Colonel Paul Otto Geibel, commander of the SS and police units in the Warsaw district, the most concrete information about the planned Polish action came about 4:00 P.M. in a telephone call from a *Luftwaffe* officer who reported that a Polish woman friend had "begged him" to leave the city because an uprising would break out at 5:00 P.M.[9] Colonel Geibel passed on this information to General Reiner Stahel, who had recently been named as commander of the Warsaw garrison, and who, disregarding suggestions of some of his aides that the source was not completely trustworthy, decided to order a general alert. He also dispatched reinforcements to beef up the guard at the three telephone exchanges and to the main post office. (Some of them arrived at their destinations under fire from insurgents.) It soon became obvious that it was too late to carry out systematically the carefully elaborated alert plan.

Neither General Stahel nor Colonel Geibel realized that, almost at the same time, the fate of Bór and of his staff was threatened by an advance of German troops on Kamler's factory over neighboring rooftops. The planned incursion was eventually beaten back—by chance—by elite units of Lieutenant Colonel Radosław, which had assembled in the nearby Telefunken factory. (The group's battle journal notes laconically: "16.00 hours: beginning of concentration. 16.20: unprovoked by us, fighting begins on the grounds of the Telefunken factory. 17:00 hours: concentration unfinished because of premature clashes."[10]) The accidental removal of the threat against the *AK* general staff and the delegate of the government-in-exile was not mentioned, presumably because at the time, the insurgents had no idea as to who they were. (The next entry in the journal is merely "18:00 hours: seizure of the school building at Okopowa [street] 55 A. The enemy, four companies strong, failed to endure the attack and withdrew.") A unit under Radosław's command also captured a large German depot filled with food and camouflage uniforms which thousands of insurgents in the suburb of Wola and in the Old Town (*Stare Miasto*) subsequently wore. A nearby school building was also seized, freeing 100 Hungarian Jews held as slave labor. The German officer commanding the makeshift camp committed suicide.[11]

Although the attacking insurgents—despite their abysmally poor weaponry—succeeded in separating the German "military area" from the "police area" (see Chapter 8), many other units were in dire straits. At W Hour some units still awaited their weapons. Among them was battalion *Odwet II*, which gathered some 600 men in a tree-shaded area of Kolonia Staszyca but had only 300 hand grenades, thirty pistols, three submachine guns, and three rifles.

The battalion was unable to link up with units south of the former airfield (*Pole Mokotowskie*) for an attack against the German "police area," including the massive SS barracks called by the Germans *Staufferkaserne*. (At the start of the 1939 war, the building housed the Polish General Staff.) Eventually it made several feeble attacks on various German positions and was decimated by machine gunfire. About fifty insurgents were captured and shot.[12]

Some 120 men of the group *Granat* attacked the nearby *Luftwaffe* barracks and the adjacent antiaircraft artillery positions and were decimated. Although attacks on German installations throughout the Mokotów area inflicted some losses on the Germans, most of them failed for lack of adequate weapons. Battalion *Bałtyk* led by Major "Burza" (Eugeniusz Landberger) surrounded and harassed with fire the SS barracks on Narbutt Street, but the action was stopped after heavy losses in the Polish ranks and the arrival of tanks.

Heavy fighting raged for hours against the barricaded area around Aleja Szucha, headquarters of *Gestapo* (the Nazi secret police) with its notorious prison where hundreds of resistance members had been tortured to death. Various buildings changed hands throughout the evening, but most of the attacking insurgents were massacred. The same pattern was repeated throughout the city, with the Germans holding on to most objectives the *AK* intended to seize. General Stahel later estimated that during that evening 500 Germans and 2,000 insurgents were killed. In a number of areas, German tanks were used, mowing down entire *AK* units.

Heavy losses were suffered by units that tried to seize Warsaw's two main bridges, Kierbedź and Poniatowski, linking the left bank of the city with the suburb of Praga. While the insurgents had some hope of local success in densely built-up urban areas, their attacks in open terrain were usually doomed to failure. An attack on the German garrison command in the Europejski Hotel near Saski Square in the city center was thwarted by the arrival of tanks. A short distance from it, Lieutenant Bohun's platoons, as well as the *Rygiel* company, attacked the bank building (*Ziemskie Towarzystwo Kredytowe*) which during the occupation served as *Arbeitsamt* (employment office), administering the procurement of men and women for forced labor in Germany. I recalled that

as gunfire raged from all directions, Bohun ordered me to leave the observation post to which I was assigned, and follow him. Outside, on the roof of a nearby building, stood a group of men with armbands on their civilian jackets, looking through binoculars. Bohun led me up a creaky ladder to a second floor window where I noticed a blood-covered man on a bed, with a priest in a black cassock at his side. Bohun told me to join several men in a room where an insurgent was firing short bursts with his Sten submachine gun at the courtyard below while two others crouched by him, loading his magazines by hand. A man lying on the parquet floor in the adjacent room pushed a hand grenade toward me. After a few minutes the Sten stopped firing and its owner struggled with the stuck weapon, swearing. Someone shouted "throw the grenade" and I hurled the powerful British Mills through the window, shattering glass on the highly polished floor. An explosion followed. I peered through the window at the courtyard and, in the falling dusk, saw several helmeted Germans running across it, stooped under their heavy packs. The Sten started firing again. Shortly afterward I heard a shrill voice shouting from downstairs "we have captured our objective." Downstairs, women were emerging from the cellar and one of them gave me a bowl of cherry preserve. An elegant man with silver hair was explaining to the women that he had just come from the headquarters and that "the news is simply excellent."[13]

In reality the news wasn't at all "excellent," and at that time several sector commanders were thinking either of leaving the city or of dismissing men who had no weapons and often turned out to be a burden. (No one actually thought how they were going to get to their homes and what fate awaited them in areas under German control.) In Kamler's factory Bór was still waiting for his radio transmitter.

At his Victoria Hotel command post, Warsaw area commander Colonel Monter was by then receiving regular situation reports, either by runners who braved the fighting or from sporadic radio contacts. Thus at dusk he knew that no major objectives, strongly defended by the Germans, had been captured but that the insurgents controlled large portions of the city where the enthusiastic population swarmed to build barricades, tearing up sidewalks and often using overturned streetcars. This led him to assess the outcome of the fighting on an optimistic note. "However, the reality was different. The German garrison suffered losses of several hundred men killed or captured but it repelled the insurgent attack, mainly due to the aid of armored units which happened to be passing through Warsaw."[14] The organizers of the uprising clearly had not included such a possibility in their planning.

The enthusiasm of the population for the uprising was unquestionable, and Monter realized that, regardless of the situation, there was no going back. The population simply "hijacked" the uprising from "the rebellious children."

A short distance from Monter's headquarters, sector commander Lieutenant Colonel Radwan climbed on the roof overlooking Dąbrowski Square. He was a roly-poly man with binoculars and a pistol strapped to his three-piece suit. He saw Warsaw in the glow of fires near the main railway station, as well as flashes of explosions all around him. He told his aides that in order to secure his sector, he had to capture the six-story telephone exchange (*PASTA*) and the central post office, both heavily defended.[15]

The insurrection appeared to be collapsing in Praga, on the Vistula's right bank. The insurgents controlled the Old Town, as well as large areas of the central part of Warsaw. In the southern suburb of Mokotów, the insurgents were dismayed by their failure to capture a single major objective and, after heavy losses in dead and wounded, began to leave the city for the nearby forests. Some unit commanders tried new desperate attacks under persistent midnight drizzle—without success. The sector command remained in Mokotów, despite the fact that out of ten companies of the best-armed *Baszta* regiment only three remained, as well as a signals unit which, during the night, laid field telephone lines between the headquarters and the areas still held by the insurgents.

The situation in the northern suburb of Żoliborz, where premature fighting had begun three hours before W Hour, was dramatic. Attacks on various German positions were simply smashed by the powerfully armed enemy. At nightfall, sector commander Lieutenant Colonel "Żywiciel" (Mieczysław Niedzielski) received reports of deadlock, shortage of ammunition, and falling morale. Having established that most of his units were incapable of further combat, he decided to leave the city for the nearby Kampinos forest, an area where there was a strong partisan unit, as well as a facility to receive parachuted supplies from England and Italy.

The departing column consisted of some 1,000 insurgents, 450 of whom carried weapons; they left shortly after midnight. Despite several clashes with German patrols, the forest area was reached by dawn under driving rain after what Żywiciel described as a "nightmarish march in chaotic conditions."[16] At 9:00 A.M. Żywiciel dispatched a runner (Ludmiła Janotowna) with a report to Monter explaining his decision. The young woman walked some ten miles to reach the outskirts of the city and then, almost miraculously, made her way through various skirmishes to Monter's headquarters at the Victoria Hotel. During the evening of August 2, Żywiciel received an order from Monter to return to his assigned sector of Warsaw.

After that first night of fighting for control of the Polish capital, an estimated 5,000 members of the *AK* left the city. Most of them returned during the following days.

In the morning of August 2, the *AK* propaganda department managed to activate the street loudspeaker system used by the occupation authorities and suddenly the stunned capital, still pelted by rain, heard the Polish national anthem "Poland Is Not Yet Lost" (*Jeszcze Polska nie Zginela*)—for the first time in nearly five years. Later in the day, the loudspeakers broadcast Bór's appeal to "the soldiers of the capital," in which he said:

After nearly five years of continuing and difficult struggle waged in the underground of conspiracy, you are now standing openly, weapons in hand, to restore freedom in our country and punish the German criminals for the terror and atrocities committed on Polish soil.[17]

Although one of his aides described the situation of the insurgents as "awful," Bór was determined to continue the uprising. At 9:00 A.M. on Wednesday, August 2, his radio transmitter began working, and Bór, a trim figure in a pale beige raincoat and porkpie hat, was able to report to London the start of the uprising and the results of the fighting. He requested "immediate" drops of weapons on the Jewish cemetery and Napoleon Square areas and the dispatch of the Polish parachute brigade to the suburb of Wola, where he had established his temporary headquarters. The undaunted cavalry general apparently still believed in success.

Ominously, there was no sign of Soviet tanks to help the uprising persistently urged by Moscow. The Soviet steamroller, which had swept across eastern Poland with amazing speed, had suddenly halted some fifteen miles outside the embattled Polish capital.

NOTES

1. Emil Kumor, *Wycinek z Historii Jednego Życia* (Warsaw: Pax, 1969), p. 229.
2. Bór in conversation with the author in New York, 1952.
3. Adam Borkiewicz, *Powstanie Warszawskie 1944* (Warsaw: Pax, 1957), p. 28.
4. Ibid., p. 46.
5. Ibid., p. 35.
6. Situation report of July 14, no. 243.
7. Situation report of July 21, no. 244.
8. Kumor, *Wycinek z Historii Jednego Życia*, p. 230.
9. Borkiewicz, *Powstanie Warszawskie 1944*, p. 57.
10. Radoslaw's battle journal.
11. Borkiewicz, *Powstanie Warszawskie 1944*, p. 73.
12. Henryk Haber in *Ekspres Wieczorny*, no. 43, 1947.
13. Author's notes written in October 1944 at the hospital of the prisoner-of-war camp in Germany, *Stalag* XI A, Altengrabow.
14. Borkiewicz, *Powstanie Warszawskie 1944*, p. 81.
15. The author overheard the remark.
16. In conversation with the author in a hospital ward, *Stalag* XI A, October 1944.
17. Author's translation of the Polish text.

CHAPTER 8

"Kill Anyone You Want"

Shortly after 5:00 P.M. on August 1, 1944, a brief mortar barrage fired by Polish insurgents on his headquarters forced Police Colonel Paul Otto Geibel to move to his "combat position" located in the cellar of the heavily protected building. Fighting continued to rage in the so-called police district, and Colonel Geibel, in an impeccable *feldgrau* uniform with a stiff collar, began contacting various outposts under his command.

As commander of SS and militarized police units in the Warsaw district, Colonel Geibel directly controlled a combat group of *Schutzpolizei*, reserve units of other police formations, two battalions of *Waffen SS*, and smaller SS units scattered throughout Warsaw—all told some 6,000 men. Contacted by telephone, various outposts reported merely that they were "engaged in fire exchanges." But after a while, the so-called *Abschnittwachen*—"sector guard posts"—described their situation as "serious." Two units could not be contacted, including one manning the city's main power plant.

A police patrol in armored cars sent to reach the Warsaw garrison commander, General Reiner Stahel, in the "military district" less than two miles away, turned back, reporting that all major intersections were under fire and that trying to force them would cause heavy losses.[1] Both, General Stahel and Colonel Geibel realized then that the situation was indeed becoming "serious."

In addition to Colonel Geibel's police and SS units, the German garrison consisted of some 6,000 men of the *Luftwaffe* and antiaircraft artillery, various *Wehrmacht* units including training and replacement depots, auxiliary services such as *Bahnschutz* (railway guards) and *Werkschutz* (factory protection), militarized Nazi party units (*Sonderdienst* and *Sonderabteilungen*), as well as some 4,000 Russians of General Andrei Vlasov's "Russian Liberation Army." Known generally as "the Vlasov Army," it was mainly recruited among Soviet prisoners. Also stationed in Warsaw was a battalion of the *Ost-Legion* (Eastern Legion), another turncoat formation. Thus the garrison normally consisted of some 20,000 men in the Warsaw urban area and perhaps another 20,000 in its vicinity. According to Colonel Geibel (who was subsequently promoted to general), the German command envisaged using 36,000 men (*Wehrmacht, Luftwaffe, SS,* and police) to deal with an eventual Polish rising.[2]

In evaluating the German forces immediately available to face the Polish uprising, the *AK* command totally ignored the fact that large elements of three *Panzer* divisions were transiting through Warsaw to prop up the crumbling Central Front. At General Stahel's request, many such units were asked to help stifle the insurgent attacks—in fact they were instrumental in containing them. (According to some German accounts, the armored units were used despite objections by General Nicolaus Vormann, commander of the 9th Army, who felt that such action was a "police matter.")

Despite some postwar accounts claiming that at the time of the uprising the German garrison was considerably depleted and weakened, most Polish analyses point to its combat value. A study by the General Staff of the Polish Forces Under British Command in London said the training and equipment of German units in Warsaw was "on a high level, corresponding to the general level of the German armed forces. The *Wehrmacht* units have maintained full discipline. According to all indications these units would fulfil their duty until the end in a calm and disciplined manner."[3]

At the time of the uprising, the *AK* command felt that leaders of the Nazi Party and paramilitary units were more committed to the regime than those of the *Wehrmacht* and were determined to fight "with confidence and brutality." The Polish resistance army believed that General Vlasov's and the *Ost-Legion*'s predominantly Russian troops were of a considerably lower caliber and that they would use the fighting against the Poles mainly as an opportunity to plunder and rape. The subsequent events proved this assessment to be accurate.

According to Viktor Suvorov, a former Soviet career officer, General Vlasov's army

was the largest of all the anti-communist forces, drawn from the inhabitants of the pre-revolutionary Russian Empire. . . . By the end of the war it consisted of approximately one million Russian soldiers and officers who had chosen to fight against the Soviet Army. Vlasov himself with unbelievable short-sightedness embarked upon a bloodthirsty campaign of terror against the inhabitants of the territories occupied by his armies.[4]

Since 1943 the German occupation authorities believed in the strong possibility of a Polish uprising, mainly on the basis of intercepted documents and confessions of tortured prisoners. What was not clear was the extent of such an operation. Although the *Wehrmacht* counterintelligence service scrupulously informed all authorities of preparations—as it perceived them—by the Polish resistance movement, neither Heinrich Himmler, head of the SS and of the "home forces," nor the command of the Central Front "took such reports seriously."[5]

Nonetheless, toward the end of 1943 Himmler declared the entire area of occupied Poland "partisan territory," organizing large units for "pacification purposes," including elements of the Vlasov Army, volunteers drafted among Soviet Muslim prisoners as well as Ukrainians and Latvians, known to have pro-German sympathies. In all cities—and particularly in Warsaw—special German areas were created, protected by bunkers and barbed wire. In 1943 a total of 24,222 Germans, including civilian occupation personnel and *Volksdeutsche*, lived in Warsaw. This number was considerably reduced after a hurried evacuation, particularly of women and children, when the eastern front approached in July 1944. The city's population after the destruction of the ghetto in April and May 1943 was 974, 745.

Every German office and institution had its own "self-defense" unit. Warsaw was divided into five defensive blocks, each given specific instructions and equipped with stocks of food and ammunition. The carefully elaborated plans considered several possibilities of Polish offensive action. Sporadic attacks were to be dealt with by police and the SS. In the event of a general uprising, the army would take over, and all Germans in the city would be under the orders of the garrison commander.

Yet, as the front approached and there was no unusual activity by the Polish resistance organizations—either by the *AK* or the small communist *AL* (*Armia Ludowa*—People's Army), according to SS General Ernest Rode "Himmler became completely convinced that under the circumstances there will be no uprising."[6] Consequently, on July 9 Himmler stripped Warsaw of a *Schutzpolizei* regiment trained for street fighting, as well as several SS units, sending them to the vicinity of the northeastern town of Grodno where there was considerable activity by partisan units. One SS battalion from Warsaw was sent to reinforce the protection of Hans Frank, Poland's occupation governor, in Cracow.

According to Adam Borkiewicz, a Polish military historian and a senior member of the *AK*, on July 15 Colonel Geibel reported that, in the

event of a major uprising, he would not be able to control the situation
with the forces under his command. He then proceeded to reduce the
number of police outposts (*Abschnittwachen*) but increased the units
guarding such key installations as the power plant and the water supply
system.[7] In the meantime the garrison's strength was increased by the
arrival of various German units retreating from the front, although few
of them were immediately ready for further combat.

Late on August 1, when it was reasonably determined that most of
Warsaw was indeed affected by the fighting, General Stahel proclaimed
a state of siege and put all Germans, military and civilian, under his
command. His appointment to Warsaw by Hitler had given him total
authority, and, as far as the civilian population was concerned, the right
to "use all available means necessary for the maintenance of calm, security and order."[8]

Himmler, who was in East Prussia, received the first report on the
situation in Warsaw from General Stahel at approximately 5:30 P.M. on
August 1. Although phrased in a careful, routine, and low-key manner,
it alarmed Hitler's *Wolfsschanze* (wolf's lair) East Prussian headquarters
at Rastenburg, as well as the German authorities in Cracow, the capital
of occupied Poland. The Nazi *Oberdienstleiter* (supervisor on duty) in
Cracow immediately cabled the party's head office in Munich that
"rioting" had broken out in Warsaw and that several police stations as
well as the main post office had been attacked. This initial report pos-
tulated that the attack might have been the work of "communist rebels
because they have red armbands." (Apparently some Germans thought
that the armbands worn by the insurgents were red.)

While the military and police commanders were trying to ascertain the
extent of the uprising, General Stahel ordered that an appeal to the population be broadcast through the megaphones placed throughout the
city, asking for calm and rejection of "criminal and irresponsible elements." The appeal warned that every building from which shots were
fired would be destroyed. It was the last time the occupying power used
the loudspeaker system which soon fell under control of the *AK* propaganda department.

By nightfall, in his Brühl Palace headquarters on the edge of Warsaw's
Old Town (*Stare Miasto*), General Stahel was in contact with most military outposts which reported repelling attacks either immediately or "after prolonged fire exchanges which caused losses." In a postwar
statement to the Polish Historical Institute, General Stahel said the
German garrison "proved to be inexperienced and tactically helpless in
street fighting and in the reaction of the defending personnel [*Mann-
schaft*]. The weaker outposts were destroyed, the stronger ones lacked
the initiative to quickly clear the foreground." General Stahel particularly
pointed out his surprise—not by the outbreak of the uprising but by its

extent, that is, the organization and determination of the insurgents "in sudden and well-coordinated attacks by groups assembled during the night and in the morning hours in private apartments."[9] (By contrast, a number of *AK* commanders complained about poor coordination, lack of more effective cooperation between units, and an unsatisfactory liaison system.)

Barricaded in the police district which had eventually repelled all *AK* attacks, in a telephone conversation with German police authorities in Cracow, Colonel Geibel asked for help and was promised Himmler's special "attack units," including heavy tanks. When informed of this development, General Stahel decided to "remain on the defensive" pending the arrival of the promised reinforcements. Meanwhile the daily situation report of the Central Front for August 1 stated briefly that "In Warsaw, at 17:00 hours, the Polish resistance movement began an uprising [*Aufstand*]. A number of German establishments was surrounded and help could be sent only to some of them."[10]

While the highest Nazi party officials and security apparatus were becoming increasingly concerned about the situation in Warsaw, General Heinz Guderian, the German chief of staff and in effect commander of the ground forces in the east, considered the developments from a strictly military point of view. A brilliant *Panzer* strategist who spearheaded the concept of *Blitzkrieg* in 1939 against Poland and then, in 1940, in France, he was now preoccupied by the situation along the entire front which was crumbling, rather than by the action of the Polish resistance. In a postwar statement to the commission investigating Nazi atrocities in Poland and published under the title *Zburzenie Warszawy* (The Destruction of Warsaw), General Guderian is quoted as saying:

On 21st of July 1944 I was appointed chief of staff of the German land forces on the eastern front. . . . After my appointment, the entire front—if it could still be considered as such—was barely a cluster of separate remnants of armies withdrawing toward the line of the Vistula. Twenty-five divisions had been entirely destroyed. . . . At the beginning, Warsaw was a small matter compared to the collapse along two thousand kilometers. . . . The Warsaw uprising was merely one episode in our terrible situation on the eastern front.[11]

It was a particularly difficult—and frequently traumatic—period for the senior German officer corps, especially in view of the Allied invasion of France and the assassination attempt on Hitler in his East Prussian headquarters. That abortive attack was followed by some 7,000 arrests, 500 executions, purges, and the imposition of Nazi ideology on the entire armed forces—during its waning months. Even the traditional military salute was replaced with the Nazi greeting of a raised arm "as a sign of

the army's unshakable allegiance to the *Führer* and the close unity between army and party."

Guderian himself, who until then had made no publicized political
statements, called on his officers to "take the lead in being good Nazis."

Every General Staff officer must be a National Socialist officer-leader . . . by ac-
tively cooperating in the political indoctrination of younger commanders . . . I
expect every General Staff officer immediately to declare himself a convert or
adherent to my views and to make an announcement to that effect in public.
Anyone unable to do so should apply for his removal from the General Staff.[12]

Whether the Warsaw uprising was a "mere episode" in the deteriorating situation, the highest Nazi Party officials looked at it with deadly
seriousness. Thus, bombarded by alarming and nervous telephone calls,
within hours of the Warsaw outbreak General Guderian revised his initial assessment. His main concern was that Warsaw was in the immediate vicinity of the crumbling front and that the action was in a city
vitally important to the German supply system.

The military situation was indeed threatening—from East Prussia in
the north to the Carpathian Mountains in the south. On July 24 the armies of Marshal Konstantin Rokossovsky seized Lublin and Lukow and
those of Marshal Ivan Konev were fighting near Lvov and crossed the
San River at least at one point. The German armies of the southern group
of the eastern front, *Heeresgruppe Sud*, were defeated. The remnants of
the 4th *Panzer* army were being pushed toward the town of Sandomierz,
and the 8th army as well as the Hungarian army were retreating in the
direction of the Carpathians. In the north, on July 25, Soviet divisions
crossed the Bug River and headed in the direction of Warsaw. The following day they seized Białystok about sixty miles northeast of the Polish capital. The central part of the line of the Vistula was hardly manned,
and during the following days, Soviet point units crossed the river in
several areas south of Warsaw. On July 28 Brest Litovsk (Brześć in Polish), where the Polish General Staff had sought refuge in 1939 after
leaving Warsaw, was seized and its German defenders taken prisoner.
The main barrier between the advancing Soviet armies and the western
part of occupied Poland was the 2nd German Army consisting of about
ten divisions. The German command counted on stiff resistance in the
north on the heavily reinforced fortifications in East Prussia. For the Germans the Warsaw uprising could not have come at a worse time—as-
suming that the Soviet armies intended to continue their seemingly
unstoppable advance.

The attack by the Polish resistance in Warsaw was given total attention
the day after the outbreak at a meeting of the top council of the *Generalgouvernement* in Cracow. The account of that meeting demonstrated

particular concern that the Polish action might spread to Cracow, and emergency measures were ordered. They included a general alert of all army and police units stationed in the ancient historic city—including announcements in movie theaters ordering soldiers to return immediately to barracks. (There were six cinemas in occupied Cracow at the time—for a population of some 200,000. They showed recent German films with Polish subtitles or prewar Polish films provided they had no political message. The resistance movement frowned on Poles going to the movies, mainly because the films were preceded by propaganda newsreels and income from the proceeds went directly into German coffers. In each theater the best seats were roped off for German military personnel and occupation officials. In the summer of 1944 the German public applauded a film with actress Marika Rök singing *"Ich binn heute ja so verliebt"*—Today I Am So in Love.)

The official account of the events in Warsaw at the *Generalgouvernement* meeting underlined the seriousness of the situation. It spoke of

spontaneous attacks during which government buildings were fired upon. . . . The rebels are heavily armed with weapons of all kinds and particularly striking is the number of submachine guns. Hand grenades were used as well as weapons for combatting armor. The commander of the security force . . . demanded that the strongest means of repression be used, including *Stuka* dive bombers. Of particular importance is the fact that the Poles are seized by fury affecting even those who had been considered as loyal.[13]

The "fury" of the Poles caused a much stronger reaction in the German headquarters in Rastenburg in East Prussia, Hitler being present at the time. Hitler immediately demanded to "raze Warsaw completely." (The phrase subsequently quoted by General Erich von dem Bach-Zelewski was *"Warschau wird glattrasiert,"* while others claim he used a more simple *"Zerstören Warschau"*—destroy Warsaw.) To achieve it he ordered the withdrawal from the city of all Germans, civilian and military, and an all-out attack, with all aircraft available on the eastern front. Thus, according to General von dem Bach's version, Hitler wanted to create "a terrifying example for Europe."[14] The German dictator apparently was inspired by the conquest of Carthage by the Romans, particularly with the order of Scipio the Africanus who had the ruins leveled and then "the land ploughed over and sown with salt to make it barren."[15]

The order to mobilize the entire air fleet in the east for a devastating attack on Warsaw had already been sent to its commander, General Robert Ritter von Greim, when the General Staff pointed out to Hitler that, basically, most military units as well as all remaining German civilians in Warsaw had been trapped and would have to fight their way out— with heavy losses. Hitler then ordered Himmler and Guderian to jointly organize a rescue operation, at the same time proceeding to smash the Polish uprising. "Upon stifling the uprising with all available means, Warsaw was to be wiped off the face of the earth, all inhabitants were to be killed, there were to be no prisoners." The *Luftwaffe* was to be used once it had been ascertained "which parts of the city were in German hands and which were controlled by the rebels."[16] The task of defeating the Polish insurgents was assigned to General von dem Bach, a Prussian who claimed he had been brought up in the "Polish tradition" in Pomerania and first fought the Poles during their 1918 uprising in Silesia.[17] At the time of the Warsaw uprising, he no longer used the "Zelewski" part of his original name.

At Guderian's instructions, sent via General Walther Model, commander of the central front, the 9th Army of General Nicolaus Vormann was to immediately fortify all bridges on the Vistula, if necessary fighting for their control, and to secure all communication lines west of Warsaw. The problem was that General Vormann had no combat-ready reserves. Informed during the evening of August 1 of "large-scale disorders" in Warsaw, General Vormann's first reaction was that, because of his army's difficult situation, "the rebellion of Polish bands should be dealt with by the police." But his chief-of-staff, General Helmut Staedtke, pointed out that the army's role would become even more difficult if the uprising was allowed to continue. After an all-night conference in their headquarters in Skierniewice, a colorless town some thirty miles west of Warsaw, the two generals agreed that there was also a strong possibility of action by Polish resistance groups in adjacent areas. By then a barrage of orders from Guderian, inspired by Hitler's reaction, had taken the situation out of their hands. The 9th Army had to find the necessary troops to cope with the unruly Polish capital and satisfy the *Führer*.

Its first action was to order a Vlasov Army cavalry regiment and an infantry battalion to create a cordon that would isolate Warsaw from the west. An armored train with cannon and heavy machine guns was sent to the northern part of Warsaw to secure a railway bridge. A two-battalion 4th East Prussian regiment (some 1,000 men) was given the task of opening and securing the passage along the broad boulevards from the Poniatowski Bridge to the main railway station. Another regiment (the 608th) was sent to Warsaw's western suburb of Wola—where General Bór still hoped for a landing of the Polish parachute brigade from Scotland.

In addition to these military dispositions by General Vormann, Himmler himself issued additional directives from his headquarters in Grossgarten in East Prussia. Almost immediately after the first news of the Warsaw uprising, he cabled the commander of the Sachsenhausen concentration camp to execute General Stefan Rowecki, former commander-in-chief of the *AK* known as "Grot," who was held there after his arrest in 1943. The execution was carried out during the night of August 1 to August 2.[18] He then ordered a special brigade commanded by *SS Obersturmbahnführer* (a rank equivalent to that of army colonel) Oskar Dirlewanger, which was in the process of reorganization near the East Prussian border, to rush to Warsaw—also with Wola as its first destination. According to the Nuremberg trial testimony by SS General Ernest Rode, Himmler wrote the order personally by hand, adding that Warsaw should be razed and authorizing Dirlewanger to "kill anyone you want, according to your desire."

According to a postwar statement by General von dem Bach, the brigade at that time consisted of 860 men, most of them released criminals whom German officers used to describe as "a herd of pigs." During its operations in Warsaw, the brigade was eventually increased to between 1,700 and 2,500 men, mostly of similar caliber, some of them renegade Russians.

Dirlewanger, a man with cruel eyes, thin lips, a prominent nose, and a scar across his cheek, was described by General von dem Bach in the following terms:

Veterinarian by profession, typical mercenary, before joining the SS he served in the Spanish Foreign Legion. According to rumors, had spent time in prison for various offenses before embarking on a military career. A clever organizer but only average as a tactician, fearless and courageous. A habitual drunkard and liar, he knew how to cover up his offenses. . . . Both Hitler and Himmler had limitless confidence in him.

Another man who was to make a terrifying impact on the Poles in carrying out Hitler's order to "raze Warsaw to the ground," was SS General Mieczysław Kaminski, an anticommunist Russian of Polish ancestry. According to General von dem Bach,

Kaminski was a political brawler [*Raufe*] who spouted theories about a great fascist Russia under his leadership [*Führerschaft*]. Women and alcohol dominated his life. He left military matters to his regiment commanders. He had no regard for anyone's property and hated no nation more than the Poles, of whom he spoke only in insulting terms. He did not want to join Vlasov's army, on the contrary, using his relationship with Himmler he tried to oust Vlasov.[19]

Kaminski was in charge of a brigade of the Russian National Liberation Army (*Russkaya Osvobodityelnaya Narodnaya Armya–RONA*) which at the time of the outbreak of fighting in Warsaw was in Silesia at Himmler's disposal. On August 2 the brigade received orders to send the bulk of its troops to Warsaw. Kaminski selected 1,700 unmarried men and formed a regiment of infantry with a group of artillery. The unit left for Warsaw in trucks in the morning of August 3.

With the Soviet front reaching the center of Poland by the middle of 1944, Russians fighting for the Germans in German uniform but with specific insignia had little hope left. The motivation of those unhappy soldiers varied. Some were genuinely opposed to the communist system, and some simply wanted to avoid the misery of German prison camps, where Soviet captives had no protection under the Geneva conventions which Moscow had never signed. The result was a mixed bag of patriots and mercenaries. If captured by the Soviets, they were immediately shot or shipped to Arctic gulags. Few of them survived the war. In the occupied territories, they were hated by the population and known for the drunkenness and cruelty that often characterizes desperate men. They were also despised by the Germans who considered them inferior—as human beings and as soldiers.

Himmler himself left his East Prussian headquarters for Poznań (Posen to Germans), a city in western Poland annexed by the *Reich* and forming what the Germans called *Warthegau* (land of the river Warta). There he mobilized two regiments of special police with heavy machine guns, as well as two companies equipped with the latest flamethrowers, and put the unit under the command of Heinz Reinefarth, an SS *Gruppenführer* and police general. Before loading the men and their materiel onto trains, Himmler personally instructed Reinefarth "how to deal with Poles." An additional unit with 150 flamethrowers followed later.

This "rescue army," consisting of disparate but mostly fanatical—or mercenary—troops, was put under the overall command of General von dem Bach, who had acquired a reputation in fighting partisan units in Russia and Poland. Thus was formed what became known as *Korpsgruppe von dem Bach*. Its components began to converge on Warsaw, mainly from the west, without any interference by the Polish resistance movement either scattered throughout the country in partisan units or held in readiness in conspiracy. The *AK* command in Warsaw had no idea of the planned German reaction. It was more concerned with keeping the uprising going in the city—while awaiting the arrival of Soviet forces and the rather illusory help of the Western Allies.

During the two days that followed the outbreak, the insurgents were able to consolidate their hold on several areas, carried out a number of attacks on German positions, and captured weapons, ammunition, and prisoners among German and Vlasov Army troops. The main post office defended by eighty Germans was finally captured, and police units sent by Colonel Geibel to rescue several besieged German outposts were scattered with heavy losses. On the second day of the fighting, the insurgents faced what was to become a widespread practice: attacks by German tanks preceded or surrounded by groups of Polish civilians, often tied to ladders to prevent their escape. Such tactics in effect paralyzed defense, as the insurgents were unable to use their inflammatory bottles or antitank grenades. Even before von dem Bach's "rescue army" arrived, the police and army units carried out a number of executions, particularly of men, regardless of whether they belonged to the *AK*. The arrival of anticommunist Russian units in German service, traditionally hostile to the Poles, considerably increased rape, looting, and mass executions.

After three days of fighting, and particularly because of the diminishing supplies of ammunition, Colonel Monter decided to concentrate on defensive action

reserving offensive operations against targets which were either important or necessary from the point of view of the situation as a whole. German resistance, initially sporadic and uncoordinated but everywhere tough, became reorganized into unified action. . . . The sound of the German-Soviet battle reaching Warsaw from the east and initially violent, weakened on August 3rd. From August 4th, there was complete silence in the east.[20]

Early on August 3, General Stahel, who by then had excellent telephone and cable connections with all the troops under his command as well as with the headquarters of the 9th army, felt that

in the city center the enemy [insurgents] seized control of entire areas and specific strongpoints, blocking linkage [of German troops]. In suburban areas there is freedom of movement not only by big but also by smaller [German] units. Lack of heavy weapons and, above all, of necessary training were responsible for the fact that all energetic sallies [by Germans] resulted in heavy losses.[21]

On the Polish side, at his headquarters in the Victoria Hotel, Colonel Monter remained optimistic. "Time is working for us," he insisted to his staff. In a message to Bór—who was still in Kamler's factory amid heavy fighting in suburban Wola—he asked the commander-in-chief of the *AK* to "urge a speedy arrival" of Soviet troops. But Bór had no contact with the Soviet armies, and there were no indications that he intended to establish any, leaving the matter to the government-in-exile in London, which was basically powerless. The fires in Warsaw were burning with increased intensity and the German planes were readying to come with more fire, from the skies.

NOTES

1. General Stahel's report to the headquarters of the Central Front.
2. Colonel Geibel's postwar account to a Polish government investigative commission.
3. *Polskie Siły Zbrojne* (London: General Sikorski Historical Institute, 1950), Vol. III, p. 687.

4. Victor Suvorov, *Inside the Soviet Army* (London, Glasgow, Toronto, Sydney, Auckland: Grafton Books, 1984), p. 365.

5. Testimony at the Nuremberg trials by SS General Ernest Rode.

6. Ibid.

7. Adam Borkiewicz, *Powstanie Warszawskie 1944* (Warsaw: Pax, 1957), p. 38.

8. Documents of the Central Front, *Fernschreiben* no. 65004/I of July 31, 1944.

9. Borkiewicz, *Powstanie Warszawskie 1944*, p. 92.

10. Report *HG Mitte* no. F 3955/44, submitted at the Nuremberg trials.

11. *Zburzenie Warszawy* (Katowice: Awir, 1946), p. 128.

12. William L. Shirer, *The Rise and Fall of the Third Reich* (New York: Simon & Schuster Inc., 1960), p. 1403.

13. Translation from the German of document OKMW I of August 2, 1944, *Generalgouvernement*.

14. Statement from Nuremberg trials quoted in *Zburzenie Warszawy*, p. 34.

15. Andrew Borowiec, *Modern Tunisia* (Westport, CT: Praeger, 1988), p. 12.

16. Ibid., pp. 121–127.

17. Borkiewicz, *Powstanie Warszawskie 1944*, p. 693.

18. Ibid., p. 96.

19. General von dem Bach's statement to the Polish Historical Institute, February 2, 1947.

20. *Polskie Siły Zbrojne*, Vol. III, p. 712.

21. Central Front records, *HG Mitte* no. F 3981/44.

CHAPTER 9

A Battle for Survival

Joseph Vissarionovich Stalin looked hard at the Polish visitor. Poland, he said, behaves as if the Soviet Union was an enemy. The "fascist" underground organization is concealing weapons for a struggle against the Soviet Union and its members are murdering communists.

It was 9:30 P.M. on August 3, 1944, and the conversation took place behind the twelve-foot thick Kremlin walls. The visitor was Stanisław Mikołajczyk, prime minister of the Polish government-in-exile in London, who had traveled to Moscow as a supplicant. The Soviet Union broke off relations with the Polish exiles in April 1943, but Mikołajczyk needed help. He was prepared to deal with the Soviet dictator to save Warsaw from annihilation.

"I cannot trust the Poles," Stalin told him.

"I rejected his accusations," Mikołajczyk wrote later in a radio message to his delegate in embattled Warsaw.

I eventually made him acknowledge that the Home Army [AK] has large numbers in its ranks, that it is motivated by a desire to fight the Germans and generally wants good relations with the Soviet Army. We did not discuss his claims of collaboration with the Germans and on the whole I found him more positively inclined toward the AK than on previous occasions.[1]

In Warsaw, the rain had stopped in the morning of that day and by late afternoon *Luftwaffe* planes appeared in the sky. They strafed and bombed *AK* units fighting in the western industrial suburb of Wola where the *AK*'s commander-in-chief, General Bór, was still stuck in Kamler's furniture factory, unable to move to a more central location. Several bombs were dropped on the city center, in the vicinity of the Victoria Hotel, headquarters of the Warsaw area commander, Colonel Monter. The *Luftwaffe* also showered the capital with leaflets bearing Bór's signature, calling on *AK* members to return to their "alert quarters" and urging the population to demand capitulation.

The bombs damaged a corner building at Kredytowa Street facing one of the telephone exchanges, towering over the area and stubbornly defended by more than a hundred Germans. The *AK*'s local sector commander ordered his fighters to reinforce barricades with the help of the population. When youthful insurgents of platoon no. 101 started looking for volunteers, they found several men dressed in tuxedos and women in long dresses in the cellar of Kredytowa 9. The bombs had obviously interrupted a celebration.[2]

Monter was still without detailed news from all sectors in the southern and northern suburbs (Mokotów and Żoliborz), as well as from the working class suburb of Praga on the Vistula's right bank. He was not quite certain which areas were controlled by the insurgents and appealed to the population, through the megaphones, to hang out Polish national flags to signal they had been liberated. As it turned out, the flags also facilitated the *Luftwaffe*'s subsequent raids.

Monter was encouraged by a report that a major German police stronghold at the crossroads in the western part of the city (intersection of Chłodna and Żelazna streets) had been captured. He also received a message that a column of trucks filled with troops had arrived at Narutowicz Square in southwestern Warsaw—the first component of General von dem Bach's "rescue army." By nightfall a second column reached Okecie Airport, carrying 1,700 men of Kaminski's Russian brigade, some of them drunk.[3]

The command of the German Central Front described the day's activities in the Polish capital in one sentence: "In Warsaw, despite the deployment of two fresh battalions, it was still impossible to secure a transit route through the city."[4]

Meanwhile, in Moscow Mikołajczyk continued his pathetic visit, still hoping for some sort of compromise with Stalin. The strategy of the Soviet dictator was clear from the beginning: by confronting Mikołajczyk with accusations of anti-Soviet activities and collaboration with Germany, he tried to exact a maximum of concessions and basically reduce the unhappy prime minister to the role of an embarrassed petitioner and not a partner. It is still unclear why Stalin bothered to talk to Mikołajczyk at all: The Soviet leader had already thrown his total support behind the communist Lublin committee (which he had set up in the first place) while large numbers of Soviet officers were being seconded to the Polish army formed throughout the liberated Polish territory. Given these two major factors, it was in Stalin's interest to eliminate the *AK* as a potentially dangerous opponent to the communist system he had carefully mapped out for Poland.

Some Polish historians, freed from the shackles of censorship after communism's collapse, claim that Stalin simply had to listen to Mikołajczyk because of the cables from Churchill and Roosevelt accumulated on his desk. To refuse to see the emigré prime minister would be too blatant for a man with Stalin's keen sense of history and could offend Moscow's powerful Western allies, they argue. But in the end, Mikołajczyk's Moscow visit produced no result and did not affect Stalin's plans for Poland.

Mikołajczyk became prime minister of the government-in-exile following Sikorski's death in a plane crash in July 1943. According to an American historian,

No wartime leader stepped into a hotter caldron that Stanisław Mikołajczyk. His public image as a farmer from Poznań and a spokesman for peasant interests was reinforced by a quiet, reserved, almost self-effacing manner.[5]

Although lacking Sikorski's looks and *savoir faire*, Mikołajczyk inspired confidence. It was thought that he would bring fundamental strength to the exiled government, so badly needed as the war and Poland's relations with the Soviet Union entered a crucial stage.

Mikołajczyk's strength was based on a wide support of peasants who constituted some 70 percent of Poland's prewar population. He lacked charisma and worldly charm but had a reputation as a capable organizer and an extremely pragmatic politician—both rare qualities among Polish leaders. But coming from the western part of Poland which for years had lived under Prussian and not Russian domination, he was not as obsessed by the Russian threat as were his ministers and senior Polish officers. In August 1944, his abilities and humble origin constituted no significant assets in his desperate talks with Stalin.

It is hard to determine whether the Western allies believed in any tangible outcome from Mikołajczyk's trip while a new communist authority was already asserting itself in those parts of Poland freed from the German occupation. Perhaps they felt that the unhappy Polish visitor was capable of achieving some form of palatable compromise. (Churchill was said to have described Mikołajczyk as a "man who looks like a fat, slightly bald old fox.")[6]

But almost immediately after Sikorski's death, Mikołajczyk made it abundantly clear that he intended to follow the general's path, particularly as far as foreign policy was concerned. And that meant complete faith that Great Britain and the United States would be instrumental in obtaining a satisfactory compromise in Polish-Soviet relations. "That trust was at one and the same time the Poles' only hope and a prime cause of their downfall.[7]

While in Moscow, Mikołajczyk's aim was not to argue about Poland's claims to the territories beyond the Curzon Line. That idea was reluctantly accepted earlier by Mikołajczyk and his foreign minister, Tadeusz Romer, under strong pressure from Churchill—and to some extent because of their pragmatic attitude. (The rest of the cabinet totally opposed this concession.) Already in February 1944, as the Red Army began disarming *AK* units participating in Operation Storm, Churchill told the House of Commons that Stalin favored "a strong, integral independent Poland as one of the leading powers in Europe." (The British statesman's illusion about the Soviet ally did not last long. Two years later, in a speech at Fulton, Missouri, Churchill said, "Nobody knows what Soviet Russia and its Communist international organizations intend to do in the immediate future and what are the limits, if any, to their proselytizing tendencies." In 1947 Churchill was the first to speak of the establishment of an "Iron Curtain" across Europe.)

On August 9, 1944, Stalin gave a farewell banquet for the unhappy Mikołajczyk, after which the Polish prime minister concluded on a more cheerful note:

During an hour-long conversation held in a very pleasant atmosphere, Stalin showed a greater understanding of the battle for Warsaw, whose importance I repeatedly stressed. Stalin had counted on the entry of Soviet troops into Warsaw on August 6, but his plan was thwarted by a counter-attack of four newly arrived German tank divisions, including the *Herman Goering* division brought from Italy. A flanking maneuver across the Vistula . . . was also delayed by two German tank divisions. This created the necessity of regrouping and bringing forward Soviet artillery. Despite the unexpected delay, Stalin had no doubt about the final outcome. He fully realizes the consequences [of the delay] for our struggle in Warsaw and promises the support of his air force within the limits of his possibilities. He asked us for details and an authoritative statement about the extent of the fighting in Warsaw, which I provided.[8]

The relative optimism emanating from Mikołajczyk's report was transmitted to the Polish General Staff in London, which immediately informed the *AK* command in Warsaw that "Stalin promised Premier Mikołajczyk to provide aid quickly to Warsaw, particularly in drops of weapons." The message also quoted Stalin as saying that a Soviet liaison officer was to be parachuted into the city, with the latest ciphers to facilitate instant communication.

To save time, and without consulting the *AK*, the head of the Polish Forces Under British Command, General Sosnkowski, cabled the Soviet government via the British embassy in Moscow that parachuting an officer into Warsaw was not safe "for technical reasons" and instead proposed an area in Kampinos forest near Warsaw where partisans were well implanted and gave all required indications, such as the password and signals in the drop zone. The officer would then be led by Polish guides to the city. Sosnkowski also specified that Warsaw needed automatic and antitank weapons and German-type ammunition (7.92 millimeters and 9 millimeters) and requested air attacks on several key targets in the area.

The Soviet government never acknowledged receipt of the message, recorded in the Polish General Staff archives under no. 6548/secret/44 and given to the British Foreign Office for relay to Moscow. It is highly unlikely that the Foreign Office or the British embassy in Moscow would either ignore the message or delay it.

There was another message to Moscow from Warsaw relayed by London, addressed to "Marshal Comrade Stalin" and dated August 5. It was written by Captain Konstantin Kalugin who, on August 4, contacted the *AK* command and identified himself as a Soviet intelligence officer sent to observe the situation and report to the commander of the Soviet front facing the Polish capital. Initially, Kalugin said, he had been accompanied by a radio operator, but, in the turmoil of the uprising, the two separated. (See Chapter 7.) Thus he submitted his message to the *AK*, proposing to send it *en clair* without explaining why it was addressed to Stalin himself. In it he wrote:

I have established contact with the commander of the Warsaw garrison which is engaged in a heroic national struggle with Hitlerite bandits. Having been informed of the general military situation, I have come to the conclusion that, despite the heroic attitude of the army and of the civilian population of Warsaw, there are certain requirements which, when fulfilled, would speed up the victory in the struggle against our common enemy. There is a shortage of automatic weapons, ammunition, grenades and anti-tank rifles.

The message listed the areas where supplies should be parachuted, to be identified by red-and-white sheets. It said that "the German air force is destroying the city and the population" and asked for air attacks on specific targets, including the two airfields. It concluded:

The heroic population of Warsaw firmly believes that you will give it the most effective military help in the immediate future. Please facilitate my contact with Marshal Rokossovsky. Capt. Kalugin Konstantin from the Black Group.[9]

The request was couched in standard communist phraseology, and its tone did not surprise the uprising's leadership. It is not clear whether it was radioed in Russian or Polish, but since it was *en clair* no codes were involved. The text (or its translation) kept in the Polish military archives in England was in Polish. To be on the safe side, Colonel Monter, the *AK*'s Warsaw area commander, decided to send a copy to Marshal Rokossovsky as well. An experienced woman courier was given the task of crossing the Vistula and finding the Soviet headquarters, but there is no record that she reached her destination or delivered the Polish request.

On August 8, or three days after Kalugin's original message was radioed to London, and having consulted Bór, Monter decided to address Marshal Rokossovsky himself via London and Moscow.

Since August 1st 1944, I have been engaged in combat against the Germans in Warsaw with the help of the entire population and all military organizations grouped in the *Armia Krajowa*, and others which joined since, such as the Workers' Militia, *Armia Ludowa* and others.

We are in the midst of heavy fighting. To clear their routes of withdrawal, the Germans are burning the city and destroying its population.

At this moment we are still tying up major German armored and infantry units but we are also suffering from a shortage of ammunition and heavy weapons. Consequently, the help of your troops is a vital necessity. Attached to my staff is a Soviet officer, Capt. Kalugin. I request radio codes that would facilitate his contact with you and thus would give me the possibility of coordinating operations.

It was signed "Nurt" (one of Monter's pseudonyms) who identified himself as the "Commander of the Warsaw region."[10]

This matter-of-fact message barely camouflaged the dire straits of the uprising which began to lose its initial offensive vigor and now had to face a massive multifaceted attack by the *Korpsgruppe von dem Bach*. It also represented a dramatic change in the attitude of the *AK* leadership: the embattled insurrection was directly asking for Soviet help, disregarding previous mistreatment of *AK* units and deportation of its officers in eastern Poland. Nonetheless, at least for the time being, Bór preferred not to be personally involved—he assigned the role of the supplicant to Monter. It was also likely that he felt that Rokossovsky might snub the commander of the "fascist *AK*" and would be more inclined to deal with the "commander of the Warsaw region."

At the same time, and particularly in view of total silence from the Russians, the Polish General Staff in London started wondering whether Kalugin still enjoyed Moscow's confidence. Concern increased after Mikołajczyk's report, quoting Stalin's proposal to send a "liaison officer with the latest ciphers," as if Kalugin's mission was no longer of any consequence.

(Kalugin remained in Warsaw virtually until the end of the uprising. He traveled freely throughout the liberated areas and contacted the underground Polish Communist Party, whose armed wing, the People's Army [*Armia Ludowa*] eventually joined the uprising. He subsequently proposed an appeal for help to Stalin via London by all left-wing Polish parties. The *AK* refused to transmit the message, feeling it represented an effort to bypass the government-in-exile. Late in September Kalugin crossed the Vistula to join the Soviet forces deployed on the right bank of the river. There is no record of his further activities.)

If the Poles in Warsaw and London had any optimism about Soviet intentions, it should have been dissipated by the communiqué of the official Soviet agency TASS of August 13, which read:

There have been reports in the foreign press, based on the Polish radio (?) and Polish press, of an uprising in Warsaw Aug. 1st ordered by the Polish emigrés in London. The Polish press and the radio of the emigré government in London, claim that the Warsaw insurgents are in contact with the Soviet command which has refused to help them. TASS has been authorized to state that such foreign press reports are either a misunderstanding or an insult against the Soviet high command. TASS has been informed that the Polish emigré circles responsible for the uprising did not try to coordinate their action with the Soviet high command. In view of that, the responsibility for the events in Warsaw is going to be borne entirely by the Polish emigré circles in London.[11]

In this blunt official communiqué representing a footnote to his conversations with Mikołajczyk, Stalin scored several critical points: He blamed the Poles for not asking his permission to rise against the Germans, and at the same time disclaimed his responsibility for the uprising (although his radio persistently urged it). Thus, in his eyes, the Western Allies could not blame the Soviet Union for Warsaw's fate. The obvious target of the communiqué was the already isolated Polish government-in-exile, which Stalin wanted to discredit totally.

The TASS communique ended the first *AK* effort to establish communications with the Soviet command, leaving further action up to the government in London. A barrage of Soviet press and radio attacks on the exile government and the *AK* followed.

A Polish historian of the uprising believes that August 4 was a crucial date because the battle for Warsaw "had reached a certain equilibrium between the opposing forces."[12] In effect what happened was that the Poles consolidated their control of large portions of the city while the Germans waited for reinforcements to launch their attack, without losing any more ground to the insurgents. But although the Polish command had no solid basis to count on Allied help, the German side was mobilizing additional forces for its garrison in Warsaw.

Shortly after the outbreak of the uprising, Bór issued orders to units mobilized for Operation Storm to interrupt their previously assigned activities and march to bring help to Warsaw. Given the nature of the terrain and the presence of occupation troops throughout the country, Bór estimated that the first sizeable partisan units would reach Warsaw about August 14.

There was considerable euphoria among the population of the capital in areas liberated by the insurgents. *AK* units which fled the city during the uprising's first night returned to the Mokotów and Żoliborz suburbs, in most cases reinforced by better armed partisan volunteers. In some areas the mood was almost festive. The *AK*'s civilian authorities emerged from the underground with secretaries, typewriters, and detailed and well-prepared directives. Hospitals, canteens, and food distribution points were being organized. (That aspect of the uprising seemed to function better than the initial military phase.) Posters appealing "To Arms in *AK* Ranks" appeared on the walls. In addition to the *AK*'s official *Biuletyn Informacyjny*, other newspapers started publication, usually on two sheets. The citizenry was blissfully unaware of the uprising's highly precarious position and apparently not perturbed by the lack of Allied help.

During that phase of the uprising the *AK*'s activities were limited to night attacks on German positions, particularly those threatening the liberated areas. Several actions were successful, losses were manageable, and weapons were seized. But on the whole a dramatic shortage persisted. In many cases men relieved from their posts on barricades handed over their weapons to their replacements. There were strict orders to save ammunition.

An officer of the *Chrobry II* Battalion in in the western sector of the city center recalled later that

initially the shortage of weapons was catastrophic. All pre-uprising calculations failed. The reality was sad. In daily reports, inflammatory bottles were often counted as weapons, along with rifles and submachine guns. Frequently I had to persuade unit commanders to lend their weapons to men in more threatened areas.[13]

During the night of August 4 to August 5, RAF Halifax aircraft dropped a number of containers on the western suburbs held by the insurgents. A total of twelve containers were recovered, loaded with machine guns, antitank PIAT weapons, and light machine guns with ammunition.

By late afternoon on August 4, *Wehrmacht*, Vlasov Army, and militarized German police battalions were disembarking from trains and trucks near Warsaw's western city limits. On the same day, SS *Gruppenführer* Heinz Reinefarth, who was in charge of units mobilized by Himmler in Poznań, reported to the headquarters of the 9th German Army in

Skierniewice. He was told by army commander General Vormann that the uprising in Warsaw was more "threatening" than initially believed and that the troops of the garrison under General Stahel were fighting "in isolation." Although General Vormann felt that the forces available so far were too weak for any decisive action, he nonetheless ordered Reinefarth to attack the western suburb of Wola and push forward to free General Stahel, who was barricaded in the Brühl Palace in the city center.

In an analysis of the situation in Warsaw after the first four days of fighting and based mainly on the evaluation by General Stahel and reports from German agents and Polish informers, the command of the 9th German Army estimated that

The insurgents in Warsaw have suffered heavy losses but are receiving steady help from outlying areas. . . . The insurgents believe that if the uprising succeeds with the help of the Red Army, an independent Polish state would be created under Allied tutelage. The hard-core bands are fighting fiercely and stubbornly despite the burning of entire streets and air attacks. . . . After air attacks, hard-core bands fire with machine guns at intersections, killing all passersby. . . . The appearance of an armored unit was reported from the ghetto. [The report apparently referred to two captured German tanks used by insurgents]. . . . In northwest [of the city] shooting stopped, apparently as a result of leaflets dropped by the 9th Army. The result of the leaflets in the remaining areas could not be determined. . . .

Virtually the entire population lives in cellars. . . . There is increased conviction that many people do not participate in the uprising and long for it to end.[14]

The report also referred to a "Polish priest" who sheltered captured German soldiers from an antiaircraft unit, as well as to the release by Poles of thirteen other German prisoners following assurances by a German commander that the twenty-five Poles held by his unit had already been freed. To the author of the German analysis, this was proof that "Poles absolutely believe words of a German officer." (According to the *AK* version, the twenty-five Poles allegedly released belonged to Platoon 1139 and were executed on August 3.)

The German analysis appears superficial and to a great extent influenced by wishful thinking. The 9th Army had obviously little concrete information about the organization and equipment of the *AK* or of its tactics. It persisted in referring to "bands" and "bandits."

At 7:00 A.M. on August 5, Reinefarth's force of some 5,000 men backed by tanks began a massive attack on the suburb of Wola, pushing the insurgents toward the Old Town. Meanwhile the well-armed *AK* group *Radosław*, consisting mainly of young men and women brought up on the ideology of Robert Baden-Powell's Scout movement, was in action against German positions in the ruins of the ghetto, freeing a camp containing Jewish prisoners (324 men and twenty-four women). According to Radoslaw's battle journal, eighty-nine were Polish citizens; the others were Dutch, Romanian, and Hungarian. Many of them joined the ranks of the insurgents.[15]

By noon August 5, the attacking Germans controlled parts of the industrial and working-class suburb. From the first day of the attack, mass slaughter of the civilian population, regardless of age and sex, began in the areas seized by the Germans and their renegade Russian allies. The number of victims was estimated in the thousands. Some of Wola's 38,000 inhabitants managed to flee toward the Old Town. The entire suburb was in flames.

An insurgent wounded in the abdomen and operated on in the *Karola i Marii* hospital recalled that when he woke up after the operation late on August 4, Polish forces were leaving the hospital, and all patients capable of walking were following them. On August 6 at 10:00 A.M.,

A Russian renegade of the Vlasov army stormed into the ward and, threatening the patients with his rifle, proceeded to rob them of rings and watches. . . . Someone showed him an identity card, saying that he was a loyal German citizen working for a major German company. The soldier looked at the document and tore it into shreds. "Never mind, you will all be shot anyway," he said in Russian.

A German officer waving a pistol appeared, ordering all to leave the ward and saying the hospital would be burned. . . . We limped out of the building in a long file in hospital underclothes into a courtyard where [another] German officer separated us into two groups. . . . There were 30 to 40 wounded in my group as well as several doctors and nurses. . . . We were led into the street and started walking westward. Houses were burning on both sides of the street. The hot pavement scalded our bare feet. . . .

After a while the column was halted and we were lined up in front of a machine gun. . . . There was little doubt what was about to happen. Some of the wounded prayed, some desperately searched for a cigarette, and others—including myself—stood motionless, pale, incapable of making a move. After a while the machine gun was removed and a German officer approached and asked where the chief surgeon was. When there was no reply, he said "You have one minute, and if he is not found, all doctors will be shot." We stood there speechless, staring at the doctors in our group. Then one of them stepped out. The German took him by the arm, led him a few steps away, and signalled to a Vlasov soldier, who aimed his rifle and fired, shattering the doctor's skull.[16]

The assault of the German troops, and particularly the Oskar Dirlewanger brigade consisting of released criminals, continued unabated, backed by tanks and air strikes. The daily 9th Army communiqué of August 6 stated that "despite the use of tanks and dive bombers, the insurgents are fighting exceptionally hard. [German] attacks from the north and south managed to gain very little terrain."

On August 5 General von dem Bach reported to General Vormann, the commander of the 9th Army, and received the title of "the general commanding in the Warsaw region." He decided to establish his headquarters in nearby Sochaczew, but already at 7:00 P.M. he was in Warsaw at General Reinefarth's command post near the railway viaduct in Wola.

He found what he later described as "a chaotic situation." While "every unit fired in a different direction and nobody really knew where to shoot," Reinefarth's police units were busy executing groups of civilians. Von dem Bach issued terse orders to reduce chaos and stressed the need for determined action backed by Stuka dive bombers to relieve General Stahel in his isolated headquarters. At the Nuremberg trials, General von dem Bach said that he also halted mass executions of the population, a statement corroborated by General Reinefarth.[17] According to *AK* records, the slaughter of women and children in that area of Warsaw indeed stopped on August 5.

Shortly after dawn on Sunday, August 6, Reinefarth began carrying out the orders by attacking a large Polish force in the region of the cemeteries outside Wola while the *Luftwaffe* launched intensive raids on the Old Town and parts of the center. Smoke from burning buildings shrouded the western part of the city held by the insurgent units. The picture of disaster was heightened by the arrival on foot of large groups of people who were fleeing Wola and spreading horror stories.

By midafternoon, as the insurgent battalions of Lieutenant Colonel Radosław were pushed back, Kamler's factory found itself in the first line of Polish defenses. General Bór and his staff, as well as the deputy premier of the government-in-exile, decided to move to the Old Town across the ruins of the ghetto, accompanied by the members of Radosław's group who had no weapons.

After establishing his new headquarters, Bór dispatched an officer to Colonel Monter in the city center and asked him to relieve pressure on the insurgents fighting in Wola by launching an attack from the east. According to some accounts, Monter ignored the order, telling the envoy from the commander-in-chief that he had "no weapons or ammunition for irresponsible undertakings."

By then a battalion of the German Dirlewanger Brigade had seized Mirowski Square and its complex of market halls (similar to *Les Halles* in Paris). Sweeping aside insurgent defenses, and using groups of civilians as "living shields," the attackers reached the Saxon Park (*Ogród Saski*) adjacent to the Brühl Palace, thus relieving the besieged General Stahel. Apparently it was high time. The morale of the military police (*Feldgendarmerie*) unit in the palace was low and the hastily armed German civilian employees of the governor's office were anxious to be sent home. "There were many defenders but there was no will to fight. Everybody kept drinking and hiding in dark corners."[18] (There was no apparent reason for fear because the Polish insurgents never came close to the Brühl Palace.)

As night fell, a Polish counterattack on Mirowski Square was beaten back, and General Reinefarth reported he was in firm control of a transit route across Warsaw toward the Vistula. Reinefarth then returned to Wola in a tank, leaving the Dirlewanger brigade under General Stahel's command. The victorious Dirlewanger troops rounded up several hundred Polish civilian men to clear the barricades and the debris of fighting along the transit route. According to postwar Polish documents, all were subsequently executed.

At the same time, SS General Mieczysław Kaminski's Russian "National Liberation" (*RONA*) brigade attacked the insurgents in the southwestern Ochota suburb to establish access to the main east-west thoroughfare, the Aleje Jerozolimskie, and then to the other main bridge across the river, the Poniatowski Bridge. An insurgent officer recalled that the area was swept by fires, and the fleeing inhabitants were shot as they ran, "each victim greeted by whoops from drunken soldiers."[19] An estimated force of some 300 insurgents fought for a week before abandoning the suburb.

The insurrection forces thus became divided into four separate defensive areas which communicated with one another mainly through the sewers and field telephone: Żoliborz in the north, the Old Town, the city center, and Mokotów in the south. Each region basically fought in isolation, separated from neighbors by a German ring of steel.

NOTES

1. Mikołajczyk's coded radio message to Warsaw of August 17.
2. At the time the author was a member of the platoon.
3. A German prisoner in conversation with the author September 1944.
4. *HG Mitte* no. 4000.44/secret.
5. Allen Paul, *Katyn: The Untold Story of Stalin's Polish Massacre* (New York: Charles Scribner's Sons, 1991), p. 283.
6. Joseph Retinger, *Memoirs of an Eminence Grise* (Brighton: Sussex University Press, 1972), p. 144.
7. Paul, *Katyn: The Untold Story of Stalin's Polish Massacre*, p. 284.
8. Author's translation of the official Polish text of Mikołajczyk's statement.
9. *Polskie Siły Zbrojne* (London: General Sikorski Historical Institute, 1950), Vol. III, p. 831.
10. Entered in Polish General Staff records as 6504/secret.
11. Author's translation.
12. Adam Borkiewicz, *Powstanie Warszawskie 1944* (Warsaw: Pax, 1957), p. 137.
13. In conversation with the author in *Stalag* XIA in January 1945.
14. Central Front files *HG Mitte, Ic AO, Banden Abendsmeldung*, August 4, 1944.
15. *Biuletyn Informacyjny*, no. 43/44.

16. A postwar report submitted by "Jeleń" of the *Zośka* Battalion to the unit's veterans' association.

17. Nuremberg trial records.

18. Statement of "Franz Krug" to the German authorities, August 19, 1944.

19. Postwar statement of Lieutenant "Gustaw" to Polish investigators.

Warsaw, August 2, 1944: A Polish patrol advances into the city center after the first night of fighting.

Insurgents in one of the last actions before the fall of the Old Town.

An *Armia Krajowa* company near the Warsaw Polytechnic Institute.

Defending Warsaw's main power station.

The Old Town's last stand before a retreat to the sewers.

Fighting in the ruins of the Old Town.

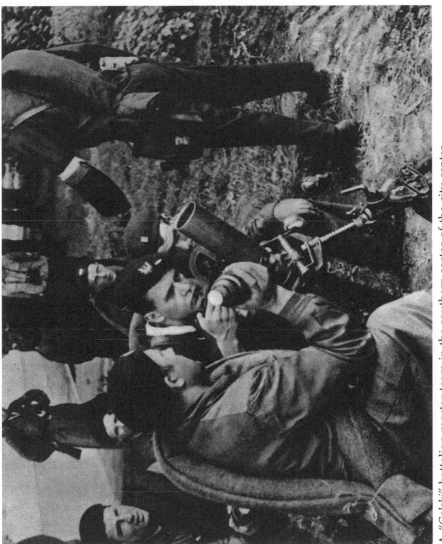

A *"Golski"* battalion mortar team in the southern sector of the city center.

CHAPTER 10

Alone in the Ruins

The German plan for wresting control of Warsaw from the hands of the Polish insurgents was an example of military simplicity combined with totally uncompromising and brutal treatment of the civilian population. It called for the establishment of secure east-west transit routes through the city and across all bridges linking the left and right banks of the Vistula, to be followed by the gradual and systematic seizure of all sectors controlled by the uprising. The attacks were to be carried out against one Polish sector at a time, using the maximum number of troops and firepower in each case. At the same time, the rest of the Polish-held areas were to be harassed by artillery fire and periodic dive-bomber attacks. One of the objectives was to break the morale of the population and thus deprive the insurgents—or "bands" in German terminology—of badly needed moral support.

The strategy was crafted by men with experience in nearly five years of war during which Nazi Germany had conquered most of Europe. For several years—at least until the battle of Stalingrad in 1943, General Erwin Rommel's defeat in North Africa, and the Allied landings in Italy and France—there was no one to effectively challenge Germany's military efficiency and superiority.

In Warsaw, the hastily mobilized German war machine was facing poorly armed and generally young insurgents, mostly without adequate training or battle experience, but seized by what German reports described as fury and determination. Their senior commanders, men in their midforties or older, had combat experience as junior officers during World War I in the Austro-Hungarian, Prussian, or Russian armies and during Poland's subsequent victorious war against the newly born Soviet Union in 1920. The disastrous monthlong 1939 campaign against Germany could hardly be considered a successful training ground. Some were graduates of France's prestigious *Ecole Supérieure de Guerre*, where, during the period between the two world wars, the stress was on the advantages of defense along fixed lines, a concept shattered by *Blitzkrieg*.

Furthermore, the senior cadres of the uprising were to a great extent affected by years of conspiracy and constant and all-pervasive efforts to avoid detection and arrest. Many, if not most, basically had lived "on the run," continually changing their identity cards, psuedonyms, and hiding places. It was hardly an environment propitious to keeping a cool head and steady nerves.

According to records of the 9th Army, the German command assessed relatively quickly the combat performance and adaptability of the insurgents to urban fighting. On August 9, after eight days of basically preliminary clashes during which the Germans did not use all means needed to quell the uprising, General Vormann, the 9th Army's commander, saw the situation with considerable misgivings. He wrote in a report that

[t]he resistance in Warsaw is growing constantly. Initially improvised, the uprising is now directed according to military rules. There are no prospects for a speedy quelling of the uprising with the means available at present.... There is also the danger that the [Polish] action might spread to a wider area, possibly throughout the country. The action can be characterized as street fighting for individual buildings in a large city.... Our losses are heavy.

The report stressed that the uprising could seriously affect the supplying of German troops, fighting east of the Vistula. General Vormann estimated that "what is needed to clarify the situation is an additional full division with a large quantity of heavy weapons."[1]

All German accounts covering the first two weeks of the fighting show concern about the degree of Polish resistance. They attributed it mainly to the insurgent tactics of allowing attacks, including by tanks, to come close to Polish positions and then of showering them with concentrated machine gunfire, grenades, and inflammatory bottles. The reports stressed that most German dead were killed by shots in the head and concluded that the insurgents disposed of a large number of well-trained sharpshooters. The German side did not notice either the paucity of automatic weapons nor the desperate lack of ammunition which was to plague the uprising throughout its duration.

In reality, although a number of sharpshooters did exist, most insurgents perfected their use of weapons while fighting. In street combat conditions, when enemies often face each other across a narrow street and frequently closer, the submachine gun became a much more practical weapon than the rifle. The Underground produced a limited quantity of such weapons based on the very simple and effective British Sten. According to an authoritative study by Adam Borkiewicz, until July 1944 Warsaw's conspiratorial workshops produced 650 "Polish Stens," as well as 2,000 similar and equally effective weapons known as *Błyskawica* (lightning). The clandestine "industry" also made some 10,000 inflammatory bottles and 200 flamethrowers.[2]

The insurgents became adept in using hand grenades, many of them produced in primitive workshops during four years of conspiracy. It was obvious that Warsaw's "rebellious children" were not afraid of fighting at close quarters—perhaps because many of them were oblivious to the potential dangers.

As the uprising spread throughout Warsaw, several other underground organizations joined in, placing their units under *AK* sector commanders. Although the command of the communist People's Army (*Armia Ludowa–AL*) left the city in July, some of its units remained. There was also a similar leftist organization known as the Polish People's Army (*Polska Armia Ludowa–PAL*) which placed its men under tactical *AK* command. Several weeks before the uprising, the command of the extreme right-wing National Armed Forces (*Narodowe Siły Zbrojne–NSZ*) agreed to join the *AK*. All told, the combined strength of these organizations participating in the uprising was estimated at 2,000. (During the immediate postwar years, the communist propaganda liked to claim that the brunt of the Warsaw fighting was borne by the *AL*.)

During the first period of fighting, the German military intelligence proved to be deficient. One of the reasons was that not many insurgents were willing to surrender, and those who were caught were summarily executed. Thus the German side relied mainly on information from a handful of agents it had managed to keep in areas seized by the uprising. And, given the conditions of urban fighting, their information was rarely accurate.

According to General Vormann's assessment of August 13, "most of the city [Warsaw] has been seized by the insurgents, who resist stubbornly and attack selected targets. They are getting supplies by air."[3] In fact, because of the intense German antiaircraft fire, parachute drops on the city from England were infrequent.

The German military machine did not take long to draw the necessary conclusions and to remedy its initial weakness in reacting to the uprising. The command system was simplified by placing the *Korpsgruppe von dem Bach*, until then responsible to Himmler, under the direct control of General Vormann's 9th Army. The group was heavily reinforced with *Wehrmacht*, paramilitary police, and specialized formations, reaching, by August 13, according to postwar Polish assessments, about 25,700 men, twenty-six tanks, thirty-eight self-propelled cannons, as well as several batteries of artillery and heavy mortars.[4] General von dem Bach's report for August 20 (*Gefechtstand den 20.VIII.44*) lists only 285 officers and 16,514 other ranks—not including some police and foreign formations, consisting mainly of Russians and Ukrainians. The *Korpsgruppe* could also count on the support of the artillery of the 9th Army estimated at 118 cannons of all calibers and of the front's air force.

General Vormann recommended that once the task of establishing unhindered "throughways" cutting across the city to the Vistula was accomplished and the heavily defended Old Town seized, further steps should depend "on the attitude of the bands." In the event that the "bands" failed to respond to capitulation appeals, they were to be "surrounded and destroyed."[5]

Although unaware of the degree of German preparations to stifle the uprising, Bór realized the approaching danger and pressed London for help, in effect accusing Poland's Western allies of failure to honor their commitments. His radio message of August 6 to London shows increasing bitterness—reflecting an alarming situation:

The Germans are bringing into action technical means which we do not possess: armor, artillery, aircraft and flame throwers. Although they are superior, we dominate spiritually. The bolshevik [sic] attack calmed down three days ago on Warsaw's peripheries without an impact on the battle in the city.

I affirm that in its present struggle Warsaw is not receiving help from the allies, just as Poland did not receive it in 1939. The balance of our alliance with Britain to date represented our help in the Battle of Britain in 1940, combat in Norway, Africa, Italy and on the western front.

We demand that you clearly spell out this fact to the British in an official statement. We are not asking for help—we are demanding that it be granted immediately. We are also demanding a halt to radio broadcasts publicizing our weakness, which is damaging to us.[6]

The exchange of statements and messages between the Polish government-in-exile and the British Foreign office, as well as between London and Warsaw, shows an enormous gap between Polish expectations and British capabilities. True, as Warsaw was fighting for survival, the Polish Second Corps of the British 8th Army was advancing beyond Ancona on Italy's Adriatic Coast, while an armored division prepared to embark for Normandy. The Polish components of the RAF were in action daily, and the parachute brigade awaited orders. However, none of this meant that the British were ready to suffer unsustainable losses in what they considered to be an exceptionally hazardous operation in distant Warsaw. They made that much clear to the Poles from the beginning, a fact that Bór steadfastly refused to accept.

On the eve of his departure for Moscow on July 25, Mikołajczyk told Churchill that the *AK* in Warsaw had been put in a state of alert in preparation for an uprising. On July 27, Count Edward Raczyński, the Polish ambassador accredited to Great Britain, informed Foreign Secretary Anthony Eden of Bór's request for the parachute brigade and air strikes on German airfields near Warsaw in the event of an uprising. Raczyński also told Eden that the exiled government would like to send four Polish RAF squadrons to Poland once the *AK* had secured the airfields. Eden promised to examine the request with military authorities but pointed out the obvious "technical problems," the foremost being the fact that Warsaw was beyond the reach of British bombers. Such distant flights were normally carried out by the U.S. Army Air Corps, landing for refueling at Soviet airfields. Apparently the Poles had not considered such details, including the defense of such airfields against the *Luftwaffe*.

The formal British reply handed to the Poles July 28 was predictable:

Quite apart from the difficulties of coordinating such action with the Soviet Government, whose forces are operating against the Germans on Polish territory, operational considerations alone preclude us from meeting the requests for assisting the rising in Warsaw. It would not be possible to fly the parachute brigade over German territory as far as Warsaw without risking excessive losses. The despatch of fighter squadrons to airfields in Poland would also be a lengthy and complicated process which could, in any case, only be carried out in agreement with the Soviet Government. It could certainly not be accomplished in time to influence the present battle.[7]

Basically what the exiled Poles and the *AK* command wanted was the assistance of the regular Polish troops and air force which would, in their minds, tilt the outcome of the uprising in their favor. Apparently the logistical and political considerations were never adequately considered although they seemed obvious, even to a layman.

While the Poles in London were rebuffed in their somewhat Quixotic quest, General Sosnkowski, the commander-in-chief of the Polish Forces under British Command, was in Italy, observing the operations of the Polish troops there. General Sosnkowski did manage to send several messages to Bór via London, one of them stating that he "categorically" opposed an uprising (see Prologue). Obviously Sosnkowski's caution was disregarded.

Although the British reply to Polish demands was painfully clear, the exile government did nothing to prevent the planned uprising. On the contrary, in its quest to reaffirm its legality in the very heart of Poland, it hoped for a miraculous success against improbable odds. The final decision and the timing to begin the action was left in the hands of the *AK* command—but the outcome depended on Stalin's goodwill.

When London realized that Warsaw was in the throes of serious fighting from which there was no easy withdrawal, the exiled Polish statesmen began bombarding Britain with requests for help—any form of help. The result was the first parachute drop of supplies in the region of the Protestant cemetery in Wola during the night of August 3 to 4. On the ground, amidst unending explosions and the chatter of machine gunfire, the drop was seen as a sign that Warsaw was not alone. But the scarcity of subsequent parachuted supplies soon brought disappointment. More and more frequent were the somber tones of the *Chorał* broadcast from London, a heart-rending nineteenth-century song about Poland's strife which had become a coded signal that no parachute drops were envisaged the following night.

After Sosnkowski's return to London from Italy and Mikołajczyk's from Moscow, the Poles launched a new series of dramatic pleas to the British and U.S. authorities. They heard the same logical explanations that the distance precluded any concerted and effective help from the West. Moreover, there was also the argument that Poland was in the Soviet operational sphere and that, basically, the Soviet side should have no difficulty in helping Warsaw. The British duly forwarded the Polish requests to Moscow—without effect.

In Italy, which the Poles considered to be a more convenient base for flights to Poland, RAF commander Air Marshal John Slessor opposed the operation as "dangerous and not promising to be successful." But faced with an offer by Polish pilots to volunteer for the mission, Slessor informed the Imperial General Staff that

Because of the desire of Polish squadrons under my command to undertake this risky operation, I see no possibility to refuse the gallant Polish commander. Consequently I agreed, although I should have maintained my objection. Weather permitting, a Polish squadron will undertake the operation and we will give it all our help.[8]

In the end Polish pilots were not the only ones to fly supplies to embattled Warsaw. They were joined by British, Canadian, and South African crews, followed by a massive daytime flight of some 110 U.S. "flying fortresses" protected by fighter planes on September 18, during which most containers fell on German-held territory. Discouraged by the fact that the areas held by the insurgents were shrinking, preventing effective high-altitude drops, the Americans discontinued further such flights. (See Chapter 12.)

While the exiled government in London struggled to convince the allies to give more effective help to the uprising, heavy fighting went on in the western part of Warsaw. Street by street, the powerfully armed German forces were pushing the insurgents from the western suburbs, the region of the cemeteries, and the ruins of the ghetto toward the Old Town. The German attacks soon isolated the Old Town from the center, prompting the *AK* command to set up "Group North" under the command of Colonel "Wachnowski" (Karol Ziemski) who found himself initially in charge of some 5,500 insurgents in a dozen units of different sizes which were mostly poorly armed. The arrival of Bór with his staff from Wola had little impact on the situation, but it obliged Wachnowski to deal directly with the *AK* commander-in-chief rather than via Colonel Monter's Warsaw command in the city center. Bór was in permanent radio contact with London, and in one of his first messages from the Old Town, he urged that the Polish parachute brigade be sent to the Kampinos forest north of Warsaw, from where it could relieve the insurgents who were under increasing pressure.

On Sunday, August 6, under clear blue skies, *AK* units staged the first and only parade of the uprising, marching through narrow streets lined with pastel-colored medieval houses which would soon be turned into rubble. (The Old Town was reconstructed with record speed after the war, with architects referring to the eighteenth-century paintings of Giovanni Canaletto.)

Within several days, Wachnowski brought under his command the embattled group of Lieutenant Colonel Radosław, by then fighting in the ruins of the ghetto, as well as the northern suburb of Żoliborz and the partisan units in the Kampinos forest. Contact with Żoliborz was established by radio and telephone, but sewers were used to carry messages, weapons, and ammunition. Several efforts to break through the surrounding Germans and link up with Żoliborz failed. Wachnowski also organized workshops to repair weapons and launched the production of explosives which supplied the insurgents with 120 hand grenades a day.

The *Wehrmacht*, SS, and Vlasov army units under the overall command of SS *Gruppenführer* (general) Heinz Reinefarth pushed irrevocably toward the Old Town, attacking the Town Hall on August 4, using as cover a group of Polish women with children and thus hampering the effectiveness of the defenders' fire. Although the attack failed, the German forces seized control of a number of adjacent buildings, rounding up the population and herding it to the nearby opera building. "Men were shot and women were used in the building of barricades or acting as a cover for riflemen."[9]

Meanwhile, after eight days of fighting and a number of counterattacks, Radosław saw the strength of his group dwindle from the initial 3,000 to barely over 1,000. His battalions originated mainly in the Scout movement (*Szare Szeregi* or Grey Ranks) and consisted of highly ideological young men and women, mostly of middle-class back-ground, many of whom had undergone conspiratorial officers' training which included combat experience in partisan units. Radosław, wounded in the leg, felt that a great potential was being depleted and suggested to Bór to gather his remaining forces and fight through the German ring to the Kapinos forest. There, he argued, his troops would serve as cadres for some 1,600 insurgents mobilized from areas near Warsaw and, bolstered by parachuted weapons, could act as a relief force to attack the Germans from outside. Bór turned down the project, fearing that removing the Radosław group would endanger the defenses of the Old Town.

Just as happened previously in Wola, Bór's headquarters in the Old Town soon found itself in the first line of defense and had to move deeper into the besieged area, to the building which before the war housed the Ministry of Justice. But there, too, he was unable to exercise systematic control over the *AK* units in the rest of the city, which were divided by the superior German forces. According to a letter from Major "Gromski" in the Old Town to Colonel "Prezes" (Jan Rzepecki) at Monter's headquarters in the city center, "Bór and his staff are in command of nothing."[10]

During the night of August 12, RAF aircraft carried out two drops of weapons on the Old Town. A brief message from Bór informed London that

On August 12 the enemy again tried to destroy our forces in the Old Town. The situation is extremely difficult. Individual buildings were lost and recovered. Enormous artillery barrage. In the evening we redressed the situation by a series of counter attacks. Heavy losses in personnel and destruction.[11]

A participant recalled that he defended a position in a warehouse, his light machine gun propped up on sacks of flour and sugar, when a German unit advanced.

I ordered the boys to hold their fire until they came closer. When I saw their faces and their fixed bayonets glittering in the sun, I could no longer wait and shouted "fire." The room shook from explosions. Some Germans surged forward, others sought cover near the wall. The noise became more deafening. Suddenly I realized that we no longer saw any targets. Downstairs, underneath our position, there was hand-to-hand fighting. . . . After a while we had the first prisoners: they had no hope of retreating under our fire. The rest of the [German] company managed to withdraw.

An hour later, another attack, this one preceded by strong artillery fire. We have more and more wounded. Our platoon now has no more than 40 people, including the girls.[12]

(According to its battle journal, on August 19 the Radosław group consisted of 659 personnel, including fifty-six officers and ninety-six women. It was armed with two heavy machine guns, twenty-five light machine guns, 124 rifles, 130 submachine guns, one mortar, and three PIAT antitank launchers.)

While the Old Town was being increasingly pulverized, *AK* forces in the southern suburb of Mokotów expanded their territory southward in an area of orchards, gardens, and suburban villas. Among their booty, the Mokotów insurgents captured stores with some 6,000 *Luftwaffe* over-alls, mostly gray or dark blue, which subsequently became the standard uniform of the *AK* battalions in the area.

Meanwhile life in the city center had become increasingly organized. There were soup kitchens and regular distributions of flour, wartime coffee, and other food supplies previously stored by the Germans. There were several open-air cafés where insurgents were entertained by singers who wore red-and-white armbands. Boy scouts in short pants carried mail within the two areas of the center—north and south—which re-quired crossing in the trench built across the main east-west avenue, Aleje Jerozolimskie. There were new postage stamps, as well as occu-pation stamps with Hitler's image crossed out.

Workshops where teams of women sewed berets and forage caps with *AK* pennants multiplied, and the insurgent army acquired a more martial look. In other factories specialists worked on converting unexploded bombs and artillery shells into hand grenades. (An average 250-kilogram bomb used by Stuka diver bombers could yield enough explosive ma-terial for 800 hand grenades.) Ammunition was still short, and new posters appeared on the walls, showing a skull inside a German helmet and the inscription "Every bullet—One German." Passes were required for civilians and insurgents traveling from one area to another. Internal barricades were manned around the clock, and anybody who moved after the evening curfew was challenged with the traditional *"Stój, kto idzie!"* (Halt, who goes there!). The password and answer changed daily and usually started with the same letters, example, *"Demokrata—doktor, Wilno—wolność."*

Insurgents who had no weapons drilled and sang military songs or quelled the increasing number of fires and struggled without adequate tools to rescue survivors from ruined houses. In the second half of Au-gust, the Germans started harassing the city with heavy mortars as well as *Nebelwerfers*—multiple launchers of large caliber incendiary shells making a characteristic sound as they were fired. (Insurgents called them "lowing cows.") Electricity was still available but water became scarce, and in parts of the city insurgents as well as German prisoners were employed digging wells. Fires frequently had to be fought with sand, passed in buckets by human chains. Half a dozen daily newspapers representing various political tendencies were distributed, usually free of charge. A few shops were still open, accepting the occupation regime's Polish *złotys*. One could get a haircut and have one's shoes repaired. But as time went by, even such institutions representing normality began to disappear.

More and more people took to living in cellars, creating a syndrome opposed by the *AK* authorities, which claimed that a *Stuka* bomb or a heavy artillery shell could easily puncture the average Warsaw apartment building and reach its cellar. By punching holes through the walls of the cellars to neighboring buildings, the insurgents created a whole underground tunnel network. Initially, while pockets of German resistance existed in the midst of areas controlled by the insurrection, traveling through the tunnels avoided sniper fire. In the later stages, while Warsaw was under quasi-permanent artillery bombardment, the "underground city" was regarded as a safer way of moving around. The tunnels were equipped with signs giving street names and arrows indicating directions.

Many people simply ignored *AK* warnings against too much reliance on cellars as shelters and continued their underground existence. One *AK* officer noted that

During the second half of the uprising, I realized that these people were suffering from the "cellar disease," which was very difficult to cure. I tried to persuade them to leave their shelters and employed them in collecting scrap for the production of grenades. . . . Some could not be persuaded. They were like cave dwellers, always terrified and pale from the lack of fresh air. Many lived in this state until the end, that is until the capitulation, and emerged from their cellars only when the Germans ordered all inhabitants to leave the city.[13]

As time went by, sewers became an essential part of the insurgent supply and communication system. Above all, when sectors surrounded by the Germans had no other hope but surrender or withdrawal, they usually withdrew through the sewers. The Germans took some time to realize their importance and eventually resorted to planting booby traps inside or raising the water level by piling up sacks of sand near some manholes.

The Warsaw sewer system dates back to the middle of the nineteenth century and was considerably expanded during the years preceding World War II. It consisted of a basic sewer network emptying the city's waste into the river and of large storm sewers, varying in height from six to eight feet. The ordinary sewers were egg-shaped and small, with an average height of between three and five feet. A large storm sewer between the city center and the Old Town was dry at the time of the uprising, but the *AK* command hesitated to use it in order not to alert the Germans when it became clear that it might be needed for a major evacuation. Meanwhile couriers—mostly boys and short women—traveled through a series of small side sewers, a trip requiring considerable effort and stamina.

The first sewer trip was a harrowing experience when I volunteered to carry mail to the Old Town in a group of five boys.

The guide was a short, stocky girl of about 19. She wore a German camouflage jacket which reached the middle of her thighs and old rubber boots. She had short hair which she had pinned tightly under a filthy beret. She showed us how to strap packages wrapped in waterproof cloth not to our backs, like rucksacks, but to the front. Each of us received a short, sturdy stick.

The sewer, the girl explained, was going to be 90 centimeters high and about 60 centimeters wide. We will be going under German positions and "occasionally they throw hand grenades inside. One peep from any of you can mean death."

We had to wait for a mortar barrage to finish before reaching the open manhole and descend along a small iron ladder, leaving behind bright August sun. The stench, total silence and feeling of isolation were overpowering. The guide counted us with the aid of her flashlight and then illuminated a dark hole. It was the entrance to the sewer.

She led us into that hole, holding her stick in front of her. The stick automatically stopped at the point where the lower part of the egg-shaped sewer narrowed, thus supporting her. She extricated it and moved forward, her back touching the top of the sewer. Her movements resembled those of a rabbit.

We followed imitating her and eventually each of us developed a certain rhythm. We advanced slowly in the slime and after a while the smell did not seem to be so overwhelming. We crossed several intersections where the sewage fluid moved swiftly and light penetrated from open manholes. Our hands, our shoes, in fact everything was covered with slime. Periodically, we rested. The trip seemed to go on forever although it did not last more than three hours.

"Old Town," finally announced the girl pointing to the growing light ahead of us. We climbed to the surface up another iron ladder. The light blinded us for a few seconds. We were in a narrow street lined with gutted buildings, some of them piles of bricks and crushed masonry. The street itself was covered with debris and tangled wires. A bored-looking man in a German military overcoat with an *AK* armband sat on a chair near the manhole, holding a submachine gun in his lap. All around us explosions followed one another with clockwork regularity. The air was thick with dust.[14]

Toward the end of August, the insurrection had little hope of holding on to the Old Town, by then a heap of rubble. Insurgents and Germans fought at close quarters in individual buildings, churches, and doorways. The center of the crumbling fortress was pounded by artillery and attacked by Stukas from the air. A battle order found on the body of a German soldier showed that General Reinefarth commanded four infantry and two engineering battalions, over twenty tanks, twenty self-propelled cannons, an armored train, a battery of six field guns, five heavy mortars on railway flatcars, and a battery of *Nebelwerfers*. During the final phase of the attack on the Old Town, the *Luftwaffe* carried out an average of twelve bombing raids a day.[15]

On August 22, with much of the Old Town in ruins, in the northern suburb of Żoliborz, General. "Grzegorz" (Tadeusz Pełczynski), together with Lieutenant Colonel Żywiciel, the regional commander, drafted a plan to relieve the pressure of the battered stronghold by attacking the Gdańsk railway station (*Dworzec Gdański*). Until then the insurgent forces in Żoliborz conducted mainly small, peripheral actions, losing only fifty killed and 180 wounded during three weeks. (Insurgents in other areas joked that their colleagues in Żoliborz "mostly played volley ball.") Bolstered by a well-armed battalion of 650 men which had arrived from the Kampinos forest, the *AK* command hoped to seize the railway station and the surrounding marshaling yards, thus linking up with the Old Town and paralyzing German rail traffic. The attack was to be helped from the south by several units from the Old Town.

The attacking forces deployed slowly in mostly open terrain, despite periodic German machine gun barrages. The insurgent attack started with precision according to watches instead of the usual signal by flares. But soon, in the darkness and without the support of heavy weapons, the attackers

were losing their commanders, tripping over weeds and clusters of bushes, creating gaps between units or dangerously grouping together. After a few minutes, the forward units were already near the railway line while others still stumbled far behind. The Germans illuminated the battlefield with flares and pounded us with machine gun and mortar fire. We were simply pinned to the ground, incapable of moving forward.[16]

The operation was a dramatic failure, with the *AK* force suffering 42 percent casualties. It was obvious that while capable of sustained and often successful sallies in built-up areas, the insurgent units simply had no capability to carry out major attacks in open terrain against a superior enemy. Amidst recrimination among officers who blamed one another for the abortive operation, several units left Żoliborz for the forests, and two or three others decided to join the defenders of the Old Town through the sewers. Because the Germans had raised the level of the sewage in two points, several insurgents drowned.

In the Old Town, Colonel Wachnowski appeared determined to resist "even in a heap of rubble," but he faced what amounted to a revolt by the tormented, dispirited, and exhausted inhabitants, packed in airless cellars with little food and only basic medical attention. The shortage of medical supplies was such that after August 20 operations were carried out without anesthesia.

The *AK* medical service estimated that toward the end of August there were some 7,000 badly wounded in makeshift hospitals, of whom 2,200 were insurgents—and were cared for by twenty exhausted doctors. The increasingly desperate inhabitants began sending delegations to *AK* sector commanders, begging them to either stop fighting or at least allow the population to leave the dying city.

On August 28 Wachnowski drafted a plan to attack Germans in an area wide enough to allow movement toward the city center by several thousand insurgents and their wounded, as well as those civilians capable of walking. Colonel Monter approved the plan, although he knew that by abandoning the Old Town, the Germans would have more troops available for action in other sectors of Warsaw.

Almost at the same time, the Germans also suffered battle fatigue, prompting General von dem Bach to inform his immediate superior, General Vormann, that his forces were unable to conquer Warsaw.

"The completion of the operation to stifle the Warsaw uprising depends on the endurance of the infantry," von dem Bach reported. He continued,

The losses of the attacking [German] units up to the evening of Aug. 28th were 91 officers and 3770 other ranks. . . . Despite support by the heavy artillery, the decisive action can be achieved only by the infantry and sapper units, in hand-to-hand fighting in the deep cellars of destroyed buildings. . . .

The Polish insurgents, obviously not as well equipped in heavy weapons as we are, can apparently replace their heavy losses with reinforcements arriving from all over Poland. After reorganization and training, these newly organized units varying in strength from companies to battalions, arrive in the city through the extensive network of sewers and underground passes. Consequently, we are suffering 150 losses daily in fighting for blocks of buildings of the Old Town.

Von dem Bach also reiterated his previous request for reinforcements in the form of a "full, and not artifically put together, division with experienced officers and soldiers."[17]

Although containing a number of accurate observations, von dem Bach's assessment, particularly of the "reinforcements arriving from all over Poland" for besieged Warsaw was far from reality. At the beginning of the uprising, Bór ordered units participating in Operation Storm to move toward Warsaw to bring aid for the beleaguered forces, but their march was slow and uncoordinated through the occupied territory. Even bringing a fully equipped battalion from the nearby Kampinos forest took eleven days, due to various local delays. South of the city, in Mokotów, the insurgents were reinforced by several hundred men from the Kabacki forest, but that was hardly enough to influence the battle.

A Polish historian of the uprising felt that Bór's initiative to mobilize a rescue operation "failed due to the lack of strong will and adequate supervision," as well as because of the incompetence of some of those carrying out the plan.[18] Eventually some of the mobilized rescue units received orders to stop their march and return to their normal areas of operation. East of the Vistula, some *AK* units heading for Warsaw were surrounded and disarmed by the Red Army. Apparently, by August 26, pinned down by artillery shells and Stuka bombs in his headquarters in the Old Town, the *AK* commander-in-chief no longer believed that the "battle for Warsaw" had any chance of success.

Colonel Wachnowski's plan to "punch a hole" in the ring surrounding the Old Town toward the city center failed after a final battle with heavy losses among the ranks of dispirited and exhausted insurgents, whose commanders did not believe in the feasibility of the operation. Already some units had begun leaving the doomed area, often pushing their way to the gaping sewer entrances through crowds of civilians and wounded. Many exhausted officers were no longer capable of leading their men into action. One of those was Major "Pełka" who gathered the surviving seven officers and thirty-eight men of his battalion, ordered them to abandon their position, and led them to one of the sewer openings, where he was stopped by *AK* military police and arrested. A court martial immediately sentenced him to death, but Colonel Wachnowski, feeling the verdict was taken too rapidly and considering the unhappy major's previously honorable record, stopped the execution.

Lacking any other option, Wachnowski asked Monter for permission to evacuate his troops through the sewers. By then Bór had already left the Old Town for the city center with his staff, radio stations, and secretaries with portable typewriters and files, by traveling through the main storm sewer. After consulting the commander-in-chief, on August 31 Monter authorized Wachnowski to abandon his sector, stressing, however, "I want the largest possible number of men with arms and ammunition. They will be needed for further combat. The wounded and those who have no weapons should remain with the civilian population."[19]

Nonetheless Wachnowski had already started evacuating some of the wounded of defenseless auxiliary units as well as some civilians. He set 8:00 P.M. on September 1 as the beginning of the evacuation of armed units in groups of fifty. Some units took their wounded with them, thus slowing down the march which under normal conditions in a storm sewer should have lasted a maximum of three hours. (The insurgents also took with them about 100 German prisoners, leaving another 100 behind.) The military police under Lieutenant "Barry" kept order at the entrances to the sewers, in several cases firing into the air to stop the surge of evacuees. By midmorning on September 2, some 3,000 unarmed *AK* members and wounded, as well as 1,500 in combat units with their weapons, had crossed to the city center, while 800 went north to Żoliborz, including members of the communist *AL* and a small unit of the Jewish Fighting Organization (*ŻOB*) commanded by "Antek" (Yitzhak Zuckerman). (See Chapter 5.) Some 2,500 wounded insurgents were left behind with the civilian population, at that time estimated at 35,000, including 5,000 seriously wounded. The preinsurrection population of the Old Town was 75,000, but some of them had left the area before the siege began.

On September 2 the German artillery laid a heavy barrage on the Old Town, obviously not realizing that it was no longer defended. The appearance of civilians brandishing white sheets halted the fire, and units of SS, Vlasov, and Ukrainian formations cautiously entered the ruins. The civilians capable of walking were escorted to the areas of the city held by the Germans; many wounded were shot. In an insurgent hospital at Miodowa Street, wounded German prisoners intervened to prevent the massacre of *AK* patients. According to records of the Reinefarth group, on September 1 and 2 a total of 1,309 people were shot and 3,695 corpses were burned.

The evacuation cut off a small unit of the elite *Zośka* battalion, which was unable to reach any sewer entrance. The battalion's commander, Captain "Jerzy" (Ryszard Białous) decided to take his group across the German-held Saxon Gardens (*Ogród Saski*), hoping that, in the dark and without armbands, the captured German camouflage uniforms and helmets worn by most of his men would save them. Indeed, the group marched in a loose formation, some periodically uttering German phrases. "We must have looked like a weary German unit returning from action," a survivor recalled.

Miraculously, it worked—until, almost within reach of the first Polish barricade at the other side of the park, a German sentry opened fire. The Poles manning the barricade answered, killing one of Jerzy's group before the others managed to shout, "Don't shoot! We're Poles! *Starówka!* (Old Town)." Jerzy succeeded in leading fifty-nine fighters (including a wounded woman) to safety—at least temporarily. "I never believed it would work but I had no other choice," he said later.[20]

Once in the relative safety of the city center, the survivors of the Old Town wearily walked in long lines to new quarters assigned to them. They marveled at the buildings which were still intact, at the glass in many windows, at the fact that men and women washed and combed their hair. One of them wrote later, "Houses still standing! The undamaged sidewalks! Well-shaped, practically elegant barricades! We still have something to fight for, something to defend."[21]

September 1 was the fifth anniversary of Germany's attack on Poland, and General Sosnkowski sent to Warsaw from London "Order No. 19" in which he wrote,

Five years have elapsed since Poland, believing in the British government and having obtained its guarantees, went to war alone against Germany's power. The September campaign gave the Allies eight months of priceless time. . . . The continuity of the Polish armed effort against German imperialism has never stopped. . . . For the past month fighters of the *Armia Krajowa* together with the people of Warsaw have been bleeding on the barricades in a lonely struggle against the enormous superiority of the opponent. . . .

The lack of help to Warsaw is being explained to us by experts citing technical reasons. . . . The loss of 27 aircraft during the past month over Warsaw means nothing to the Allies, who now have many thousands of planes of all types. We should remember that Polish airmen suffered 40 percent losses in the Battle of Britain. . . .

Warsaw is waiting. It is not waiting for words of praise, appreciation, pity or compassion. It is waiting for arms and ammunition. . . .

Your heroic commander has been accused of not having foreseen the sudden halt of the Soviet offensive before Warsaw's gates. History will be the judge and we are confident of the verdict. We are accused of lack of coordination with the general operational plans in eastern Europe. . . . For the past five years the *Armia Krajowa* has been accused of passivity and simulating war effort against the Germans. Today it is being accused of fighting too much and too well.[22]

The text was published in London on September 4 and Prime Minister Mikołajczyk asked President Władysław Raczkiewicz to demand Sosnkowski's resignation, apparently under considerable British pressure. Raczkiewicz initially resisted, and Sosnkowski remained commander-in-chief until the end of September, when he finally resigned. Bór was named as his successor, and his pseudonym was later added to his name: Tadeusz Bór-Komorowski. But at that time he was already preparing the draft of "honorable capitulation" and was obviously unable to assume any form of command in isolated Warsaw—particularly as he was about to become a prisoner. (See Chapter 12.)

The idea of surrender was discussed on September 9 when the *AK* command decided that further resistance was hopeless. Bór's assessment was based on the constantly shrinking terrain in the hands of the insurgents and diminishing prospects of help from outside, either from the west or east. He was opposed by his chief of staff, General "Grzegorz" (Tadeusz Pełczynski), and chief of operations, Colonel "Filip" (Józef Szostak), both of whom believed that such a drastic step was premature.

Also on September 9, Bór received a letter from General Ernest Rohr, commander of the southern sector, who participated in negotiations on the evacuation of the civilian population, suggesting discussions on capitulation "to spare the lives of Warsaw's numerous inhabitants." Bór replied that he would consider such negotiations only with a representative of the *Wehrmacht* and not of the SS, obviously referring to General von dem Bach. Bór also asked the German side to halt the city's bombardment pending talks which he envisaged on September 10.

Bór's correspondence and obvious despondency caused the protests of various commanders, including a formal letter from Colonel Monter, who asked for "two more days." He also suggested contacting General Michał Rola-Żymierski, the new head of the Polish forces under Soviet command, offering him "loyal cooperation." At the same time, a radio message from London informed Bór that the Allies were considering a major air drop of weapons on Warsaw. As a result Bór sent Rohr another letter asking for full "combatant status" for *AK* personnel "without any investigation of their anti-German activities before Aug. 1st, 1944." Rohr replied, addressing Bór as *"Oberbefehlshaber der AK"* (commander-in-chief of the *AK*), asking for a written confirmation of capitulation. Bór's subsequent letter made further demands, claiming that the *AK* had little confidence in German promises and asking that conditions of capitulation be broadcast on German radio.[23]

The German side did not reply to the last letter and the sudden sound of Soviet artillery on the Vistula's right bank changed entirely the mood in the besieged *AK* command.

NOTES

1. Document *AG Mitte* (Central Front) AOK, no. 4572/August 10, 1944, 1:20 P.M.

2. Adam Borkiewicz, *Powstanie Warszawskie 1944* (Warsaw: Pax, 1957), p. 33.

3. Central Front documents, AOK 9 Ia, no 3998, August 13, 1944.

4. Borkiewicz, *Powstanie Warszawskie 1944*, p. 195.

5. *HG Mitte*, AOK 9, no. 3876/4.

6. Dispatch to London entered in Polish archives as Ldz. 6436.

7. Official text.

8. According to the text published by the Foreign Affairs Ministry of the government-in-exile in October 1944.

9. Documents *Iskra DOG* (acronym for the Latin *documenta occupationis germanicae*), entry 22.

10. Correspondence between the two, carried through the sewers, survived Warsaw's destruction.

11. Text based on *Dziennik Polski i Dziennik Żołnierza*, a Polish language daily in London, no. 191/44.

12. Postwar statement by "Boruta" of the Radosław group, quoted in *Pamiętniki Żołnierzy Baonu Zośka* (Warsaw: Nasza Ksiegarnia, 1957), p. 295.

13. Emil Kumor, *Wycinek z Historii Jednego Życia* (Warsaw: Pax, 1969), pp. 285–286.

14. Description based on author's notes written in the fall of 1944, *Stalag* XIA.

15. *Polskie Siły Zbrojne*, Vol. III (London: General Sikorski Historical Institute 1950, p. 752.

16. A survivor's account to the author in *Stalag* XIA in January 1945.

17. Document in files of the Central Front, AG Mitte, no. 257 of August 29, 1944, AOK 9, Ia, 4486gh.

18. Borkiewicz, *Powstanie Warszawskie 1944*, p. 304.

19. Official text.

20. In conversation with the author in London, 1948.

21. "Leszczyc" in *Pamiętniki Żołnierzy Baonu Zośka*, collective work, p. 389.

22. Official text.

23. Borkiewicz, *Powstanie Warszawskie 1944*, pp. 504–508.

CHAPTER 11

Condemned by Stalin

The despairing population of what the Germans called "the Warsaw caldron" (*Kessel*) simply couldn't believe it: On Sunday, September 10, the forty-first day of the disastrous uprising, the thunder of Soviet artillery broke the oppressive silence to the east of the battered capital. At 11:00 A.M., Soviet fighter aircraft forced four German bombers away from the city center, and at 4:00 P.M. a German plane was shot down in a dogfight with Soviet fighters. An hour later four German planes went down over the eastern suburb of Praga on the Vistula's right bank. Praga itself had been silent since August 2, when the uprising in the sprawling working-class suburb collapsed.

"The sight of aerial combat and the growing sound of artillery raised our hearts," wrote the official *AK* organ, *Biuletyn Informacyjny*. Weary inhabitants emerged from their cellar shelters and craned their necks, looking at the sky.

Yet on the ground, it was a critical day for the northern part of the city center (*Śródmieście Północne*) where insurgents defended virtually every building under heavy attacks backed by armor, self-propelled cannons, and "goliaths"—miniature tanks packed with explosives. Guided by cable, the goliaths were capable of shattering barricades, puncturing gaping holes in buildings, and were regarded as one of the most effective weapons in urban warfare. After stubborn resistance the insurgents lost the movie theaters *Colloseum* and *Studio* while the *Cristal Cafe* passed back and forth. In several areas fighting spread to the cellars packed with civilians, causing victims among men, women, and children. The attacking German forces had been reinforced by two militarized police regiments, each accompanied by a Vlasov Army unit. According to insurgent accounts, Vlasov Army Russian renegade soldiers taking part in the fighting raped women, looted, and shot men dragged from the cellars.

Some *AK* units reported being unable to hold their positions. A typical situation report by Captain "Ognisty" said his unit's losses were 42 percent.

My men are exhausted, undernourished and suffering from lack of sleep. . . . A two day's rest would allow reorganization and create a new fighting spirit. I am worried about infectious diseases among unwashed soldiers. The weapons are in a terrible state because there is no time nor conditions to clean them.

"Only those on stretchers are allowed to withdraw," retorted the sector commander, Lieutenant Colonel "Tunguz" (Józef Zawislak).[1] The insurgents succeeded in holding most of their positions, and the following day, September 11, the intensity of the fighting subsided. It also became clear that on the other side of the Vistula, the Soviet Army had launched a massive attack on Praga, preceded by night air raids over a large area which they illuminated by flares dropped on parachutes. It seemed as though Warsaw's agony might be coming to an end. At the *AK* headquarters in the basement of a massive *PKO* (*Państwowa Kasa Oszczędności*) bank building, Bór and his staff wondered whether under pressure from the Western Allies, Stalin had indeed changed his attitude toward the dying Polish capital.

On September 12 the *AK* command reported in a radio message to London

A large-scale Soviet attack on Praga is developing. It looks successful. The Soviet air force dominates. The meager parachute drop and aerial Soviet-German battles have enormously improved the morale of the troops (*AK*) and of the civilian population. There is a will to fight in a generally optimistic mood. Strong German pressure [continues] against us, particularly in the region of Czerniaków. There is a shortage of ammunition and hence concern that we might not be able to hold out just before reaching the finishing line. Immediate help with ammunition essential.[2]

The "meager parachute drop" refers to the penultimate effort by the Western Allies to supply Warsaw by air, during the night of September 10. The Czerniaków region was the area of the Vistula's left bank below the Poniatowski Brigde viaduct, still held by the insurgents after the territory above the bridge, known as Powiśle, had been abandoned. It was on that pocket of Polish resistance that General von dem Bach decided to concentrate his next assault, mainly to prevent the attacking Soviet forces from reaching a secure area for a possible landing from across the river.

My battle plan [von dem Bach wrote later], was based on a pincer movement from the north and south along the Vistula, in order to be able, when necessary, to create a new front against the Russians. Already from the beginning, I regarded the city center as the last target. . . . An attack on Żoliborz [northern suburb] was even lower on my agenda because that opponent, although fierce in defense, basically relied on defense and never seriously attacked my permanently threatened northern flank.[3]

Considering the defense of the Vistula to be exceptionally important to the survival of the Central Front, General Vormann, the commander of the 9th German Army, reinforced General von dem Bach with the 19th *Panzer* division of General Hans Källner. In addition the *Korpsgruppe von dem Bach* also received police and reserve troops dispatched by Himmler.

The mood of Warsaw's population was reflected in an article of the *Kurier Stołeczny*, one the newspapers published by the insurgents.

We are reaching the pit of distress. Who will break down first, Berlin or Warsaw? Who will help us first? Moscow or London? How long will our nerves last and the walls of the remaining buildings stand? Will the newly dug wells help? Sunday brought a respite. Daytime the Soviet air force, British planes at night. . . . From the tombs scattered on Warsaw's streets we can hear the voices of our fallen brothers and friends: don't waste our sacrifice. . . . We are facing the key question: have we been cheated?

The mood is constantly changing, in the shelters and among highly placed politicians. Fires, the loss of homes, hunger and the problem of survival shape our opinions. Fatigue plays an enormous role. . . . In the shelters the main theme is the prospect of leaving the city. . . . They talk about capitulation: quick, as long as there is still something left. And yet other voices caution "What is the point? The population will face slavery, the city will be levelled anyway. Yes, we started too early, let us not hurry, we can hold out the last five minutes."[4]

Three other insurgent dailies printed a communiqué broadcast on the field radio station *Wawer* of Marshal Rokossovsky's command. It reported a concerted attack on Praga's residential area of Saska Kępa, as well as on German positions north of the city during thirty hours of steady pressure on the ground and from the sky. Rokossovsky's communiqué also spoke of drops of supplies to Polish insurgents in the suburb of Marymont and in the Kampinos forest. It claimed that Soviet aircraft had created a covering umbrella over Warsaw.[5]

Such was the situation in Warsaw and its immediate vicinity when

Bór proposed cooperation between Rokossovsky's armies and the insurgents fighting in Warsaw. In a radio message to London for relay to Moscow and then to the Soviet command in the field, he asked the Soviet government to "greet, in my name and in the name of my soldiers, the approaching Soviet Army and its Polish components." The message contained details of the situation and listed the areas lost since the previous such missive sent by Monter—which had never been acknowledged. It stressed the decision to continue the struggle and in no uncertain terms pleaded with Rokossovsky to parachute ammunition into the city for the German weapons of the insurgent forces, listing the areas most suitable for such an operation. The message said:

The inhabitants of the city suffer enormously from the German heavy artillery and dive bombers and I beseech you to concentrate your action on these two means of combat. Knowing our situation, you should not expect our sustained cooperation because, lacking heavy weapons, our attack possibilities are limited. Nonetheless, after supplying us with heavy weapons and indicating the direction most suitable to you, we will be able to concentrate all our effort during the decisive attack by the Soviet Army on Warsaw. Please give us the necessary elements to establish direct radio contact. With soldierly greetings, Bór, Lieutenant General.

Thus Bór, leader of a force described by Stalin as "fascist," was now clearly a supplicant, making a desperate effort to establish a working relationship with the powerful Soviet marshal. When the message was received in London for relay to Moscow, the firmly anti-Soviet Polish commander-in-chief, General Kazimierz Sosnkowski, considered the greetings to the Soviet army superfluous and suggested they be deleted. The suggestion was ignored by Prime Minister Mikołajczyk, who was preoccupied by political aspects of the problem, and the entire text was sent on to Moscow.[6]

Having halted his armies east of Warsaw shortly after the outbreak of the uprising, Rokossovsky now acted swiftly. Throwing into combat the 125th Corps of the Soviet Army, he literally pulverized the German defenses, and in heavy fighting beat back a counterattack by General Källner's 19th *Panzer* Division. Already on September 13, two days after the Soviet offensive began, units of the 1st Polish Infantry Division under Soviet command stormed into the outskirts of Praga. Some forty Soviet planes pounded the steadily withdrawing German formations. Early on September 14, General Georg Hans Reinhardt, the commander of the Central Front, admitted defeat in a report to the *Wehrmacht*'s headquarters.

After heavy fighting and heavy losses in street combat against overwhelming enemy forces, the city [Praga] found itself day and night under fire by the heaviest artillery and [German] units were under constant air attacks. In order to prevent the destruction of German units and facilitate their withdrawal over the bridges, an order was given to abandon Praga during the night of Sept. 13th to 14th.[7]

Withdrawing Germans blew up (albeit incompletely) Warsaw's two main road bridges, as well as the railway bridge between them. The Soviet forces now faced the fires and ruins of Warsaw across the Vistula, its bridges partially in the water. According to two postwar Soviet defectors, Marshal Rokossovsky could now "watch through his field glasses while the Germans destroyed insurgent Warsaw."[8]

Besides Stalin's statement on August 9 to Mikołajczyk, prime minister of the Polish government-in-exile, that the Soviet advance on Warsaw had been thwarted by a German counterattack (see Chapter 9), there has never been a satisfactory explanation about the sudden calm—for such a long period—in the middle of the eastern front. Neither has the Kremlin bothered to justify its refusal to allow the Western Allies to use Soviet airfields for refueling in their supply missions to the Polish insurgents. On the contrary some historians stress the insulting remarks about the AK by the Soviet dictator. The powerful Soviet offensive of September 10 and the virtually instant capture of Praga could hardly have been initiated by Marshal Rokossovsky himself, a man whose entire military career was based on his blind obedience to Stalin.

Born in 1896, young Rokossovsky served in the Czarist Army during World War I and went over to the Red Army almost immediately after the revolution. He fought against the "white" rebels and the Poles in 1920, and rose rapidly after the war to command a regiment, a division, and then a corps. During the sweeping purges that literally decapitated the Soviet military leadership in the 1930s, Rokossovsky shared the fate of those who were arrested and tortured. According to one account, during various interrogations

nine of his teeth were knocked out, three of his ribs were broken, his toes were hammered flat. He was sentenced to death and spent more than three months in the condemned cell. There is testimony, including his own, that, twice at least, he was subjected to mock shootings, being led to the place of execution at night, and made to stand on the edge of a grave as generals on his right and left were shot.[9]

His fortunes improved on the eve of World War II, when he was released from jail and was given the command of the 9th Mechanized Corps, one of the few tactical formations that delayed the rapid advance of the German forces into Russia's heart. Three weeks later he was promoted and given command of the 16th Army which fought in the battle of Smolensk and later succeeded in repelling the German advance on Moscow. It was the first significant Soviet success during the dramatic phase of the campaign that saw the German Juggernaut crush entire divisions and armies. In the battle for Stalingrad in 1942 and 1943, Rokossovsky commanded the Don Front, which played a key role in encircling and destroying a large and elite German formation and turned the tide of the war.

Thereafter stars rained upon Rokossovsky. They fell onto his shoulder boards, onto his chest and around his neck. In 1944 he was awarded the diamond Marshal's Star and a gold star to pin on his chest.[10]

No one suspected that the man who in August 1944 halted his armies outside Warsaw and then, six weeks later, pushed them a few miles forward, was going to be sent by Stalin to Warsaw after the war. He was to become marshal of Poland, minister of defense, deputy president of the Council of Ministers, and member of the Politburo of the Polish Communist Party.

Rokossovsky remained a favorite of Stalin's but a favorite who was under sentence of death, a sentence which was lifted only after the death of Stalin in 1953. ... The relationship between Stalin and Rokossovsky was based upon the fact that Stalin gave the orders and that Rokossovsky carried them out without question.[11]

Outside Warsaw in 1944 under Rokossovsky's command were units of the Polish People's Army, initially formed in the Soviet Union in 1943. In its ranks were men released from gulags who had been unable to reach the forces organized in 1941 under the command of General Władysław Anders, which were subsequently transferred to the Middle East and took part in the Italian campaign. After the entry into Poland of the victorious Red Army in 1944, the "People's Army" was bolstered by draftees. Because most Polish officers who found themselves prisoners in the Soviet Union were either exterminated at Katyn and elsewhere or left with the "Anders Army," Soviet officers were seconded to lead Polish troops. According to Viktor Suvorov, a defector from the Red Army, "even after the 'people's' government had been established, the Polish army did not come under its command, remaining a part of the Soviet army."[12]

That certainly was the case when the Soviet-led 1st Polish Infantry Division, named after Tadeusz Kościuszko, a hero of the American Revolution and leader of the 1794 Polish uprising against Russia, fought its way to the left bank of the Vistula—literally 600 yards across from the remaining insurgent positions in Czerniaków. The unsuccessful landing was unbeknown to the Polish insurgents desperately waiting for help. The Soviet grand design was not so much military as political. In the light of subsequent events, the doomed Warsaw uprising happened to be a helpful factor in Moscow's plans for a postwar Europe.

Poland's relations with Russia and with its successor, the Soviet Union, have rarely been friendly and most often hostile. According to some Russian specialists,

Poland has always been the most unruly of the Russian empire's subject nations. Russia had lost Poland over and over again, but each time, by force of arms, it had brought it back into its orbit. . . . There had not been a single Russian emperor—nor after the Bolshevik revolution a single Soviet *vozhd* [leader]—who had not run head on into the Polish question. . . . In 1920, Lenin, an internationalist and pragmatist, sent the newly formed Red Army into Poland to take Warsaw by storm. Stalin had taken part in that unsuccessful campaign as political commissar of the Southwestern Army Group. On two later occasions, that despot, chauvinist, and imperialist, as though wreaking revenge for the failure of the 1920 campaign, "definitively" put Poland into Russian hands.[13]

Although two Russian experts (Vladimir Solovyov and Elena Klepikova) describe the Warsaw uprising as "the result of carefully thought out Soviet provocation,"[14] it is doubtful that in 1944 Stalin acted the way he did because he was still smarting from the Soviet Union's failure twenty-four years before. He was not responsible for the outbreak of fighting in Warsaw, sanctioned from London by the exiled government and carried out by the Polish Home Army. But he certainly had no intention of giving it substantial help, and he used Warsaw's slow death to his own advantage. A success by the *AK*—and by the exiled Poles— was certainly not what Stalin had in mind for Poland.

In letters to Churchill and Roosevelt, he [Stalin] called the insurgent patriots "a gang of criminals who have taken this gamble in Warsaw with the idea of seizing power." In 1940 he had seen to it that the flower of the Polish officer corps was destroyed by his own secret police. Now, in the summer of 1944, he saw to it that the rest of the Polish army was finished off in Warsaw by Hitler, thereby making it easier to transform postwar Poland into a Soviet satellite.[15]

Some historians describe Stalin as a subtle and far-sighted strategist, a man unlikely to be given to the passion of revenge. Stalin might have disliked—or even hated—the Poles, but his earlier assessments of Russo-Polish relations were clinical. Thus, when in 1920 Polish troops had been routed after their initial victorious march on Kiev, political commissar Stalin tried to disabuse the Soviet leadership of hopes of carrying the "torch of the revolution" to the heart of Europe. When Marshal Mikhail N. Tukhachevsky told his troops in a ringing order in July 1920 that "over the corpse of White Poland lies the road to worldwide conflagration," Stalin cautioned Lenin that fighting the Poles in Poland would be more difficult than during their march into the Ukraine. Already at that time, Stalin apparently had little faith in Lenin's theory that the Polish working class—including traditionalist peasants—would welcome the Red Army. Historians quote Stalin as saying that "it is easier to saddle a cow than to establish communism in Poland."

But Stalin espoused the theory that it was feasible to create a protective belt of states, including Poland and Hungary under Soviet control. "These were countries that according to Stalin would not agree to become Soviet republics."[16]

Given the history of Russo-Polish relations and the traditional animosity between the two countries, it was virtually inevitable that the cooperation pledged by Moscow and the Polish government-in-exile in 1941 would fail. After the initial clash over the eastern territories awarded to Poland by the 1921 Treaty of Riga, there was the question of Polish military personnel—particularly officers—missing in the Soviet Union as well as the fate and number of Polish citizens who had been deported by the Soviets (well over a million). The London Poles had reasonably accurate figures of Poles, military and civilian, held in German camps and in Soviet gulags. Some of the figures were based on official Soviet statements, which Moscow subsequently denied. Thus when, after the 1941 German invasion, discussions started about forming a Polish army in the Soviet Union, the Soviets claimed that "there were no more than 20,000 Polish fighting men to be freed in Russia." Władysław Sikorski, then prime minister of the government-in-exile, retorted that the previously published Soviet documents gave the figure of 190,000 Polish soldiers captured in 1939.[17]

(In fact, Soviet data about Polish prisoners in the Soviet Union changed frequently. For example, in November 1939 Foreign Minister Vyacheslav Molotov claimed 300,000 Polish troops had been captured, but less than a year later, the official Soviet army newspaper *Red Star* spoke of 8,000 officers and 200,000 other ranks in Soviet custody.)

That question was to mar the dialogue between Moscow and the London Poles until the end of the war, exacerbated by the discovery of the Katyn graves of Polish officers in 1943. And from the beginning, the Russians systematically cast doubt on the validity of the government-in-exile, suggesting that a "Polish National Committee" be formed instead—in the Soviet Union.

Under strong British pressure, an agreement was signed by Sikorski on July 30, 1941, "in the face of enraged opposition within his own cabinet."[18] The British, of course, wanted the Poles to brush aside their ancient quarrels with Russia, but it was easier said than done, particularly when the first recruits for the planned Polish army started arriving. Their assigned camps—initially guarded by the ubiquitous *NKVD*—were around Buzuluk, an impoverished and neglected town at the southern end of the Ural Mountains about 600 miles from Moscow. The recruits consisted of soldiers captured in 1939 and deportees who had found themselves in Arctic gulags, Altai Mountains work camps, salt mines, and other places where "expendable" prisoners were used. Most were physically unfit, not only for military service but also for the arduous trip to get there. They brought with them epidemics and tales of horror. Many were so emaciated that they died after arrival. In the end, by November 1941 about 46,000 had been gathered in several camps, and the Soviets warned that rations for only 30,000 were available. There were shortages of uniforms, shoes, and medical supplies. Eventually, British uniforms, weapons, rations, and other supplies started arriving. Władysław Anders, a cavalry brigade general released by the Russians from the notorious Lubyanka prison, was named commander-in-chief of an army that gradually began to look like one.

There was no end to arguments with the Soviet authorities about every detail. Above all there was the gnawing question about a large number of missing officers for whom the Soviet authorities could not account. They included most of the officers of the 40,000-strong Lwów garrison which surrendered to the Soviets September 22, 1939, after a ten-day siege by the Germans. Where were these officers, the Poles kept asking. The discovery of the Katyn graves provided part of the answer, but for years the West preferred the version that the Nazis committed the massacre. It was certainly more convenient at the time when Russians were dying by the thousands while fighting the Nazis.

The mass graves containing 4,143 officers, some in full regalia and many wearing tight-fitting cavalry boots, were discovered in March 1943 in a forest outside Smolensk, an area under German occupation at the time. They included two generals and one vice admiral. The Germans, including Hitler, Himmler, and Joseph Goebbels, master of Nazi propaganda, immediately saw the discovery as potential dynamite capable of blowing Allied unity apart. In April journalists from neutral countries and various hastily organized commissions were flown to the scene, including that of the Polish Red Cross from occupied Poland. Letters from families found on the corpses, as well as entries in the prisoners' diaries, showed dates ending in the spring of 1940. All had been shot in the back of their heads and buried in neat rows. Apparently they had been transported to the scene of the massacre from the camps in Starobelsk, Kozelsk, and Ostashkov.

The torrent of gory details emanating from Nazi Germany was immediately countered by Moscow, which accused the Germans of being the authors of the mass murder, stating that "the Hitlerite murderers will not escape a just and inevitable retribution for their bloody crimes."

But to the Poles under the Nazi occupation, the massacre showed all signs of the permanent Soviet warfare against the "capitalist officer class." Mass crimes had been committed by the occupying Nazis throughout the war, yet Polish officers captured during the 1939 campaign—including Jews—remained in prisoner-of-war camps. During the months that followed the Katyn announcement, I did not meet or hear of a single person who—perhaps for the first time—disbelieved the Nazi version.

(When communist constraints no longer applied in Poland, an official document published by the Polish Information Agency *Interpress* in 1992 revealed that the three camps established near Smolensk—mostly in abandoned and dilapidated churches and monasteries—contained 16,500 prisoners. They consisted of officers, members of the frontier defense corps, policemen, and clergymen of all faiths, including Major Baruch Steinberg, chief rabbi of the Polish army. The document further states that on March 5, 1940, the Political Bureau of the Central Committee of the Communist Party ordered the execution of 14,700 Polish prisoners-of-war and 11,000 other prisoners. Of the 15,500 Polish military personnel held in the Smolensk area, only 450 survived. Thus the Katyn graves contained less than one-third of the victims. According to the same document, Lavrenti Beria, at the time head of the *NKVD*, admitted to Polish General Zygmunt Berling, "we have made a great mistake."[19])

When the Polish government-in-exile asked for an impartial investigation by a reputable organization such as the International Red Cross, the Western press instantly took the side of the Soviet Union, often accusing the Poles of helping the Nazi propaganda machine. The British and Americans tried to calm the Poles in what was becoming an embarrassing and damaging affair. Over lunch on April 20, Churchill bluntly told Sikorski, "If they [the officers] are dead, nothing you can do will bring them back."[20]

A day later (April 21), Stalin sent scathing telegrams to Churchill and Roosevelt, accusing the Sikorski government of collusion with Germany and announcing that "for these reasons the Soviet government has decided to interrupt its relations with that [Polish] government." Neither the United States nor Great Britain had expected such a dramatic break, which in effect was the beginning of Stalin's systematic policy of working toward Poland's incorporation into the Soviet sphere of influence. According to American historian Allen Paul,

The crisis also dramatized how little the world knew about the plight of the Poles. The war had begun as a fight to preserve their independence. But by 1943 it had become a war to defeat Germany and the initial objective was rapidly fading from view.[21]

It was obvious that the decline of the Polish government-in-exile was by then irreversible. Its uncompromising attitude led to its isolation and resulted in the Allied recognition, at the end of the war, of the puppet communist government in Poland.

On the fifty-seventh anniversary of the announcement of the gruesome Katyn discovery, April 13, 1990, Soviet President Mikhail Gorbachev officially admitted Soviet guilt in the massacre and provided additional details.

On the basis of various secret documents gradually released after World War II, it became fairly obvious that neither Churchill nor Roosevelt trusted Stalin, but both found it expedient to humor him in order to pursue the war. For example, a select Congressional Committee investigating the Katyn massacre studied a Pentagon document in 1952 which asserted in part:

Since Russia is the decisive factor in the war, she must be given every assistance and every effort must be made to obtain her friendship. Likewise, since without question she will dominate Europe on the defeat of the Axis, it is even more essential to develop and maintain the most friendly relations with Russia.[22]

By the time Marshal Rokossovsky's troops stormed Praga and established positions along the Vistula facing the embattled parts of Warsaw, Stalin was consolidating his power over Poland through the pro-Soviet "Committee of National Liberation" formed in Lublin on July 22, 1944. Most of its members had come from the Soviet-sponsored "Union of Polish Patriots" whose task was to turn Poland into a Soviet-style state. The so-called "Lublin Committee" was later recognized as Poland's government by the Western Allies.

In that context the main question is why had Stalin ordered the seizure of Praga and why, starting September 14, units of his "Berling Army" had begun crossing the river in what turned out to be a suicide mission?

According to the official history of the Polish Home Army (*AK*) written by a team of its senior officers in London after the war,

On the 14th September, the Soviet attack in the Warsaw region died down, although Soviet air force continued to appear over the city, and Soviet artillery fired on some German positions in the capital. Starting with the night of Sept. 14th to 15th, Soviet planes dropped supplies of arms, ammunition and food every night. Among the defenders [of Warsaw] new hope was born as well as an improved view of the Russians.

At the same time, a unit of Berling's troops commanded by Red Army Major Latyshonok crossed the river to upper Czerniaków. Berling's unit fought in Czerniaków as part of the *AK* under the command of Lt. Col. Radosław, and subsequently, along with the battalion *Broda*, was left there by Radosław until Sept.

23rd. It is difficult to understand for what reason the Berling unit had been sent to Warsaw as it was not followed up by any reinforcements.[23]

(Józef Kuropieska, a retired general who died in 1998, told a Polish historian that he had met several Berling Army officers in a prisoner-of-war camp at Woldenberg who admitted crossing the river without a plan or prior reconnaissance. "I then became convinced that Berling was a criminal," Kuropieska was quoted as saying.[24])

Already by the beginning of September, after the dramatic withdrawal through the sewers from the Old Town, the *AK* commander-in-chief considered upper Czerniaków to be the next target of von dem Bach's offensive. (Postwar documents showed Bór's assessment of the German general's plans to be correct.) Although discussing the prospect of capitulation with his officers and drafting letters in his perfect German to General Rohr (as a former Austrian officer Bór was bilingual), the *AK* leader desperately wanted to keep all options open. Thus it was essential that the insurgents continue holding a strip of the Vistula's bank for a possible rescue from across the river. This was made even more urgent after the Germans seized the Powiśle area between the two road bridges, which the command of the Central Front announced in a brief report of September 6, stating,

In Warsaw, today's attack achieved positive results. All of *Weichselviertel* [German translation of the Polish term Powiśle—Vistula area] is in our hands. From 11 A.M. until dusk a stream of civilian prisoners is flowing out of the city. . . . In Warsaw, 152 bandits were liquidated in one of the courtyards by two machine gunners from the Dirlewanger group.[25]

After that successful operation, General von dem Bach could muster more of his troops to attack and liquidate the insurgent hold on the remaining bank of the river south of the Poniatowski Bridge and the adjacent area known as upper Czerniaków. The assault group consisted of seven combat battalions (average strength 600 men), a unit of self-propelled cannons and two companies of heavy tanks. Among the units was a regiment of the by-then notorious Dirlewanger brigade.[26]

The *AK* strength in the area targeted by von dem Bach was defended by approximately 1,100 insurgents, some 150 of whom were recovering from wounds. Until then that part of Czerniaków had been spared heavy fighting. It was hardly touched by heavy artillery or Stuka dive-bombers. Bór decided to reinforce it with the remnants of the *Radosław* group, by then about 500 strong—from the initial 3,000.

The group—including a handful of volunteers from other units—assembled during the evening of September 5 in the garden of a once

elegant restaurant at Aleje Ujazdowskie 37—approximately where today's modern U.S. embassy is located.

The once manicured garden was littered with tables and chairs strewn about
haphazardly. Everywhere there were men in splotchy German camouflage jackets taken from SS stores at the beginning of the uprising. Rifles and machine
guns were stacked in neat piles. There was a strong smell of cooking emanating
from the restaurant kitchen, where men speaking in a foreign language were
busy preparing a meal. "Hungarian Jews liberated in the ghetto," explained a
blond girl carrying a submachine gun.
    We were fed and then led to a pavilion where boots of various shapes and
sizes were lined up like soldiers on parade. I selected a pair of German jack boots
and discarded my worn out city shoes. At dusk, groups of armed men began to
form in the garden. Firing broke out in several directions and we could see tracer
bullets overhead. To the east, a flare shot toward the sky.
    One by one the names of skeletal battalions now reduced to weak companies
were called out: *Parasol, Zośka, Broda, Czata*—units which had fought from the
suburbs of Wola, across the ruins of the ghetto and the destruction of the Old
Town to the sewer retreat. We were led by a "Lieutenant Szczerba" and a woman
introduced to us as "Pani Zofia." Both were dressed in German camouflage uniforms and carried Schmeisser submachine guns. With us was a silent, tall, and
lean officer in a perfectly fitting prewar Polish captain's uniform, the empty left
sleeve tucked into his pocket. The Hungarians with their various cooking utensils
closed the column.
    We crossed the tree-lined Aleje Ujazdowskie running as firing around us in-
tensified. There were the usual barricades, a half-burned church, an empty square
eerie in the moonlight. Soon we were in a complex of apartment buildings, then
in a park sloping down toward the river. "Pani Zofia" counted us periodically.
When we walked into a maze of cellars, she passed along the message "total
silence, Germans on upper floors." We held on to each other's belts in order not
get lost in the darkness.
    And then, as if by magic, we found ourselves in a different world, a world of
silent streets lined with small apartment houses. There were gardens and the
smell of greenery permeated the humid night. We were led into an empty apartment where we slept on the floor. In the morning we discovered that we could
wash—there was water! We stared through the intact window at an apartment
across the street: a family was eating breakfast around a table! In the street below,
several women walked carrying shopping bags. In the distance, a machine gun
fired long, seemingly pointless volleys. No one seemed to pay any attention to
it.[27]

    Four days later the bucolic atmosphere was shattered by a massive air
attack and salvoes of heavy artillery. A new German offensive had begun.
    The attacks from the north, west, and south were systematic and mur-
derous. Once more the survivors of the Old Town had to fight for every
building, courtyard, and cellar. But the area was not heavily built-up,

and the open spaces, orchards, and vegetable patches were more difficult to defend than the tightly packed houses of the Old Town. Except that this time there was some hope: every night small Soviet aircraft called by the Russians *kukuruzniks* (like the planes used for spraying Russia's sprawling cornfields) would drop supplies to the insurgents. They often appeared suddenly over the rooftops and released their cargo without parachutes: sacks of dry bread, groats, canned meat and lard, crates of weapons and ammunition. The crates often broke on impact, damaging the weapons inside. They included the long and effective antitank rifles known as *PTR*, the crude but lethal *PEPESHA* submachine guns, and other weaponry of the Soviet arsenal. But ammunition for the German and British weapons of the insurgents was running out, and soon discarded Sten submachine guns could be found in the courtyards of crumbling or burned-out buildings.

While this time the attacking German planes did not linger over their targets, fearing Soviet antiaircraft fire from across the river, the artillery bombardment was relentless. Gradually there were fewer buildings to defend, and the area controlled by the defenders diminished every day, paralyzed by the superior fire of the attackers.

A woman courier recalled that on September 12,

Air attacks became more devastating. The Germans bombed the houses that were still intact, the "lowing cows" [heavy mortars] set fire to the Mariawitow church. Okrąg street was burning. . . . Every time one had to find a new passage to reach the headquarters with a message because the old one was either covered with rubble or was burning.[28]

When one of the makeshift hospitals was set on fire on September 13,

nurses carried some 120 wounded to the city gas-works already in German hands where the Dirlewanger soldiery kicked and beat them, raping women. . . . But in the evening, when Soviet planes raided the gas-works, the Germans scattered and the nurses and civilian population managed to carry the wounded to safety.[29]

In the afternoon of September 15, Radosław summoned unit commanders to his headquarters in the cellar of Wilanowska Street no. 18/20 about 200 yards from the riverbank and outlined his options: either to fight his way north to connect with the forces of the city center or to defend the coast of the Vistula at all costs, regardless of casualties, to facilitate an expected crossing by Soviet troops. He chose the second option but also decided to evacuate the walking wounded through the sewers to Mokotów, south of his besieged sector. He sent a patrol to reconnoiter the feasibility of the sewer route and at the same time or-

dered an officer to cross the river with a letter addressed to "the Commander of the Russian forces in Praga" in which he asked for artillery
support and supplies, giving the details of the area held by his units.[30]

Virtually at the same time, General Zygmunt Berling, commander of
the 1st Polish Army under Soviet command, ordered his units to cross
the Vistula along its entire length facing Warsaw. While some divisions
were to simulate attacks in the northern part off Warsaw, the task of
helping Radosław's embattled sector was given to the 9th infantry regiment of the 3rd division. According to a Polish historian, the crossing
by an advance party had been coordinated with Radosław on September
14, and the first reconnaissance unit was accompanied by an *AK* officer.
In the early hours of September 16, a flotilla of river barges and pontoons
set off from the Praga suburb of Saska Kępa toward the coast held by
Radosław. At first unnoticed by the Germans, the last elements of the
assigned battalion landed amidst a barrage of mortar and heavy machine
gun fire. At 4:30 A.M. the regiment's commander, Major Franciszek Mierzwinski, reported to his superiors that 300 men had crossed the river
equipped with fourteen heavy machine guns, sixteen antitank rifles,
eight mortars, five antitank guns, and food for four days. The unit was
commanded by Major Latyshonok (first name not available), seconded
from the Red Army.[31] Such, at least, was the version authorized by the
communist authorities of postwar Poland.

After a sleepless night at gun emplacements in the badly damaged building at
Okrąg Street no. 2, we heard the shuffling of feet on the staircase and voices in
the soft, almost Russian, accents of eastern Poland. Mist shrouded the no man's
land and there was hardly any shooting in our immediate vicinity. The only
noise was that of a tank engine being revved up behind the ruins ahead of us.

Guided by an *AK* officer, the new arrivals carried in a powerful Soviet *Maxim*
heavy machine gun, complete with small wheels and a steel shield. They set it
on a table near the window, propped it up with bricks and a 17-year-old gunner
opened fire. He was obviously not accustomed to saving ammunition. His long
bursts were loud and devastating and soon we saw several Germans leaving
their positions directly in front of us. The young gunner grinned. Minutes later
he fell backwards, blood trickling from his mouth, victim of a German sharp-
shooter.

Our new friends wore long khaki coats of the pre-war Polish cut and large
Soviet helmets with a 12th century Polish eagle—without a crown—painted on
them. Some had the four-cornered Polish field caps. They addressed us as "brothers" or "citizens," and spoke of their "political education officer." It all made us
feel somewhat uneasy. We noticed that while they were armed to the teeth,
including the brand-new semi-automatic rifles which even the powerful *Wehrmacht* did not have at that time, their personal equipment consisted of simple
sacks hanging on their backs. They were mostly peasants from the eastern plains
and marshes conscripted only a few months before. Most had never seen a city
before—and were now looking at a ruin.[32]

Later that day artillery from across the Vistula—apparently Polish and Soviet—unleashed a powerful barrage on the German positions which lasted less than an hour. But it was said to have delayed a planned German attack. The Germans fighting for access to the river generally preferred to fight during the day, resting at night but periodically announcing their presence by bursts of machine gunfire. The insurgents were allowed little rest and some soon walked as if in a daze.

We had become almost like robots. Daytime we automatically rushed to whatever position was indicated to us, took cover and fired. Sometimes we saw the enemy and sometimes we just fired in his direction. We fought in cellars and on the upper floors of ruined buildings. Several times, while manning a position on the second floor, I heard German voices underneath shouting "Banditen Hände hoch" [Bandits, hands up]. No one ever thought of surrender.

At night we kept our eyes open by propping up the eyelids with match sticks. We ate when the girls brought us indigestible horse meat with pasta, pickled herring or sugared orange peel found in nearby stores. Men fell around us and we had become virtually oblivious to it. Officers to whom we had become accustomed were being replaced by new ones, units were constantly being amalgamated because of losses. I never understood how we managed to hold on to some buildings or why the Germans, having succeeded in entering them, often withdrew. I could only assume that those in charge of us knew why the defense of one building was more important than that of another and justified such casualties. There were no more newspapers, as in the city center, and we had no idea what went on elsewhere. Our world was the ruined buildings we were told to defend, the constant threat of deadly "goliaths" directed by cable, and fatigue.[33]

A nurse attached to Battalion Zośka (by then only a weak company), who was fifteen years old at the time, described her impressions of the fighting for control of the access to the river as the "blackest days."

When the building (at Okrąg street) was smashed by "goliaths," we could still hear the moaning of those buried underneath. We couldn't help them: the Germans had cut off access with gunfire and planes bombed us constantly. I am in despair, consoled by Zych [author's pseudonym] as best as he could. All around me are the bodies of fallen colleagues, the cellars are filled with wounded, there are no bandages, water, food. I don't know how I survived those days and nights.[34]

On September 17, from his headquarters in the city center, the AK commander-in-chief sent his second appeal to Marshal Rokossovsky via London. In it he gave details of the procedure to reestablish telephone connections between Praga and Warsaw. There was no Soviet answer and no apparent effort to contact the AK by telephone. But three days later, two Soviet liaison officers were parachuted to the city center and contacted the *AK* command. They wanted details of how the Poles imagined Soviet action on behalf of the insurgents. Because their radio station was damaged while landing, Bór's proposals could not be sent until later. Meanwhile, Soviet artillery observers were parachuted to Mokotów and Żoliborz. In the constantly pounded ruins of Czerniaków, one artillery radio operator had been active for days, apparently without effect. When I was assigned to the squad protecting Radosław's headquarters at Wilanowska Street no. 5, I distinctly heard a hoarse Russian voice shouting in the cellar: "*Elektron, Elektron*, give me supporting fire to the coordinates indicated before. *Elektron, Elektron*, why don't you answer!"

On September 19 several more boatloads of Berling troops arrived in the increasingly shrinking sector. The insurgents managed to send some wounded to Praga together with a handful of fleeing civilians. The river was under constant German fire, and some of those trying to cross it drowned. Although the Soviets launched a thick smoke screen over the area, no tangible reinforcements arrived. Exhausted and dispirited, Radosław told Major Latyshonok that he saw no prospects of a successful defense without help. At dusk, after his protective squad beat back a German attack on his headquarters, Radosław decided to take most of his men to Mokotów through the sewers, leaving some seventy insurgents under Captain Jerzy (Ryszard Białous) with Latyshonok's troops.

Near midnight on Sept. 19th, we moved toward the river bank where the sewer entrance was located. We advanced in a snake-like column but when I reached the manhole and tried to go down I saw Radosław standing in the muck, his rolled up trousers showing a bandaged leg, and he ordered me to go back. "Next convoy at 1.00 hours," he called out.

The sight of that wounded officer in the frightening cavern permeated by stench haunted me for days. Here was the leader of an elite battle group which had fought from one doomed sector of Warsaw to another and which was now reduced to a handful of exhausted survivors. Two days before I heard him shout into the telephone "how am I going to feed my 200 men?" Now he was no longer able to feed them or lead them to battle but merely to yet another loathsome sewer retreat.

We spent an hour in a building packed with exhausted insurgents, many of them wounded, while the German artillery pounded the riverside. Shortly after 1 A.M. we headed for the manhole but artillery shells exploding nearby shattered the initially orderly retreat. Men and women started pushing their way to the manhole in a chaotic crowd. Somehow I managed to get down.

It was a large storm sewer, parts of it equipped with boards to facilitate walking and some of its branches even illuminated by electric light bulbs. In other parts the level of the sewage had been raised considerably by sandbags placed by the Germans, reaching my thighs. At various sewer junctions, women guides gave us whispered directions. The last part of the trip was through a small sewer, forcing us to crawl for about half an hour (I did not have a stick to help me, as during a previous such trip to and from the Old Town).

After about four hours we emerged into a sunny morning of a peaceful suburban area. Somewhere to the east, beyond the line of trees and small houses, a
machine gun chattered and there were some mortar explosions. I emptied the
muck from my boots and sat down on a log. An insurgent in grey overalls armed
with a pistol watched us, smiling. Girls with clean hair distributed warm liquid—
tea, or maybe coffee, it didn't matter. It was warm. And I just wanted to look
at the sky.[35]

A man who watched the insurgents being helped out of the sewer
manhole later observed, "They gave the impression of people who were
totally exhausted. They dozed while sitting in the garden although it
was daytime and the area was under fire."

The arrival of the remnants of the *Radosław* group was reported briefly
to General Monter in the city center by Lieutenant Colonel Karol, Mokotów's commander:

Because of the exhaustion of men and the lack of food and ammunition, Radosław today after midnight began evacuation to me. Details tonight. Disorgan-
ized Berling troops have remained on the coast. I ordered Radosław to reorganize
his force (about 200, of whom 50 percent wounded).[36]

The day Radosław's exhausted troops reached the precarious safety of
Mokotów, the headquarters of the 1st Polish Army under Soviet command in Praga "had become convinced that, on the basis of the experience of the fighting near the Vistula, the leadership of the Warsaw
Insurrection did not intend to cooperate with the 1st Army nor give it
any effective help." In view of that appraisal, General Berling decided
to maintain his units in Czerniaków "as long as possible although the
prospects of reinforcing those units appeared dim."[37] It was obvious that
despite the dispatch of liaison officers and various messages, Berling, a
general appointed by Stalin, envisaged no further cooperation with the
Warsaw insurgents. In effect the Warsaw uprising had been condemned
to death.

The fighting—or slaughter—in Czerniaków continued three more
days. Despite repeated promises by General Berling himself, the promised boats to transport the last defenders to the Soviet-held side of the
river never turned up. Major Latyshonok and some of his soldiers were
captured as they tried to fight their way toward the insurgent positions
in the city center. After the last remaining buildings fell, the surviving
civilian population was escorted on foot to transit areas in the German-
held western suburbs. En route, SS guards and soldiers of the Vlasov
Army robbed them of jewelry and watches while young men and women
suspected of being members of the *AK* as well as several priests were
taken out of the column and shot. In reporting the victory by telephone,

a Major Fischer, of the staff of the *Reinefarth Group*, asked that the soldiers who had taken part in the action be given special praise because "the fight for the last building lasted only 24 hours."[38] (In 1957, Major Fischer was still in a Polish jail for crimes committed during the uprising.)

A brief communiqué by the German Central Front of September 23 noted that "in the southern part of the Warsaw caldron [*Kessel*] near the Vistula, the 9th Army broke the last resistance by the insurgents, who fought until the last bullet."[39]

A work detail consisting of Polish civilians was ordered to collect bodies after the battle. They found some 200 corpses with *AK* armbands and also the bodies of 200 women and men, apparently civilians. In addition thirty members of the *AK* were found hanged in a riverside shack. The captured Berling Army soldiers were usually treated as prisoners-of-war—although some *AK* members from Czerniaków also ended up in German *Stalags*.

Captain Jerzy, the undaunted commander of the *Zośka* battalion who was left behind by Radosław with a handful of his troops, refused to consider surrender even as the remaining buildings filled with corpses and the dying wounded fell one by one. "I will personally blow out the brains of any man who mentions capitulation," he said hoarsely in the cellar of a half-ruined house near the bank of the river. In a last and somewhat macabre meeting with Latyshonok punctuated by explosions, Jerzy heard the Soviet officer explain that his task was merely "fraternal help" for the fighting Poles, that his unit had lost 500 dead and wounded, and that he was full of admiration for the insurgents, many of whom would be given "officers' ranks in the people's army."[40]

The two men then parted company, with Jerzy succeeding in repeating his earlier exploit when he led his unit from the Old Town across a German-held park. Accompanied by his woman courier, two insurgents, and a Berling Army sergeant, moving at night and successfully clashing with German sentries, the small group literally fought their way to the city center.

NOTES

1. Adam Borkiewicz, *Powstanie Warszawskie 1944* (Warsaw: Pax, 1957), p. 493.

2. Dispatch no. Ldz 8235/tjn, September 12, 1944.

3. "*Gefahr der Vereinigung der Russen mit dem Aufstandischen in Warschau*," document of the German Command no. 6516/44 of September 24, 1944.

4. Author's translation of *Kurier Stołeczny* of September 12, 1944.

5. Newspapers *Barykada*, *Wiadomosci z Miasta*, and *Biuletyn Informacyjny*.

6. *Polskie Siły Zbrojne* (London: General Sikorski Historical Institute, 1950), Vol. III, p. 838.

7. Central Front situation report for September 13, *HG Mitte*, Ia no. F 4770/44, September 14, 1:00 A.M.

8. Vladimir Solovyov and Elena Klepikova, *Inside the Kremlin* (London: W. H. Allen, 1987), p. 101.

9. Viktor Suvorov, *Inside the Soviet Army* (London, Glasgow, Toronto, Sydney, Auckland: Grafton Books, 1987), pp. 3–31.

10. Ibid., pp. 31–32.

11. Ibid., pp. 32–33.

12. Ibid., p. 35.

13. Solovyov and Klepikova, *Inside the Kremlin*, p. 99.

14. Ibid., p. 100.

15. Ibid.

16. Allen Paul, *Katyn, The Untold Story of Stalin's Polish Massacre* (New York: Charles Scribner's Sons, 1991), p. 53.

17. Ibid., p. 157.

18. Ibid., p. 160.

19. *Dokumenty Katynia* (Warsaw: Interpress, 1992), pp. 155–156.

20. Paul, *Katyn, The Untold Story of Stalin's Polish Masssacre*, p. 213.

21. Ibid., p. 227.

22. Official text.

23. *Polskie Siły Zbrojne*, Vol. III, p. 839.

24. Jerzy Jaruzelski in a letter to the author, June 2000.

25. Central Front records Ia no. F 464/449, September 6, 1944, signed by General Heidkampner.

26. *Ordre de Bataille* listed by the Central Front on September 7, 1944.

27. Description based on author's notes.

28. "Krystyna" of the *Zośka* battalion in a postwar statement.

29. Statement by Lucja Stanisławska of March 15, 1947, quoted in Borkiewicz's *Powstanie Warszawskie 1944*, p. 569.

30. Borkiewicz, *Powstanie Warszawskie 1944*, p. 573.

31. Ibid., p. 582.

32. Description based on author's notes.

33. Ibid.

34. Lidia Markiewicz-Ziental in collective publication edited by Andrzej Czarski, *Najmłodsi Żołnierze Walczącej Warszawy* (Warsaw: Pax, 1971), p. 103.

35. Description based on author's notes.

36. Borkiewicz, *Powstanie Warszawskie 1944*, p. 599.

37. Postwar statement by Colonel J. Horodecki in Warsaw.

38. Documents of the Headquarters of the Central Front of September 23, 1944.

39. *HG Mitte* Ia F 4924/44, September 23, 1944.

40. Jerzy in conversation with the author in London, 1948.

CHAPTER 12

The End of Agony

On September 18, 1944, Warsaw saw the last tangible proof of Western interest in the dying uprising, when an impressive flotilla of 110 U.S. aircraft appeared in the clear skies over the city at approximately 1:45 P.M. Most of them were Liberator bombers, assisted by fighter aircraft. Almost immediately the numerous antiaircraft batteries placed throughout the German-held territory of the city opened fire, and the planes flew in their impressive formation surrounded by black puffs of exploding shells. (Postwar accounts published in communist-ruled Poland claimed the U.S. planes were assisted by Soviet aircraft bombing German artillery positions.)

The spectacle was incredible. We stared at the clearly visible large planes when suddenly the sky was covered by a mass of colored parachutes descending toward the city. We weren't sure what they were and a hysterical officer, his nerves obviously shattered by days and nights of fighting, shouted "open fire to support the landing operation." We obeyed automatically, and began spraying the German positions in front of us with a sustained cannonade, wasting precious ammunition. After a while we realized that the parachutes were not carrying men but containers and that the wind was sweeping them toward the German-held parts of the city.[1]

According to the records of the Polish Forces under British Command in London, out of several hundred containers dropped on the city, the insurgents managed to intercept only fifteen. The *AK* organ *Biuletyn In-formacyjny* claimed the weight of intercepted supplies was 16 tons, which seems highly improbable.

Since the first parachute drop of supplies for the Warsaw uprising on August 4 until the massive U.S. effort of September 18, the Western Allies had used a total of 228 aircraft to help the insurgents, thirty-four of which were shot down. The supplies included ten mortars, 100 light machine guns, 200 PIAT antitank launchers, 100 rifles, and 700 pistols. From the low-altitude Soviet drops over twelve nights in September, the insurgents recovered five heavy machine guns, 700 submachine guns, 143 antitank rifles, forty-eight light mortars, and 100 rifles.[2]

Considering the paucity of weapons received by the *AK* from the large American drop, the United States decided to discontinue the supply action for the Polish capital. Britain followed suit. It was clear that the area controlled by the insurrection was becoming too limited for effective parachute operations from Italy or Britain. It certainly was not like the relatively close mountains of Bosnia-Hercegovina where Josip Broz Tito's partisans survived mainly on the supplies provided by the Western Allies.

The increasingly dispirited Polish insurgents felt abandoned by the West, left at the mercy of the Soviet Union. They knew that Paris and Rome had been liberated but that Warsaw's liberation was in Soviet hands. The abortive landings of the Berling Army in Czerniaków and, subsequently, in parts of upper Powiśle and Żoliborz, should have shown them that nothing concrete could be expected from that "ally." Nonetheless the *AK* command continued fuelling hope.

In his "order of the day" coinciding with the American parachute drop on the city, Bór told his weary troops:

The battle against the Germans in Warsaw is coming to an end. . . . We have survived for seven weeks and we will survive until the entry into the capital of the victorious Red Army . . . and quickly reconstruct the Polish Armed Forces to avenge on German soil the damage, humiliation and losses inflicted upon us by the German criminals. To achieve that aim you must overcome your fatigue with fighting.[3]

While the Warsaw insurgents continued their hopeless battle, the exiled Polish politicians seemed to have been preoccupied with plans for Poland's future and its relations with a powerful and victorious Soviet Union. Various projects envisaged cooperation among prewar political parties, free elections, plans for the administration of the German territories that were to be ceded to Poland, the granting of legal status to the banned Communist Party, and other ideas basically irrelevant in the face of Soviet power.

Given the record of the Soviet Union's actions in the liberated Polish territories and the volumes of radio messages illustrating them, one cannot escape the feeling of complete irrationality by the men claiming to represent Poland. But then there was little else they could do—other than outright capitulation before the Soviet fait accompli. Moscow had its own plan for Poland, and its limited help to the Warsaw uprising, as well as arrests and deportations of *AK* partisan units, demonstrated that plan clearly. And the West preferred to stay out of what looked like a very difficult and insoluble situation.

The various proposals prepared in London were duly relayed to the *AK* commander-in-chief and the "Council of National Unity" (*Rada Jedności Narodowej*), a coalition of the four main political parties acting in Poland as an extension of the government. But whenever the government-in-exile made some gestures toward the Soviet Union in its statements, it encountered strong and uncompromising opposition from its organs in Poland.

Thus the Council of National Unity proposed that the relations between the Home Army and the Soviet authorities should be based "on the same principle as those between Britain and the United States and the authorities in liberated France." Furthermore, it demanded withdrawal of the Soviet troops from Poland once the hostilities with Germany were ended and the immediate release of all Poles who had been deported to the Soviet Union.

This voluminous radio traffic between half-ruined Warsaw and the Poles in London went on in the absence of any official communication between Marshal Rokossovsky and the Polish insurgents. The Soviet marshal simply ignored messages from Warsaw while Moscow was systematically going ahead with its own plans. In retrospect the Polish suggestions and demands seemed pathetic at a time when Polish communists appointed by Moscow had been installed on Polish territory (in Lublin) and already acted as a de facto government.

Bór himself described the plans of the government-in-exile as tantamount to capitulation because they were based "on the good will of the Soviet Union."

It is my duty to state, in the name of the Home Army under my command and undoubtedly in complete agreement with the views of all patriotically motivated Poles, that Poland did not fight for five years, in extremely difficult circumstances suffering horrible sacrifices, in order to capitulate to Russia. . . . Our combat against the Germans has shown that we are capable of proving our desire for freedom, which we value more than our lives.[4]

For its part, Moscow reacted relatively early to the proposals from the London Poles. A communiqué of the official Soviet news agency TASS on September 6, 1944, simply stated that the proposals had been transmitted to the Polish (communist) Committee of National Liberation "because such problems can only be dealt with by the Poles themselves."

The only question constantly brought up by the exiled Poles which received total support from the Western Allies was that of full combatant rights for the members of the *AK* and its recognition as part of the Polish Armed Forces under British Command. Already on July 30, after a number of its units in the field had been forcibly incorporated into the communist Berling Army and officers deported to the Soviet Union, the Polish government-in-exile pleaded for Allied intervention and a formal announcement of the *AK*'s recognition.

Britain and the United States at first tried for a tripartite statement that would include the Soviet Union, but without success. Finally, on August 30—a month after the outbreak of the Warsaw uprising—a formal statement of such recognition was read in the House of Commons by Foreign Secretary Anthony Eden and was subsequently published in the press and broadcast by the British Broadcasting Corporation (BBC). However, it referred only to the German and not Soviet treatment of Polish prisoners.

The statement stipulated that the Home Army was "a fighting force which is an integral part of the Polish Armed Forces." Members of the Home Army

have received instructions to carry out their military operations according to the rules of war. . . . They act in units under the orders of responsible commanders. They wear distinct badges or Polish uniforms. In such circumstances, repression against members of the Polish Home Army constitutes a violation of the laws of war also binding Germany. His Majesty's Government warns all Germans who participate in such outrages, or are responsible for them, that they will be held responsible for such crimes.[5]

A similar statement was issued by the government of the United States. But during most of September, with minor exceptions, the Germans regarded captured *AK* members as "bandits" subject to immediate execution, and referred to *AK* units in their communiqués as "gangs" or "bands" (*Banden* in German).

In view of the exceptionally high losses suffered in Warsaw, the German command intensified efforts to persuade the insurgents to give up their struggle. Such feelers, which increased in September, were mostly directed at Polish sector commanders, frequently using Red Cross personnel or Poles persuaded to carry such messages, often accompanied by promises of treating the insurgents according to the Geneva conventions. Particularly persuasive were messages from General Rohr, commander of the German troops in the southern sector, who invariably invoked the suffering of the civilian population exposed to bombing and starvation. The German offers were either ignored by Polish commanders or rejected, particularly when it seemed that the long-awaited Soviet help was coming.

The *AK* command, including the headquarters of General Bór, by then billeted in the telephone exchange building in the southern part of the city center, and the Warsaw area command under Monter (promoted to general's rank) felt that capitulation was becoming the only option.

"The last food reserves were running out in the city center," recalled a chronicler describing the situation on or about September 20. For the population of 260,000, which remained under insurgent control in the heart of Warsaw, and the 18,000 *AK* members in the central area, the uprising's civilian administration had 100 tons of barley, 50 tons of wheat, and stocks of sugar estimated to last four days. Consequently, at a meeting of senior officers, "for the first time Gen. Monter mentioned the problem of capitulation threatening his corps, recalled the losses suffered until then in action, the fate of 70,000 members of the intelligentsia massed in the city center and the need to save the rest of the population."[6]

A representative of the communist *Armia Ludowa* (*AL*) objected to such a posit, claiming that, because of the intensity of Soviet arms supplies, the combat performance of the insurgents had improved. Instead of capitulating he proposed to decrease the insurgent-held territory accompanied by an intensive effort to seize the largest possible area along the Vistula to facilitate contacts with the Red Army. But at that time the surviving insurgents in Czerniaków were trapped in suicidal defense of the few remaining buildings near the riverbank; Radosław's exhausted troops were crawling through the sewers toward Mokotów; and Soviet artillery spotters were shouting into microphones their pleas for fire support which were rarely acknowledged.

On September 20, in a move seen by some as "legalizing" the *AK* in preparation for a capitulation, Bór announced a reorganization of his units into a part of the regular Polish Army—and for the first time announcing the names of the key commanders in addition to their pseudonyms. Thus the *AK* forces in Warsaw had become "the Warsaw Army Corps" under the command of Monter (identified as Antoni Chruściel), with Colonel Wachnowski (Karol Ziemski) as deputy commander.

The components of the corps carried the same numbers as the divisions that had their components based in Warsaw before the war: the 8th Infantry Division in Żoliborz, the 10th in Mokotów, and the 28th in the center. The divisions were divided into "regiments," also with prewar numbers. To maintain the tradition of the insurrection, various units were authorized to keep their original names. (In fact, most insurgents were unaware of the changes that did not affect their limited scope of operations.)

Meanwhile, profiting from a pause in the fighting on the Soviet front, General von dem Bach proceeded to regroup his forces for a decisive attack on the remaining insurgent strongholds. A quick end to the operations against the *AK* was also urged by the new commander of the German 9th Army, General Smillo von Luttwitz, who feared that "in the Warsaw region the enemy, the Polish 1st Army, is regrouping in order to launch new attacks using new forces."[7] Unknown to General von Luttwitz, on the previous day the 1st Polish Army had received orders from the Soviet command to organize "defense along fixed lines" rather than repeat its previous attempts to cross the Vistula.

After preliminary skirmishes and some seizure of territory from the insurgents on the outskirts of Mokotów, on September 24 General von dem Bach threw his forces into action, bolstered by the SS *Panzer Herman Goering* division. By 8:15 A.M., the sprawling area of suburban villas, gardens, and modern apartment blocks was hit by a storm of heavy artillery shells accompanied by the terrifying whine of Stuka dive-bombers.

Our rest after the sewer retreat from Czerniaków was shattered within minutes. Shells exploded in front and behind our billets in a two-story housing complex. Terrified inhabitants rushed to the cellars, clutching their belongings. Our unit commander also ordered his men to follow suit, leaving me on the upper floor as "observer." I wasn't sure what I was supposed to observe. All I could see were explosions, smoke and units of Mokotów defenders in their grey overalls from captured *Luftwaffe* stores running in small groups along a tree-shaded street—toward the exploding shells.[8]

After a two-hour artillery barrage accompanied by raids involving up to thirty planes, a German force estimated at three infantry battalions backed by armor and "goliaths" stormed the insurgent positions from the south and west. The impact of von dem Bach's attack was immediate. The terrain, once again, did not favor the insurgents without heavy weapons. Open areas, orchards, and municipal parks did not facilitate urban warfare. Amidst the exploding shells of heavy mortars and bombs from the attacking aircraft, the Germans seized the outlying areas of Ksawerów and Królikarnia. Smoke billowed toward the sky from Warsaw's latest battlefield.

A massive school building on Woronicza Street, used during the war as German barracks and painted in camouflage colors, was captured by the Germans but was recovered in an immediate counterattack. Once more Radosław's weary troops were sent into battle to bolster the units ordered to recover other positions.

In the basement of the school building battered by artillery shells we were told, once again, that a "last effort" was required. Late in the evening we were deployed along with other units in open terrain pock-marked by craters caused by bomb explosions. I was with Lt. "Mały" and several others in such a hole, waiting, when a flare knifed across the sky. "Attack!" shouted the lieutenant, cupping his hands around his mouth. We heard a "hurrah" from the first line, grenade explosions and some shouts of triumph. Then a forest of German flares illuminated the battlefield while heavy machine gun fire swept it from one end to another. Several wounded men began crawling to the rear.[9]

When this insurgent effort was beaten back by the Germans, Mokotów's commander Lieutenant Colonel Karol came to the conclusion that the heavy losses suffered during the first day of the attack precluded effective defense of the existing lines. Thus, on September 25 he decided to abandon a large portion of the suburb and barricade himself in the more heavily built-up northern area, where large apartment blocks offered the possibility of continued resistance. As night fell on September 25, Karol's last reserves found themselves in the front line. Seeing the obvious withdrawal from the outlying areas, crowds of civilians burdened by their belongings followed. But the loss of the area containing large vegetable gardens immediately created a food problem. It was clear that Mokotów could not resist much longer.

On September 26 under continuing pounding by the victorious German attackers, Karol decided that his only option was to abandon the suburb and retreat to the solidly defended heart of Warsaw through the sewers. In the afternoon, during a two-hour cease-fire agreed by both sides, some 9,000 civilians left the Polish sector for the German lines. Radosław's survivors were among the units deployed to cover the retreat which started in the afternoon although the sewer route had not been completely reconnoitered. The first to leave were some lightly wounded insurgents, members of the civilian administration, and remnants of several units which no longer had ammunition. (Wounded twice by a hand grenade and a mortar shell the previous day, I remained in the billet assigned to my unit rather than in one of the makeshift hospitals. The building was twice bombed by Stuka aircraft.)

In the evening Karol and his staff entered the sewer, putting Major "Zryw" (Kazimierz Szternal) in charge of the last fighting units grouped in half a dozen apartment blocks.

The night was cool and a persistent drizzle pelted the units heading toward the sewer entrance at Szustra Street. I limped along, helped by two young girls. When we reached the manhole protected by a barricade, I realized that with my leg and hand wounds and fever I could not face the prospect of another sewer retreat. I told my immediate commander that I preferred to remain in Mokotów, regardless of what the Germans might do with me. I watched as my companions descended into the dark pit wishing me luck and then was left alone, leaning on a stick.

Suddenly firing broke out in the vicinity and someone shouted that the Germans were attacking, chasing Polish civilians ahead of their tanks. I saw Lt. Mały in his Soviet helmet round up the few remaining men with arms and run in the direction of the attack.

Walking with increasing difficulty across the courtyards and gardens of a large apartment block I saw a Red Cross flag over a doorway. When I entered I was met by a grey-haired woman with an air of authority. I explained that I had been in sewers before and could not face another sewer experience. "Child," she said, "come and tell those idiots what sewers are like." I then realized that the basement where I found myself was filled with young men with *AK* armbands, some on crutches and some with bandaged arms and heads. Dutifully, I described the various types of sewers, the stench, filth and claustrophobia. It made no impact. Some of the men said they would rather die in sewers than be shot by Germans. They continued waiting for a guide while I was given a mattress in one of the rooms of what turned out to be a "hospital."[10]

For those who were trying to make their way to the central part of Warsaw, it turned out to be the most terrifying sewer retreat in the uprising's history. The organizers envisaged groups of fifty people, just as from the Old Town and Czerniaków, but within several hours the sewers had become packed with some 800 men and women trying to find their way in the underground labyrinth. Some guides were lost, some led people to manholes in German hands. *AK* accounts estimate that some 150 insurgents who emerged in the German sector were shot, and seventy-six others survived, although no completely accurate figures are available. An unspecified number of people died of exhaustion or from gas dropped into manholes by the Germans.

Before Lieutenant Colonel Karol reached the city center, he stumbled into a patrol heading toward him with Monter's "categorical orders to return to his positions in Mokotów." A member of the patrol described the situation in the sewer as "filled with ghost-like creatures in various positions—standing, kneeling, sitting or crawling in the slime. Some of them were already dead. . . . The whole scene looked eerie and reminded one of a lunatic asylum."[11] Many people in the sewers were trampled to death or lost their senses during a thirty-six-hour search for exits. Some were lucky. Lidia Markiewicz-Ziental, wounded in the face while attending to my wounds two days earlier, said after the war that her successfully concluded trip lasted only fourteen hours.[12]

When Karol started his return march, his party was showered with hand grenades dropped through a manhole and was forced to turn back. Meanwhile, during the morning of September 27, the last group of 150 wounded insurgents entered the sewer in Mokotów where Major Zryw tried to persuade his dispirited troops to return to their positions. Some refused, although the German attack continued. To stop the slaughter, Zryw dispatched Major "Burza" (Eugeniusz Landberger) and two other officers with a white flag to the Germans. The German commander (General Rohr) guaranteed that members of the *AK* would have prisoner-of-war status under international law but gave the insurgents only fifteen minutes to make up their minds. Major Zryw accepted his terms.

The firing stopped suddenly in mid-morning after periodic bombardment throughout the night. Earlier, in anticipation of surrender, a nurse took away parts of my German equipment, including helmet, camouflage jacket and trousers, as well as photographs and documents showing my membership in the *AK*. A doctor then announced that "Major Burza surrendered" and that the civilian wounded will be taken to hospitals in occupied Poland and *AK* members to Germany. I thought of slave labor and concentration camps (where many Warsaw civilians ended up) and decided that the promise of protection by the Geneva convention offered a better chance of survival. After the civilians were carried out, two German soldiers, armed, helmeted and in what looked like brand new uniforms, walked into the cellar and asked "*Hier alle Soldaten*?" [All here are soldiers?] The nurse said yes.

I was carried out of the cellar on a stretcher into a grey autumnal day. A middle-aged *Wehrmacht* soldier stood by a pile of abandoned weapons. We were grouped on the ground floor of a building equipped with mattresses and even some beds. There was a commotion in the corridor and a German general appeared, dressed in a long, perfectly tailored coat with red lapels. He spoke briefly, praising our combat performance and regretting that "such brave opponents" did not fight communism on Germany's side. Just as he finished, artillery salvoes exploded nearby. "Your Russian friends," the general said and left.[13]

The *AK* members taken prisoner in Mokotów were the first large group treated by the Germans as regular army combatants.

According to a Central Front report for September 27,

The insurgents in Mokotów have surrendered. Taken prisoner were 2000 members of the *AK* and also seized were 5000 civilians. Thirty-six *Wehrmacht* soldiers held as prisoners were freed as well as 60 civilian Germans. . . . According to reports by agents, the insurgents and the population suffered heavy losses. . . . The capitulation of the insurgents in Mokotów was a real success in efforts to suppress the uprising in Warsaw.[14]

Before leaving Mokotów for a sewer trip to the city center, Lieutenant Colonel Karol received a message from General von dem Bach, carried by Polish negotiators, proposing a meeting with Bór "on neutral ground." Karol had left the message unanswered. On September 28, the day after the fall of Mokotów, von dem Bach repeated his proposal, this time suggesting a meeting to agree on the terms of surrender. At that time the insurgents controlled only the center of the city and the northern suburb of Żoliborz.

According to the official history of the *AK* published after the war in London,

The news from London was bad. The Americans declined to undertake further flights to Warsaw, invoking the paltry results of the Sept. 18th expedition, early dusk and technical obstacles. The Russians, while fueling the struggle with propaganda statements, were not eager to establish permanent contact with the insurrection's command. Nothing indicated that they were about to launch an offensive in the Warsaw region. . . . The situation of the defenders was becoming hopeless; they were increasingly plagued by the shortage of ammunition and other means of combat, the population starved in the ruins, the first spell of cold weather had arrived. It seemed likely that the two main centers of resistance would fall within several days.[15]

During the evening of September 28, Bór summoned his key commanders, as well as the delegate of the government-in-exile, for a decisive conference. After a terse review of the situation, all present agreed to begin contacts with the German command to discuss the conditions of surrender.

Meanwhile, using the previously suggested procedure for radio communications, the *AK* command informed Marshal Rokossovsky that Warsaw's garrison saw no prospects of holding out longer than October 1. Unless a Soviet attack took place before then, Warsaw would be forced to lay down arms. This time receipt of the message was confirmed by the Soviet radio station.

The following day (September 29), having studied the relevant parts of the 1929 Geneva conventions, Bór dispatched two officers to von dem Bach with a proposal to begin exploratory negotiations. The SS general agreed and submitted German conditions, stressing that although they expired on October 2, Bór had to deliver his agreement to begin talks on September 30. Thus the *AK* command had basically one day to make up its mind. The terse German demand was unquestionably caused by procrastination of the Polish side during previous contacts, when the Poles were still expecting Soviet help.

Bór immediately informed London—and still suggested breaking off the talks in the event of Soviet help.

We have determined that the paltry food rations will last only three days. We see no prospects that during that period the Red Army would be capable of occupying Warsaw or giving it sufficient protection or support to continue [the struggle]. . . . I have informed Marshal Rokossovsky about the situation, asking for help. But unless I receive it in substantial form, I will be forced to capitulate.[16]

Bór also told London that he had agreed with the Germans to start evacuating the civilian population from the besieged city, that Żoliborz was under intense bombardment, and that the Germans expected to occupy the northern suburb in three days. He stressed, "In the event of an attack by the Red Army in the immediate future, evacuation [of the population] will be interrupted and I am prepared to resume hostilities."

There was no reply from Rokossovsky before the German deadline and no sign of activity on the Soviet front facing Warsaw. Bór informed von dem Bach that he was sending officers on October 2 to begin negotiations with the German command.

German preparations for a general attack on Żoliborz had already begun on September 22 with the arrival of the elite 19th *Panzer* Division of General Hans Källner, who took command of all German forces in the northern sector of Warsaw. They included two infantry regiments, units of the Vlasov Army, Cossacks in German service, and various support units with about thirty artillery pieces and eighty heavy machine guns. The Polish insurgent force consisted of 2,500 men and women, 1,500 of whom were in combat units, many armed with recently supplied Soviet weapons. The Russians, as usual flying at a low altitude, also dropped some food and tobacco on Żoliborz. On the whole the suburb suffered an acute food and water shortage and was cut off from the Vistula by the German 25th *Panzer* Division, subsequently assigned to the 2nd German Army.

General Källner was a former Austrian cavalry officer "of the old school," and had met Bór when both served the Habsburg Emperor Franz Josef in World War I. Afterward they met occasionally at international horse shows. According to von dem Bach, Källner was proud of his elite division, resented being assigned to fight Polish "gangs," and regarded every resistance fighter as a "common criminal."[17]

With the German troops of General Källner massing for a decisive attack, two Soviet artillery spotters equipped with a radio station were parachuted into Żoliborz. As a result, the Żoliborz *AK* commander, Lieutenant Colonel Żywiciel (Mieczysław Niedzielski), was able to establish contact with the Soviet command on the Vistula's right bank and received supporting artillery fire. It was perhaps the only example of effective cooperation between the Soviet forces and the *AK* in Warsaw.

Żoliborz had been under intensive artillery fire and tentative infantry attacks basically since September 19, but the insurgents managed to hold their positions. As usual the civilian population suffered most. In such an atmosphere, General Källner proposed, in writing, an organized exodus of the population and the capitulation of the insurgent units. Żywiciel refused all suggestions to lay down arms and accused the Germans of murdering women and children during the fighting in the nearby area of Marymont. After this exchange, on September 29 and 30,

Källner's troops advanced street by street, systematically reducing the area under insurgent control.

During the evening of September 29, Żywiciel summoned all unit commanders for a conference, which was held in the cellar of a burning building at Mickiewicz Street. All reports were abysmally pessimistic: the number of dead and wounded increased every hour, entire units were being massacred. A month later, in the hospital of *Stalag* XIA, Altengrabow, Żywiciel recalled,

I established that, with what I had under my command, I could fight a defensive action for a day or two more but was incapable of any substantial offensive operation. Some of my officers suggested that we abandon the population and fight our way through the German cordon to the Kampinos forest. Others proposed contacting the Russians and asking their help in crossing the river to Praga. I accepted the second option as more feasible.[18]

Żywiciel contacted the Soviet headquarters by radio and received agreement to provide a smoke screen over the river, as well as boats to carry the insurgents to the other side. The Soviet command set 7:00 P.M. of September 30 as the beginning of the planned rescue operation.

However, unbeknown to Żywiciel, this plan coincided with the decision by Bór to begin talks with the Germans about Warsaw's capitulation—including the Żoliborz garrison which the *AK* commander believed incapable of further action. On the morning of September 30, Colonel Wachnowski (Karol Ziemski), accompanied by one officer, crossed to the German lines and was taken to General von dem Bach's headquarters in Ożarów outside Warsaw. According to the version recorded by the *AK* command, the Germans demanded the immediate capitulation of Żoliborz, but Wachnowski insisted that he had to refer the matter to Bór. Meanwhile the two sides decided that further talks concerning the fate of Żoliborz would be carried out directly with General Källner, whose troops were tightening their armored noose around the burning suburb. Thereupon Wachnowski was taken back to Warsaw where he was allowed to reenter the Polish sector of the city.

Bór then instructed Wachnowski to conduct further negotiations about Żoliborz with General Källner—in coordination with Żywiciel. But as Källner and Wachnowski sat down to discuss the technical details of capitulation, the German general said his staff had intercepted radio signals about Żywiciel's plans to cross the river to the Soviet side and that he intended to prevent the operation.

Källner proposed a one-hour cease-fire at 5:00 P.M. during which Wachnowski would cross the Polish lines in Żoliborz and contact Żywiciel. The Polish envoy followed an attack by German tanks on foot, and eventually, when the tanks halted for the planned truce, by shouting across a barricade, persuaded the insurgents to stop their fire. He found Żywiciel, wounded, lying in his command post, who told him he intended to continue resisting. Żywiciel also informed him that he had received a message from the Soviet side that the requested smoke screen and boats would be available at 11:00 A.M. However, when nothing happened, another Soviet signal said the operation would take place later, at dusk.

By then neither Żywiciel nor Wachnowski believed the Soviet intentions, and, given the shrinking area held by the insurgents, Wachnowski authorized Żywiciel in writing to capitulate. The German side pledged to treat the insurgents and the population "according to international law."[19]

Shortly after Żywiciel told his units to lay down their arms, he was handed a radio message from Praga, informing him that the smoke screen had been blown away by wind but that boats would be available later. "Fight your way through to the Vistula. We will facilitate your crossing," the Soviet message said. By then most of Żywiciel's troops had surrendered.

Some, however, refused to capitulate and tried to fight their way to the river. Only a handful of members of the communist AL succeeded in reaching the other side. A small unit of the Jewish Fighting Organization (ŻOB) refused to believe German guarantees of combatant status and hid in a cellar with a stock of food and water. It remained there undetected, and after six weeks they reached the Kampinos forest. Among them was deputy commander of the ŻOB and one of its founders, Yitzhak Zuckerman. (See Chapter 5.)

A German communiqué announced that after stubborn street fighting the last Polish units had surrendered in Żoliborz and "efforts to flee eastward across the river were thwarted, inflicting heavy losses on the enemy." The communiqué listed the number of prisoners as "60 officers, 1300 armed insurgents, 130 women fighters and 400 wounded." It said that between one and three hundred members of the AL did not join the capitulation and "either intend to continue fighting or escape across the Vistula."[20]

Colonel Wachnowski's role in persuading the commander of Żoliborz to capitulate was decried after the war by the Polish communist regime and its press. The campaign intended to show that although the AK had the means of crossing the river to join the Soviet forces, it preferred to capitulate to the Germans.

When the defense of Żoliborz collapsed on September 30, the AK command was already engaged in intense negotiations with General von dem Bach. In addition to the AK envoys, participating in the talks were representatives of the Polish Red Cross and of the refugee agency known by the initials RGO (Rada Główna Opiekuńcza). Their main concern was to facilitate an organized exodus of some 250,000 civilians still remaining in the areas controlled by the insurgents and suffering from hunger and lack of adequate medical care, who were living in primitive conditions in cellars and the few buildings that were still intact. A cease-fire was decided during the daytime hours of October 1 and 2, to allow the population to leave the ruined city.

The departing inhabitants were allowed only as much baggage as they could carry. The sick and wounded were transported by horse-drawn carts mobilized in villages in Warsaw's immediate vicinity. All were grouped in several abandoned factories around Warsaw (Ursus, Włochy, Pruszków, and Piastów) from where they were to be sent to labor camps in Germany or "other assigned destinations."

Yet during the first day of the evacuation, only 8,000 people left the ruins, mostly women and children. The mood of the population was thus summed up in one of the last articles in the insurgent press:

We have given Poland all those who have fallen on the battlefield, we have given it our suffering, our possessions and the roofs over our heads.

We are now facing more misery. But we will not spread lament and tears throughout Poland, nor don the laurels of heroes. We are leaving filled with the bitter Polish truth and yet confident that our suffering was not in vain. . . . And those who will try to diminish the value of our folly will have to face the specter of the fists of those who died in the ruins.[21]

During the evening of October 1, at the *AK* headquarters on Pius Street no. 19, four officers were designated to begin formal capitulation negotiations. Their directives were drafted as artillery shells exploded around them, marking the end of the first day of the civilian evacuation. The following day they crossed the Polish lines and were taken to General von dem Bach's headquarters in Ożarów.

According to a Polish historian, von dem Bach discussed the situation at length, praised the bravery of the insurgents, and admitted that the uprising was a major obstacle paralyzing German communications and the freedom of action against the Soviet Army. He then telephoned the commander of the 9th German Army, informing him about the start of the negotiations, as well as Himmler, who cautioned him that in the event of a Soviet attack the Poles would break off the talks. Von dem Bach also told the Polish officers that in order to grant them the status of combatants on the basis of the Geneva convention of August 17, 1929, he himself had to travel to Hitler's headquarters.[22] The Poles agreed to dismantle some their main barricades on the same day (October 2) and release all German prisoners. The first *AK* units were to march out of the city on October 4, the rest the following day. The Poles also succeeded, after prolonged discussion, to persuade the Germans to consider members of the communist *AL* as "part of the Warsaw Army Corps."

Meanwhile the Germans were facing an unusual situation: When, in London, General Sosnkowski resigned as commander-in-chief in view of the Warsaw disaster, the government-in-exile appointed Bór in his place. Thus the Germans were about to take as prisoner the commander of all Polish forces under British Command of which the *AK* was a part. Although the exiled Poles had undoubtedly made the symbolic appointment as part of the effort to increase the stature of the insurrection and its commander, the Germans saw in it an opportunity to discuss a cessation of hostilities by *AK* units throughout Poland. The Polish envoys refused to be drawn into a discussion on the subject, and von dem Bach did not insist.

The capitulation act was signed for the German side by General von dem Bach and for the *AK* by Colonel Kazimierz Iranek-Osmecki (known in the *AK* as "Heller") and Lieutenant Colonel Zygmunt Dobrowolski ("Zyndram"). It consisted of twenty-three articles, confirming the status of *AK* members, including women, as prisoners-of-war and guaranteeing immunity for their anti-German activities while in the Underground before the uprising. It was an unprecedented and enormous concession by the Germans who until then treated resistance fighters as "bandits." It was never applied to the resistance movements in other countries of occupied Europe.

The evacuation of the wounded prisoners was to be carried out in cooperation with the *AK*'s chief surgeon and his German equivalent. The Germans agreed that the transport and supervision of Polish prisoners would be in the hands of the *Deutsche Wehrmacht* (the German Armed Forces) and would not include members of other nationalities serving Germany (such as Russians, Ukrainians, or Cossacks). The German side was adamant that the entire civilian population of Warsaw would have to leave the city. Article 10 of the first part of the act of capitulation specified that

the evacuation will be carried out in a manner sparing the population unnecessary suffering. Transport of objects with artistic, cultural or religious value will be facilitated. The German command will undertake to secure the public and private property remaining in the city.[23]

Three *AK* companies armed with submachine guns and rifles would remain in the city for "housecleaning duties" until the evacuation of the wounded and the civilian population was completed.

The crowds of dejected civilians were already pouring out of the ruined city toward the Western Railway Station (*Dworzec Zachodni*). They were herded onto trains, according to one evacuee, "while guards fired on those who attempted to flee, shouted insults and distributed blows."[24]

(My experience was different. Although captured in Mokotów six days before the formal capitulation agreement and with only a verbal guarantee from General Rohr, myself and several hundred other *AK* wounded were neither harassed nor insulted. Taken in a convoy of horse-drawn wagons to a railway siding south of the Warsaw racetrack, we spent an uncomfortable day under a persistent autumn drizzle waiting for transport, and were given the standard thick *Wehrmacht* soup and bread.)

On October 3, in his final order of the day announcing the capitulation, the cavalry general who has gone into history as Bór-Komorowski, bade farewell to all those who had fought under his command and to the population. He said that the insurrection was overwhelmed by the enemy's technical superiority, which had shrunken the area controlled by the insurgents, and that there was no food left.

Facing the prospect of the total annihilation of Warsaw's population and of burying under its ruins all those who fought and hundreds of thousands of inhabitants, I decided to stop fighting. I thank all soldiers for their splendid and unswerving performance in combat. To all who have died I pay the tribute which their sacrifice and suffering deserve. I offer my thanks to the population and beg it to forgive all improper acts which, inevitably, must have been committed during the long period of our struggle. . . . I reiterate my faith in the final victory of our just cause.[25]

The ruined capital was shrouded by an eerie and oppressive silence as the last wounded were carried out, and one after another streets were emptied. Soon German demolition teams moved in to destroy those public buildings that had survived the battle intact while the occupation authorities looted all movable property left behind. There was no one to protest or invoke the clause of the capitulation agreement guaranteeing their preservation.

There was also silence on the other side of the Vistula, where all military activity by Soviet troops and their Polish communist allies halted for more than three months.

NOTES

1. Based on author's notes in *Stalag* XIA, fall of 1944.

2. *Polskie Siły Zbrojne* (London: General Sikorski Historical Institute, 1950) Vol. III, pp. 799–800.

3. Excerpts from the official text cited by Adam Borkiewicz, *Powstanie Warszawskie 1944* (Warsaw: Pax, 1957) p. 592.

4. Official text.

5. Ibid.

6. Borkiewicz, *Powstanie Warszawskie 1944*, p. 600.

7. Central Front Records, Ia no. F 4924/44 of September 23, 1944.

8. Author's notes written in *Stalag* XIA, fall of 1944.

9. Ibid.

10. Ibid.

11. Borkiewicz, *Powstanie Warszawskie 1944*, p. 636.

12. In conversation with the author.

13. Author's notes written in *Stalag* XIA, fall of 1944.

14. Central Front records Ia no. F 4986/44.

15. *Polskie Siły Zbrojne*, Vol. III, p. 868.

16. Bór's dispatch of September 29 entered in *AK* files Ldz 9313/tjn.

17. Von dem Bach's statement published in *Dzieje Najnowsze*, Warsaw, 1947, Vol. I, p. 313.

18. In conversation with the author.

19. Borkiewicz, *Powstanie Warszawskie 1944*, p. 663.

20. Documents *HG Mitte Ic A Banden Tagesmeldung*, October 1, 1944.

21. From *Kurier Stołeczny*, no. 45/44.

22. Borkiewicz, *Powstanie Warszawskie 1944*, pp. 688–689.

23. Official text.

24. Borkiewicz, *Powstanie Warszawskie 1944*, p. 693.

25. From official text.

Epilogue

The last radio signal from Warsaw to London was recorded under the number 1936 at 9:40 P.M. on October 4, 1944. In it, Lieutenant General Tadeusz Bór-Komorowski informed the Polish government-in-exile that, because of the possibility of German reprisals against the *AK* and the civilian population, he could not avoid captivity, but, once in the prisoner-of-war camp, he would attempt to escape "regardless of personal risk and toil."

The general reported:

Today I visited General von dem Bach with whom I agreed on the terms of capitulation. I was invited to lunch with representatives of the German Army and civil administration. I declined, but in discussions with Gen. von dem Bach I obtained the best possible conditions for the *AK* prisoners and for the civilian population of Warsaw.[1]

By dusk that day, the first column of *AK* prisoners had left the ruins of Warsaw. According to German records, it consisted of 375 officers, 1,227 other ranks, and 221 women. At 10:00 A.M. the following day, six men, three wearing civilian hats and overcoats and three others in prewar Polish uniforms, approached the German lines near the gutted and half-burned Warsaw Polytechnic Building. They were saluted at the last Polish barricade by General Antoni Chruściel (Monter), who was wearing a Polish uniform with medals from the 1920 war against the Soviet Union. The autumnal day was gray with clouds massed over Warsaw's low skyline.

The Poles advanced toward a group of waiting German officers. Those in civilian clothes, including Bór-Komorowski, removed their hats; the others saluted. A German major stepped forward and raised his arm in the Nazi salute by then adopted by all of the German Armed Forces. Addressing Bór as *"Herr General,"* the German officer informed him that "according to my orders, I have the honor of taking you into captivity" (*Ich habe den Befehl und die Ehre Sie in Gefangenschaft zu nehmen*).

Accompanied by one of his officers, Bór walked slowly toward the nearby monument known as "the sapper," where his headquarters company stood at attention, many of the men weeping.

Only a handful of "official" German journalists recorded this chilling farewell, paralyzing in the silent drama of a general who had lost an army and a city he intended to liberate, after sixty-three days of torment, death, and unanswered pleas for help. The scene was only a few years away from applauding crowds at international horse shows or the glistening sabres of his 9th Lancers with crimson bands on their square-shaped caps. Around Bór, a whole world had collapsed.

He slowly put his felt hat on again, was seated in an open German staff car, and driven away from the ruined city. His last guard of honor on Polish soil then proceeded to lay down its arms.

Throughout the day a long column of prisoners, including five generals (promoted by London during the uprising), marched along a previously decided route. One of the *AK* staff officers who watched the procession recalled later that "although they carried weapons, it was not a military march. They walked like convicts or a funeral cortege. Their faces reflected pain and overwhelming, heart-breaking sorrow. Many wept."[2] All weapons were laid down before the column left the city and marched to transit centers along a road guarded by *Wehrmacht* troops; a soldier was placed every fifty yards.

During the time between the formal capitulation and the departure of the first column, the Warsaw garrison performed a number of "house-keeping" chores which included promotion entries in battle journals (some of which were then buried) and the payment of seven dollars to each insurgent going into captivity—their only pay since the uprising began. An estimated $1 million in dollar bills was removed for further conspiracy by *AK* officials who left the city with the civilian population.

The prisoners were dressed in a variety of clothing, but parts of German uniforms worn during the uprising had been carefully discarded to avoid friction with the captors and possible accusations of looting German equipment. Thus the column moving into captivity did not resemble the units that had resisted for sixty-three days. Many wore berets and forage caps instead of the captured German helmets used during the uprising, civilian overcoats, and ill-fitting suits taken from abandoned apartments; they carried rolled blankets, rucksacks, or even suitcases. Some had damaged their weapons before turning them over, and, in several cases, broke them in front of the German officers supervising the surrender. Such demonstrations of bitterness stopped when the Germans warned that they violated the act of capitulation, and threatened sanctions.

According to German figures, 11,668 insurgents, including women, had gone into captivity from Warsaw's city center by the end of October 5. Left behind were 4,000 wounded in the central part, 500 wounded in Mokotów and 400 in Żoliborz, who were subsequently evacuated and sent to several different prison camps. Between October 1 and 7, the Germans counted 155,519 civilians leaving the city, but the figure appears incomplete. Hidden among the civilians were a number of *AK* officers who intended to carry on the Underground struggle, as well as members of the insurrection's civil authorities, including the deputy prime minister of the government-in-exile.

Treatment of the *AK* prisoners varied, depending on the commanders of the *Wehrmacht* units handling their evacuation. Some were shouted at, pushed with rifle butts, and crowded without food or water into cattle wagons. The wounded from Mokotów (including myself), after a cursory examination of their injuries by Russian and other prisoner doctors at the Skierniewice transit camp, were loaded into freight wagons equipped with wooden cots and lavatories. The *Wehrmacht* guards—one soldier armed with a rifle and hand grenades for each wagon—did not prevent groups of Polish civilians from reaching the train with baskets filled with food.

The fate of the civilian evacuees was apparently much worse. According to Polish accounts, many were shipped to forced labor centers in Germany, and an estimated 40,000 who were regarded as "dangerous elements" ended up in concentration camps.

Bór and some twenty senior officers—selected by the Germans—were driven to a railway station escorted by General Ernest Rode. Then, in a first-class railway carriage, they were taken to a camp in East Prussia.

According to some Polish historians, this unusual treatment was meant to show that the Germans respected their prisoners, particularly the man who was the titular head of all Polish Armed Forces (except, of course, those under Soviet command). There was also speculation that the Germans might have tried to persuade the officers, embittered by the failure of Russian help for the uprising, to form a "Polish legion" similar to other ethnic formations fighting on the German side. There are no records of such conversations, and there was no possibility that the Poles would even consider the idea (suggested previously by various German commanders in the field). After a short stay in East Prussia, the selected group was sent to the *Offlag* (*Offizierslager* or prisoner-of-war camp for officers) in Murnau in Bavaria, where they joined hundreds of other Polish officers held there since the 1939 campaign.

On October 5, the day when the leadership of the Warsaw uprising went into captivity, British Prime Minister Winston Churchill paid tribute before the House of Commons to "the heroic stand of the Polish Home Army" and of Warsaw's population. The exiled Polish community in Britain, the Polish General Staff, and the forces at the time fighting in Italy and in France were stunned when they heard or read his words that "despite all efforts by the Soviet army, the German fortifications on the Vistula could not be forced and the rescue could not come in time."[3] The "German fortifications" along the Vistula were installed only after the uprising, and the inactivity of the Soviet forces all throughout the uprising was obvious to most Poles. The refusal to allow British and U.S. planes to use Soviet airfields for supplying Warsaw was outspoken enough. To many Poles, Stalin wanted Warsaw destroyed as much as Hitler did.

The last German communiqué referring to the uprising was issued on October 10, stating tersely that "after repeated searches of the blocks of houses in the central caldron [*Kessel*], it can be concluded that the entire population has left Warsaw."

According to *AK* historian Adam Borkiewicz, the communiqué of the German Central Front was not completely accurate. Apparently a number of people had remained in the maze of Warsaw's underground hideouts, perfected during the uprising. Borkiewicz claims that a group of the Jewish Fighting Organization (ŻOB) had remained hidden at Promyk Street, and another ŻOB unit in the cellars under the ruins of the Queen Jadwiga secondary school, as well as in several other places. An *AK* unit of more than thirty fighters commanded by "Major Bicz" had remained in the Jewish cemetery at Okopowa Street until October 16.[4]

Shortly afterward a massive, organized looting campaign of the remnants of the Polish capital began in earnest. Delegations from a number of German—as well as Polish municipalities under German occupation— were allowed to enter the ruins and strip them of anything of value which had not been taken by the *Wehrmacht*, SS, and their Russian and Ukrainian allies. Postwar Polish assessments claim that some 33,000 railway wagons filled with furniture, personal belongings, and factory equipment were taken out of Warsaw. Entire blocks of abandoned houses were set on fire, and a number of monuments as well as official buildings were blown up by special German troops known as *Verbrennungs und Vernichtungskommando* (Burning and Destruction Detachment).

Warsaw in those days was a "sinister desert of ruins," some smouldering for a long time. Entire streets were covered with fallen buildings;

large areas—such as the Old Town—were literally pulverized. According to postwar Polish assessments, 10,455 of Warsaw's 24,724 buildings—or 42 percent—were completely destroyed, and most of the remaining ones required major repairs. Twenty-five churches and synagogues were destroyed, as well as sixty-four secondary and eighty-one primary schools. A Polish author commented that "under the ruins, in the flames of fires or in the hands of the looters disappeared centuries of our cultural and economic patrimony."[5]

Estimates of human losses during the uprising vary between 150,000 to 200,000 people—killed in action and in mass executions, buried under the ruins, drowned in the sewers, dead of wounds, disease, malnutrition, or exhaustion. The *AK* command assessed its losses at 15,000 killed and about 25,000 wounded from among close to 50,000 men and women who served in the uprising either in fighting or in auxiliary capacities. (Many of those who suffered light wounds preferred to remain with their units rather than go to makeshift hospitals established mainly in the cellars.) Only a handful of invalids survived from such elite units as Lieutenant Colonel Radosław's Scout battalions which fought in the uprising's most deadly battles.

Considering the enormous technical superiority of the German forces involved in the quelling of the uprising and the paucity of weapons of the Polish insurgents, German losses were exceptionally heavy. The command of the 9th German Army listed the number of its dead and wounded in Warsaw from August 1 until September 16, 1944, at 8,951. In his official postwar statement on the uprising, General von dem Bach used the figures of some 10,000 dead, 7,000 missing (and considered to be dead), and 9,000 wounded.[6]

During the sixty-three-day battle, the Polish insurgents captured four German tanks, two armored cars, twelve mortars, four antitank guns, 102 heavy and light machine guns, as well as several hundred submachine guns and rifles. Close to 200 tanks were either destroyed or damaged.[7]

Considering the battle for Warsaw as one of the most difficult during World War II, the German command awarded its participants a special badge known as *Warschauer Abzeichnung*. According to a study published in Great Britain, "the Warsaw Shield was issued to commemorate the suppression of the Warsaw rising. Permission for its use was granted on 10 December 1944, but it was never actually distributed to the troops."[8] Addressing an SS officers' training course in the fall of 1944, Himmler, one of the main authors of Warsaw's destruction, described the battle for the Polish capital as one of most stubborn of the war, comparable only to that of Stalingrad.

In a number of postwar analyses of the Warsaw uprising, questions were raised about various missed opportunities by the *AK* command.

According to military critics, the successes achieved during the first two weeks were never adequately exploited and the relatively well-armed concentration of partisan units in the nearby Kampinos forest was never properly used to reduce German pressure on the insurgents fighting in the city. Others note poor tactical cooperation between various *AK* sectors and the lack of energy by their commanders in carrying out initiatives, usually too late. Plans to bring rescue from underground units mobilized throughout Poland were never fully carried out.

There is no question that the *AK* command and its prewar cadres were exhausted by the five years of conspiracy and psychological pressure. They started the uprising in a state of nervous tension, and many of them doubted its success. Once made, their decisions were rarely changed, regardless of the consequences. The confusion created by the sudden change in the timing of the uprising was disastrous; the complete lack of heavy weapons thwarted all attacks in open terrain. The insurgents were stubborn in defense and successful in a number of persistent attacks on some of the key objectives. But the strategy of the headquarters eventually became that of holding as much territory as possible and fighting a desperate rear guard battle for virtually every building—while awaiting Soviet help. The fifteen-year-old couriers who raced with messages through heavy machine gunfire and mortar barrages were awarded medals and military ranks. Children hurled Molotov cocktails at tanks or cut the cables guiding the deadly "goliaths." To some it was almost a game—until the city crumbled, block by block, around them. Still they continued singing patriotic songs and regarded a gun as a prize possession.

The blunt fact is that given the power and the technical means of the German forces, which included bombers, heavy mortars, and the most sophisticated weapons of street combat, and without the help of the Soviet Army, the insurrection was doomed from the start. It is hard to believe that the Soviet steamroller that swept through the eastern part of Poland would suddenly halt at Warsaw's gates just when the insurgents began their combat. The lack of contact between Marshal Rokossovsky and the *AK* command was glaring. The political cards were stacked against the *AK* even before the uprising began. The Russians intended no concessions to the exiles in London or to their anticommunist army battling the Germans in Warsaw. They had created a de facto communist government of their own in Lublin, and *AK* partisan units in areas freed by the Russians were being either incorporated into the Polish Army under Soviet command or deported to the Soviet Union. According to most postwar Western assessments, the decision to allow Warsaw to be destroyed and its population to be massacred was made at the highest level of Soviet power.

To the Poles, once the insurrection had begun, there was no retreat.

The gradual elimination by the Germans of the various insurgent bastions was relatively slow, and experts were amazed that it lasted sixty-three days. This could only be explained by the stubbornness of the resistance fueled by an accumulation of hatred against the Germans during the five years of occupation, increased by such brutal methods as attaching women to tanks during attacks. There was also an incredible euphoria at being able to confront the enemy in open combat. The atmosphere of the doomed city was thus summed up by one newspaper published during the uprising:

We are free. Around us a battle is raging—and there is the senseless cruelty of the enemy. Most of us don't know the fate of our kin. Life is becoming more and more difficult, we are suffering growing losses not merely in combat but in the search for water and food. . . . But there is a thriving life behind the barricades. . . . There are no regrets and no fear. And we are determined to die in the Polish Thermopylae, in the ruins of our city, rather than abandon the independent life and the values gained in the general enthusiasm.[9]

On January 14, 1945, two Soviet armies, the 61st and 47th, as well as the First Polish Army under Soviet command, stormed Warsaw from three directions and forced the 9th German army to abandon what the Germans called *Festung Warschau* (Fortress Warsaw). The 6th Polish Infantry Division crossed the Vistula by pontoon and rubber boats and became the first unit to enter the ruins of Warsaw on January 17. Demining teams followed, and engineers cleared away enough rubble to allow the holding of a military parade in one of the city's main arteries on January 19. The Polish troops in their Soviet helmets marched in parade step before a group of Polish and Soviet generals and hastily summoned communist officials. There were no applauding crowds or even civilian spectators because Warsaw was a dead city.

During the three months that followed the uprising, the *AK* continued its activities in the part of Poland still under German occupation. It was a low-key operation aimed mainly at "protecting the population." The new commander, General "Niedźwiadek" (Leopold Okulicki) was appointed by Bór and left Warsaw with the civilian population to establish headquarters in the vicinity of the southern town of Częstochowa. His task was not easy. One by one area commanders reported bitterness at the tragic uprising and dissatisfaction with the *AK* command. Okulicki busied himself with organizing payments to the families of *AK* prisoners-of-war and considerably increased allowances for active resistance members. Just before the Soviet offensive in January, various *AK* units carried out several sabotage operations and attacks on German installations.

On January 19, 1945, the government-in-exile in London ordered the *AK* dissolved. Some 50,000 *AK* members in partisan units announced their identity to the arriving Soviet units, and most were deported to the Soviet Union. Others continued normal lives without revealing their former membership in the Underground. Okulicki himself and his staff were invited to a banquet by a senior Soviet commander, where they were arrested, sent to Moscow, and tried before a Soviet court on charges of "antistate activities." They were eventually released.

Other *AK* members formed an anti-Soviet underground organization named "Freedom and Independence" (*Wolność i Niezawisłość–WIN*). One of them was Lieutenant Colonel Radosław (Jan Mazurkiewicz), whose elite battalions fought some of the uprising's toughest battles. Mazurkiewicz was arrested in the summer of 1945 and, after "interrogation," appealed to the members of the organization to stop the pointless struggle. Newsreels during the early period of postwar communist Poland were filled with images of partisan units surrendering their weapons— and of trials of arrested leaders who had decided to continue the resistance. Mazurkiewicz himself was appointed to what was known as the "*AK* Liquidation Commission" through which the communist authorities tried to establish detailed records of the former Underground. (I saw Radosław briefly at the Warsaw Military Cemetery in November 1945 during a ceremony commemorating the uprising's dead. He was stooped and silent and gave the impression of being a broken man.)

Bór-Komorowski was taken to London shortly after his prisoner-of-war camp's liberation. He assumed the largely titular role of commander-in-chief of the Polish Forces under British Command. Because the components of these forces were dispersed—as part of the British 8th Army in Italy, the 1st Canadian Army in Germany, and the Scottish Command in the United Kingdom—the commander's role was limited. He and a number of other Polish generals—including Władysław Anders, commander of the 2nd Polish Corps in Italy—were stripped of Polish citizenship by the communist authorities, a measure rescinded after the fall of communism in Poland in 1990. Between 1947 and 1949, Bór was prime minister of the emigré government in London, which stubbornly continued its isolated existence. He died in 1966.

Stanisław Mikołajczyk, prime minister of the government-in-exile at the time of the Warsaw uprising, joined the postwar Polish communist government which was internationally recognized shortly after the war's end. He said his decision was intended to "save the biological substance of the Polish nation" because he feared that Stalin was ready to "drown Poland in a sea of blood."[10] He escaped to the West in October 1947.

General Zygmunt Berling, who founded the Polish Army with Soviet backing and led it to the gates of Warsaw in 1944, ended his military career as a three-star general in communist Poland and head of the General Staff Academy. In 1953 he became deputy minister of state farms and "inspector of hunting."

Adolf Hitler and Heinrich Himmler, the two men who wanted Warsaw razed to the ground and all of its population killed, both died by suicide: Hitler in his bunker in besieged Berlin in April 1945, Himmler by swallowing a cyanide capsule when captured by the British forces.

SS General Erich von dem Bach, who was assigned the task of leveling the Polish capital but later pleaded with Hitler for the combatant status for the insurgents, served a prison sentence in Germany for his wartime acts. He was brought to Poland several times to give testimony at trials of war criminals. He subsequently cooperated with Polish historians who assembled material on the uprising's demise.

Joseph Stalin, born Iosif Vissarionovich Dzhugashvili, whose obsession with Poland's anticommunism helped Hitler destroy Warsaw, died of natural causes in March 1953. He was subsequently exposed by his own compatriots as one of the century's most ruthless dictators responsible for the deaths of an estimated 20 million people.

Not many members of the so-called ethnic armies in German service survived long after their "tour of duty" in Warsaw. When captured later by the Soviets, they were immediately shot. Even those Vlasov Army soldiers, Ukrainians, or Cossacks lucky enough to have found themselves on the western front were handed over under escort by the Allies to the Soviets.

After the war Soviet Marshal Konstanin Rokossovsky, who "watched through field glasses while the Germans destroyed insurgent Warsaw," was given the title of "Marshal of Poland" and became a de facto "military governor of Poland, senior watchdog over the Polish government and supervisor of the Polish politburo."[11] When demonstrations swept Poland in October 1956 amidst the first signs of a growing anticommunist opposition, hundreds of thousands in Warsaw chanted "Rokossovsky to Moscow." The marshal and his Soviet generals in Polish uniform were showered with medals and financial awards and sent back to the Soviet Union. But freedom had to wait a long time—until a simple shipyard electrician by the name of Lech Wałęsa and his *Solidarność* (Solidarity) labor movement started a chain of events in the 1980s which eventually shattered the communist regimes which Stalin had envisaged as a protective shield around Russia.

NOTES

1. Official text.
2. Emil Kumor, *Wycinek z Historii Jednego Życia* (Warsaw: Pax, 1969), p. 291.
3. Official text.
4. Adam Borkiewicz, *Powstanie Warszawskie 1944* (Warsaw: Pax, 1957), p. 697.
5. S. Podlewski, in Warsaw's *Dziś i Jutro* periodical no. 31/47.
6. Von dem Bach quoted in the Polish publication *Dzieje Najnowsze*, Warsaw, 1947, p. 322.

7. Borkiewicz, *Powstanie Warszawskie 1944*, p. 703.

8. Guido Rossignoli, *Army Badges and Insignia of World War 2* (London: Blandford Press, 1972), p. 216.

9. Newspaper *Barykada*, no. 9, August 20, 1944.

10. Allen Paul, *Katyn, The Untold Story of Stalin's Polish Massacre* (New York: Charles Scribner's Sons, 1991), p. 328.

11. Viktor Suvorov, *Inside the Soviet Army* (London: Grafton Books, 1984), p. 32.

Appendix A: Significant Dates

August 23, 1939   Nazi Germany and the Soviet Union sign a non-aggression treaty, with a secret clause on Poland's partition. German troops mass along the Polish borders.

August 30, 1939   Poland announces a general mobilization starting the following day.

September 1, 1939   German troops attack Poland from several directions.

September 8, 1939   German armor reaches the outskirts of Warsaw. The siege of the Polish capital begins.

September 17, 1939   Soviet troops enter Poland along the entire eastern border to link up with the Germans. The Polish government flees to Romania. Poland is divided between Germany and the Soviet Union.

September 28, 1939   Warsaw surrenders to the Germans after a twenty-day siege.

October 5, 1939   Resistance of the last remaining Polish units collapses.

October 14, 1939   The first formal meeting of the embryo command of the Underground meets in Warsaw. The Underground eventually becomes the Home Army (*Armia Krajowa*), gradually growing to some 350,000 members.

Winter 1939   Mass expulsion of Poles from Poland's western areas, formally annexed by the *Reich*.

1940   Forced resettlement of Poles by the Russians to the eastern Soviet regions. The Auschwitz (*Oświęcim*) concentration camp is built by the Nazis.

Fall of 1940   Ghettoes for Jews are established in all major towns under the German occupation.

June 22, 1941   Germany launches "Operation Barbarossa," a massive attack on the Soviet Union. The Polish territories awarded the Soviet Union soon fall into German hands.

July 30, 1941   The Soviet Union and the Polish government-in-exile now in London sign a cooperation agreement. Difficulties arise over missing officers initially held in Soviet camps.

February 3, 1943   Surrender of the German army in Stalingrad changes the tide of the war in Soviet favor.

April 13, 1943   Berlin radio announces the discovery of mass graves of Polish officers at Katyn and blames the Russians. The Polish government in London asks for an independent investigation. Moscow breaks off relations with the exiled Poles shortly afterward.

April 19, 1943   An uprising breaks out in the Warsaw ghetto as the Nazis begin a final attempt to liquidate it. After a month of fighting, the ghetto is razed, and its remaining inhabitants killed.

June 30, 1943   General "Grot" (Stefan Rowecki), commander-in-chief of the Home Army, is arrested by the Gestapo and imprisoned.

July 4, 1943   General Władysław Sikorski, prime minister of the government-in-exile, dies in a plane crash off Gibraltar.

January 11, 1944   The Soviet Union announces it considers annexation of the Polish eastern territories as resolved. Soviet troops enter the territories in pursuit of the retreating Germans. Some Polish partisan units are disarmed and deported to the Soviet Union.

July 22, 1944   A "Committee of National Liberation" is formed in Lublin with de facto powers in the territories liberated by the Soviet Union. It is gradually transformed into a full-fledged communist government.

August 1, 1944   The Home Army begins "Operation Storm" in Warsaw to wrest control of the city from the German occupation forces.

August 2, 1944	Adolf Hitler orders Warsaw destroyed and its inhabitants killed. A special force is set up to deal with the uprising. A Soviet offensive halts outside Warsaw.
August 3, 1944	Stanisław Mikołajczyk, prime minister of the Polish government-in-exile, pleads with Stalin to help the Warsaw insurgents. Stalin procrastinates but issues a vague promise.
August 4, 1944	The Royal Air Force carries out its first parachute drop to the Polish insurgents in Warsaw.
September 2, 1944	The last insurgents evacuate the Old Town through the sewers after a murderous battle that left the entire area in ruins.
September 4, 1944	In London, General Kazimierz Sosnkowski, commander-in-chief of the Polish Forces under British Command, openly accuses the Allies of sacrificing Warsaw.
September 9, 1944	The Home Army command in Warsaw for the first time discusses the possibility of capitulation.
September 12, 1944	The Soviet Army attacks the Warsaw suburb of Praga on the Vistula's right bank, eventually forcing out its German defenders. Soviet planes begin dropping supplies to the Polish insurgents.
September 16, 1944	The first units of the Soviet-formed Polish People's Army cross the river and join the Home Army insurgents in the area of Czerniaków. The landing turns into a prolonged and disastrous battle, with some insurgents withdrawing south through the sewers.
September 18, 1944	The United States carries out a massive air drop of supplies to Warsaw. Most parachuted containers fall into German hands.
September 24, 1944	The Germans launch an attack on the suburb of Mokotów, which falls three days later. For the first time, captured Home Army members are treated as prisoners-of-war. Contacts and correspondence between the *AK* and German commands increase.
September 30, 1944	Defense of the northern suburb of Żoliborz collapses. The city center is isolated.
October 1, 1944	Formal capitulation talks begin and are concluded the following day. Crowds of civilians begin to leave the ruined city.
October 4, 1944	Under the terms of the capitulation, Home Army units march into captivity.

January 17, 1945   Soviet and Soviet-backed Polish troops capture the empty
                    ruins of Warsaw after a brief offensive.

January 19, 1945   The Polish government-in-exile in London orders the
                    Home Army disbanded. Soviet troops advance westward
                    across Poland.

Appendix B: Military and Paramilitary Formations

1. POLISH (PRIOR TO AND DURING THE 1939 CAMPAIGN)

Army *Kraków*
Army *Łódz*
Army *Pomorze*
Army *Poznań*
Army *Prusy*
Army Group *Warsaw*
6th Infantry Division
13th Infantry Division
25th Infantry Division
9th Lancers Regiment
Nowogrodzka Cavalry Brigade

2. UNDER BRITISH COMMAND 1940–1944

1st Parachute Brigade
2nd Polish Corps
Royal Air Force (RAF)

3. HOME ARMY PARTISAN UNITS

5th *Armia Krajowa* Division
27th *Armia Krajowa* Division
30th *Armia Krajowa* Division
Garda Battalion

4. HOME ARMY UNITS IN THE WARSAW UPRISING

Bałtyk (battalion)
Baszta (regiment)
Bohun (company)
Broda 53 (battalion)
Chrobry II (group)
Czata 49 (battalion)
Granat (group)
Group North
Kolegium "B" (company)
Odwet II (battalion)
Parasol (battalion)
Platoons 101, 112, 116, 1139
Radosław (group)
Rygiel (company)
Warsaw Army Corps
Zośka (battalion)
Żyrafa (group)
8th Infantry Division
10th Infantry Division
28th Infantry Division

5. UNDER SOVIET COMMAND

1st Polish Army
1st Polish Infantry Division
3rd Polish Infantry Division
6th Polish Infantry Division
9th Polish Infantry Regiment

6. SOVIET

16th Soviet Army
47th Soviet Army

61st Soviet Army
9th Mechanized Soviet Corps
125th Soviet Corps

7. GERMAN

2nd German Army
6th German Army
8th German Army
9th German Army
Central Front Headquarters
Dirlewanger Brigade
4th East Prussian Infantry Regiment
Heeresgruppe Sud
608th Infantry Regiment
Korpsgruppe von dem Bach
33rd Motorized Infantry Regiment
Ost Legion
4th *Panzer* Army
4th *Panzer* Division
19th (Saxon) *Panzer* Division
25th *Panzer* Division
SS *Panzer* Division Herman Goering
SS *Panzer* Division *Totenkopf*
654th *Pionier* (Engineering) Battalion
Reinefarth Group
RONA (Russian National Liberation Army) Brigade
SS *Standarte* Adolf Hitler Regiment
16th *Wehrmacht* Corps

Bibliography

BOOKS

Beevor, Antony. *Stalingrad*. London: Penguin Books, 1999.

Bielecki, Zygmunt. *Wojsko Polskie, 1939–1945*. Warsaw: Interpress, 1984.

Borkiewicz, Adam. *Powstanie Warszawskie 1944*. Warsaw: Pax, 1957.

Browne, Harry. *World History, the Twentieth Century*. Cambridge: Cambridge University Press, 1970.

Czarski, Andrzej. *Najmłodsi Żołnierze Walczącej Warszawy*. Warsaw: Pax, 1971.

Drozdowski, Marian. *Alarm dla Warszawy*. Warsaw: Wiedza Powszechna, 1964.

Kirchmayer, Jerzy. *Powstanie Warszawskie*. Warsaw: Czytelnik, 1959.

Kopański, Stanisław. *Moja Służba w Wojsku Polskim, 1917–1939*. London: Veritas, 1965.

Kryska-Karski, Tadeusz. *Piechota 1939–1945*. London: Polish Institute. 1974.

Kumor, Emil. *Wycinek z Historii Jednego Życia*. Warsaw: Pax, 1969.

Kuropieska, Jozef. *Wspomnienia Oficera Sztabu*. Kraków: Krajowa Agencja Wydawnicza, 1984.

Ordon, Stanisław. *Łuna nad Warszawą*. London: Thomas Nelson and Sons, 1941.

Paul, Allen, *Katyn, The Untold Story of Stalin's Polish Massacre*. New York: Charles Scribner's Sons, 1991.

Retinger, Joseph. *Memoirs of an Eminence Grise*. Brighton: Sussex University Press, 1972.

Rómmel, Julian. *Za Honor i Ojczyznę*. Warsaw: Wiedza Powrzechna, 1959.

Rossignoli, Guido. *Army Badges and Insignia of World War 2*. London: Blandford Press, 1972.

Rowecki, Stefan. *Wspomnienia i Notatki Autobiograficzne*. Warsaw: Czytelnik, 1988.
Shirer, William L. *The Rise and Fall of the Third Reich*. New York: Simon and
     Schuster, 1960.
Solovyov, Vladimir, and Elena Klepikova. *Inside the Kremlin*. London: W. H. Al-
     len, 1987.
Stahl, Friedrich. *Heereseinteilung 1939*. Bad Nauheim: Wehr Kund, 1954.
Suvorov, Viktor. *Inside the Soviet Army*. London, Glasgow, Toronto, Sydney,
     Auckland: Grafton Books, 1984.
Vasold, Manfred. *August 1939*. Munich: Kindler Verlag, 1999.
Weygand, Maxime. *Memoires: Mirages et Realité*. Paris: Flammarion, 1957.
Zable, Arnold. *Jewels and Ashes*. New York, San Diego, London: Harcourt Brace,
     1991.
Zuckerman, Yitzhak. *A Surplus of Memory: Chronicle of the Warsaw Ghetto Uprising*.
     Berkeley, Los Angeles, Oxford: University of California Press, 1993.

OFFICIAL DOCUMENTS AND PUBLICATIONS

Armia Krajowa records (Polish).
Central Front records (German).
Dokumenty Katynia (Polish).
Dzìeje Najnowsze (Polish).
Foreign Affairs Ministry records (Polish).
Gefahr der Vereinigung der Russen mit dem Aufschtandischen in Warschau (German).
Generalgouvernement documents (German).
General Staff records (Polish).
High Command Records (German).
Iskra DOG (Polish).
Nuremberg Trial documents (United States).
Polskie Siły Zbrojne (Polish).
Radosław Battle Journal (Polish).
Zburzenie Warszawy (Polish).

NEWSPAPERS AND PERIODICALS

Barykada (Warsaw)
Biuletyn Informacyjny (Warsaw)
Dziennik Polski i Dziennik Żołnierza (London)
Dziś i Jutro (Warsaw)
Ekspres Wieczorny (Warsaw)
Kurier Stołeczny (Warsaw)
Robotnik (Warsaw)
Wiadomości z Miasta (Warsaw)

Index

Members of Poland's Home Army are listed in this index by their pseudonyms, in italics, and cross-referenced with their real names when known. Some names, particularly of those killed in action, have never been revealed.

Names of major military and paramilitary organizations are also in italics, except for internationally known terms such as Nazi and Nazism. The names or numbers of military units mentioned in the text are listed in Appendix B.

Adriatic, 122
Africa, 119, 122
Altai Mountains, 145
Altengrabow, 168
Ancona, 122
Anders, Władysław, general, 142, 145, 182
Angers (France), 25, 42
Anglo-American Allies, 3, 67, 71, 72, 102, 107, 111, 122, 134, 138, 139, 160; parachute drops to Poland, 3, 45, 63, 68, 73, 90, 112, 122–23, 124, 138–39, 157–58, 159. *See also* Great Britain; London; Poland, under British Command; Warsaw Uprising
Anielewicz, Mordechai, 61, 64

Antek (Zuckerman, Yitzhak), 57, 60, 61–65, 133, 169
Arctic gulags, 102, 145
Armia Krajowa (*AK*–Polish Home Army), 2, 47, 51, 57, 60, 105, 106, 109; and arrests by Soviets, 4, 74–77, 110, 132, 181; capitulation of, 170–72, 176–77; command of, 4, 5, 67, 68, 71, 72, 76, 81, 87, 94, 108, 109, 138, 161, 166, 168, 179; created, 46; dissolved, 181; and Great Britain, 68, 138; and Jews, 50, 57, 61, 62, 65; mobilization of, 82–84; in Operation Storm, 68, 69, 70, 72–77, 111, 131; recognition of, 160; and the Red Army, 70, 73, 74–77, 108,

109, 110, 151, 166–67, 168; reorganization of, 161; sabotage by, 47; and
the Soviet Union, 47–49, 70, 71, 105,
107, 109, 143; strength of, 47; supplies by air to, 45, 68, 157–58, 166;
uprising plans of, 48, 69; before
Warsaw Uprising, 2, 6; in Warsaw
Uprising, 79–90, 95–96, 106, 112,
132–33, 161, 179; weapons of, 84,
121. *See also* Bach; *Bór*; Warsaw Uprising
Armia Ludowa (*AL*–People's Army),
46, 62, 65, 95; in Warsaw Uprising,
110, 111, 119, 121, 161, 168, 171
Arnhem, 3
Aryan, Aryans, 23, 60
Auschwitz (Oświęcim), 36, 65
Austria, Austrian, 28, 42, 59, 148, 167
Austro-Hungary, 2, 16, 42, 52, 120
Axis (powers), 147

Bach, von dem Bach-Zelewski, Erich,
general, 99, 100, 101, 115, 131, 148,
162, 183; corps of, 102, 106, 110,
121, 122; views on Warsaw Upris-
ing of, 131, 138–39; and Warsaw's
capitulation, 135, 166, 167, 169–71,
175
Baden-Powell, Robert, 113
Baltic Sea, 29
Baltic States, 30, 33
Barry (Kozakiewicz, Włodzimierz),
lieutenant, 132
Bataliony Chłopskie (*BCH*–Peasant Bat-
talions), 46
Belgium, 34
Beria, Lavrenti, 146
Berlin, 29, 35, 50, 51, 139. *See also* Ger-
many
Berling, Zygmunt, general, 71, 74,
145, 148, 151, 154, 181
Berling Army. *See* Soviet Union, and
Polish Army under Soviet Com-
mand
Białous, Ryszard. *See Jerzy*
Białystok, 98
Bicz, major, 178
Bielany, 69

Biuletyn Informacyjny, 52, 63, 112, 137,
158
Black Sea, 29
Bohemians, 58
Bohun, lieutenant, 80, 88
Bojowe Szkoły (*BS*–Battle Schools), 46
Bolsheviks, 48, 50, 122, 143
Bór, Bór-Komorowski, Tadeusz, general (also *Lawina*), 2, 67, 70, 71, 72,
74, 77, 168; as *AK* commander-in-
chief, 52–53, 134, 171, 182; contact
with London by, 3, 90, 122, 123,
125, 138, 140; decision on the War-
saw Uprising, 2–6, 85; pessimism
of, 132; and Soviets, 138, 140, 152,
158, 159; trapped in Old Town, 125,
132; and Warsaw's capitulation, 134–
35, 148, 161, 166, 167, 168, 172, 175–
76, 177, 182; during the Warsaw
Uprising, 81, 87, 90, 103, 106, 111,
115, 126, 132, 148. *See also Armia
Krajowa*; Warsaw Uprising
Borkiewicz, Adam, 95, 121, 178
Borowiec, Andrew. *See Zych*
Bosnia-Hercegovina, 158
Brandenburg, 58
Britain, British. *See* Great Britain
British Broadcasting Corporation
(BBC), 160
Broniewski, Władysław, 65
Brześć (Brest Litovsk), 13, 14, 98
Bug River, 15, 29, 39, 49, 70
BUND (General Jewish Workers' Un-
ion), 59, 66
Burza, (Landberger, Eugeniusz), ma-
jor, 88, 165
Buzuluk, 145
Byelorussia, Byelorussian, 25, 29, 30,
38, 59, 75; republic of, 72

Canada, Canadian, 124
Canaletto, Giovani, 125
Canaris, Wilhelm, admiral, 31
Carpathian Mountains, 12, 98
Carthage, 99
Casimir the Great, King, 58
Catholic, Catholics, Catholicism, 10,
34, 36, 58, 59

Chamberlain, Neville, prime minister, 28
Christians, Christianity, 9, 10, 12, 23, 33, 34
Chruściel, Antoni. *See Monter*
Churchill, Winston, prime minister, 53, 71, 72, 107, 108, 123; and Katyn, 146; and Warsaw Uprising, 143, 178
Communism. *See* Poland; Russia; Soviet Union
Constantine, Grand Duke, 9
Cossacks, 167, 171, 183
Cracow (Kraków, Krakau), 35, 37, 52, 85, 95, 96; as capital of occupied Poland, 24, 26, 32, 96, 97, 98
Curzon, Lord George, 71
Curzon Line, 15, 49, 71, 73, 76, 108
Czechoslovakia, 28, 32, 57
Czerniaków, Adam, 61
Czerniaków. *See* Warsaw Uprising
Częstochowa, 181
Czuma, Walerian, general, 8

Dachau, 14
Daladier, Edouard, prime minister, 28
Dirlewanger, Oskar, general, 101, 114, 115, 148
Dobrowolski, Zygmunt. *See Zyndram*
Doktor (Karaszewica-Tokarzewski, Michał), general, 20–22, 42
Don front, 142
Draza (Sotirovic, Dragan), 75
Dutch, 114

East Prussia, 12, 96–97, 98, 99, 100, 178
Edelman, Marek, 65
Eden, Anthony, foreign minister, 123, 160
England. *See* Great Britain
Erazm (Tatar, Stanislaw), general, 53, 69
Europe, 20, 27, 28, 33, 48, 134, 143; conquered, 119, 171; Iron Curtain in, 108; and Soviets, 147; and Warsaw, 99

Filip (Szostak, Józef), colonel, 134
Filipkowski, Władysław. *See Janka*
Finland, 48
Fischer, major, 155
Foerster, Wolfgang, 32–33
France, 12, 13, 19, 25, 27, 28, 32, 67, 120, 178; conquered, 34, 42, 47, 57, 97; against Germany, 29; liberation of, 119, 159; treaty with Poland, 28
Frank, Hans, governor, 30–32, 35, 36, 39, 95
Franz Josef, emperor, 167
Fulton, Missouri, 108

Galinat, Edmund, major, 22
Gdańsk (Danzig), 28
Geibel, Paul Otto, colonel, 86, 87, 93, 95, 102
Generalgouvernement (government of occupied Poland), 24, 26, 30, 34, 35, 37, 44; and Warsaw Uprising, 98–99
Geneva conventions, 21, 102, 166, 167, 170, 171
Germany, Germans, 1, 12, 48, 59, 160; army of, 1, 97–98, 119; Central Front of, 1, 5, 85, 94, 95, 97, 98, 106, 139, 148, 155; foreign policy of, 27–29; garrison in Warsaw, 2, 5, 84, 86, 93–95, 100–102, 120; Germans in Warsaw, 95, 99; invasion of the Soviet Union by, 34, 47; losses in Warsaw, 179; minority in Poland, 11, 22; in 1939 campaign, 7, 8, 12–16, 29, 30, 85, 97; Poland's occupation by, 27, 29, 30–39, 99; Soviet offensive against, 97; treaty with the Soviet Union, 28, 29; and Warsaw Uprising's assessment, 113, 119–20. *See also* Frank; Himmler; Hitler; *Oberkommando der Wehrmacht*; Warsaw Uprising; *Wehrmacht*
GESTAPO (*Geheime Staatspolizei*), 11, 20, 32, 39, 42, 51, 52, 68, 88
Ghetto. *See* Cracow; Great Britain; Himmler; Warsaw
Gibraltar, 53
Gluecks, Richard, 36
Goebbels, Joseph, 145

Goering, Hermann, 57
Gorbachev, Mikhail S., president, 50, 147
Great Britain, British, 3, 12, 27, 28, 43, 56, 108–9, 145, 146, 159, 160, 178; Polish exiles in, 43, 44, 48, 56, 76, 122, 144, 178, 182; treaty with Poland, 28, 122; supplies to Poland by, 45, 63, 68–69, 73, 90, 112, 121, 122–23, 124, 138–39, 158, 178; war on Germany by, 12, 29, 44; and Warsaw ghetto, 56, 65; and Warsaw Uprising, 122, 123, 124, 134, 139, 160. *See also* Anglo-American Allies; London; Poland under British Command
Greim, Robert Ritter von, general, 99
Grodno, 95
Gromski (Wardejn-Zagórski, Tadeusz), major, 126
Grossgarten, 100
Grot (Rowecki, Stefan), general, 42, 43, 48, 49, 50, 67, 69; arrest of, 51–52; commander-in-chief of the *AK*, 42, 43; execution of, 99; and Jews, 63
Grupy Szturmowe (*GS*–Assault Groups), 46
Grzegorz (Pełczynski, Tadeusz), general, 130, 134
Grzybowski, Wacław, 30
Guderian, Heinz, general, 97–100

Habsburgs, 167
Halder, Franz, general, 31
Heller (Iranek-Osmecki, Kazimierz), colonel, 5, 69, 171
Hesse, 58
Heydrich, Reinhard, 57
Himmler, Heinrich, 31, 33, 36, 100, 145, 183; and the Warsaw ghetto, 55, 56, 64; and Warsaw Uprising, 95–96, 99, 100, 101, 102, 170, 179
Hitler, Adolf, 1, 7, 10, 27, 145, 183; assassination attempt against, 85, 97; intentions toward Poland, 27, 30; and Jews, 57; and Warsaw Uprising, 96, 99, 100, 143, 170
Holy Roman Empire, 58

Home Army. *See Armia Krajowa*
Hungary, Hungarian, 41, 87, 98, 114, 144, 149

International Red Cross, 146
Iranek-Osmecki, Kazimierz. *See Heller*
Italy, Italian, 3, 119, 122, 123, 158, 178, 182

Janka (Filipkowski, Władysław), colonel, 75–76
Jankowski, Jan Stanisław. *See Soból*
Janotowna, Ludmiła, 90
Jerzy (Białous, Ryszard), captain, 133, 153, 155
Jewish Fighting Organization. *See ŻOB*
Jews, Jewish, Judaism, 33, 146; and anti-Semitism, 46, 58–60, 63; in Cracow, 35–36; liquidation of, 31, 33, 35, 55–56; settled in Poland, 58–59; in Warsaw, 10, 12, 23, 24, 57; in Warsaw ghetto, 50, 55–66; and Warsaw Uprising, 65, 87, 114, 149

Kabacki (forest), 132
Källner, Hans, general, 2, 139, 140, 167–68
Kaluga, 75
Kalugin, Konstantin, captain, 81, 109–11
Kaminski, Mieczysław, general, 101, 106, 116
Kampinos (forest), 21, 90, 109, 125, 126, 130, 131, 139, 168, 169, 180
Karaszewicz-Tokarzewski, Michał. *See Doktor*
Karol (Rokicki, Jozef Wacław), lieutenant colonel, 154, 163–65
Karski, Jan, 60, 77
Katyn (forest), 38–39, 50, 52, 56, 142, 144–47
Kazakhstan, 38
Kiev, 9, 143
Kirchmayer, Jerzy, lieutenant colonel, 53
Kiwerski, Wojciech. *See Oliwa*
Klepikova, Elena, 143

Klimecki, Tadeusz, general, 49
Komorowski, Tadeusz. *See Bór*
Konar (Chruściel, Antoni), colonel, 63.
    See Monter
Konev, Ivan, marshal, 98
Korbońska, Zofia, 56–57
Kosa, lieutenant, 80
Kościuszko, Tadeusz, general, 9, 142
Kowel, 73–76
Kozakiewicz, Włodzimierz. *See Barry*
Kozelsk, 145
Krajewski, Henryk. *See Trzaska*
Kraków. *See Cracow*
Królikarnia, 162
Krzemieniec, 30
Krzyżanowski, Aleksander. *See Wilk*
Ksawerów, 162
Kumor, Emil, captain, 21, 22
Kurier Stoleczny, 139
Kuropieska, Józef, general, 148
Kutno, 14, 15, 21
Kutrzeba, Tadeusz, general, 16
Kutschera, Franz, 47

Landau, Ludwik, 12
Landberger, Eugeniusz. *See Burza*
Laszcz (Skroczynski, Albin), general, 5
Latvia, Latvians, 95
Latyshonok, major, 147, 151, 154
Lawina. See Bór
Lenin, Vladimir Ilich, 143, 144
Libourne, 43
Lithuania, Lithuanian, 55, 56, 58, 72,
    75
Łódz, 65
London, 57, 67, 76, 144, 171, 180, 181;
    communications via, 108, 110, 111;
    and the Polish Underground, 2, 3,
    48, 52, 53, 67, 69, 70, 71, 72, 85, 147;
    and Warsaw ghetto, 56; and War-
    saw Uprising, 81, 90, 103, 122, 123,
    138, 143, 159, 166, 167, 175. *See also*
    Bór; Great Britain; Warsaw Uprising
Lublin, 4, 76, 77, 98, 106, 147, 180
Lubyanka prison, 42, 145
Luftwaffe (German air force), 44, 47,
    123; and Warsaw Uprising, 79, 86,
    87, 94, 99, 100, 105, 115, 125, 127

Lukow, 98
Luttwitz, Smillo von, general, 162
Luxembourg Gallery (*Galeria Luksem-
    burga*), 20, 21
Lwów (Lvov), 32, 41, 42, 71, 75–76,
    98, 145

Mały, lieutenant, 163, 164
Markiewicz-Ziental, Lidia, 164
Marymont. *See* Warsaw Uprising
Mazurkiewicz, Jan. *See Radosław*
Middle East, 25, 53
Mierzwinski, Franciszek, major, 151
Mikołajczyk, Stanisław, prime minis-
    ter, 53, 72, 182; and Warsaw Upris-
    ing, 105, 106–8, 109, 111, 123, 140,
    141
Model, Walther, general, 100
Mokotów, 9, 52, 65. *See also* Warsaw
    Uprising
Molotov, Vyacheslav, foreign minis-
    ter, 15, 29, 144
Molotov-Ribbentrop Line, 15, 69
Mond, Bernard, general, 63
Monter (Chruściel, Antoni), general, 5,
    62–63, 80, 82–83, 89, 90, 103, 106,
    110, 115, 125, 154, 161, 164; contacts
    with Soviets, 110, 140; and Old
    Town, 126, 131, 132; and Warsaw's
    capitulation, 161, 175
Moscow, 35, 102, 105–9, 143; and Po-
    land, 4, 27, 29, 30, 39, 46, 49, 50, 67,
    69, 72, 76, 77, 144, 145, 182; and
    Warsaw, 139. *See also* Russia; Soviet
    Union; Warsaw Uprising
Munich, 96
Murnau, 178

Napoleon, emperor, 9, 86
Narodowe Siły Zbrojne (*NSZ*–National
    Armed Forces), 46, 121
Narvik, 43
Nazi, Nazism (National Socialism), 2,
    11, 27, 28, 31, 35, 39, 46, 47, 50, 59,
    96, 98; atrocities of, 23, 97, 145–46;
    concentration camps of, 21, 36; and
    Warsaw Uprising, 96, 97. *See also*

Germany; Himmler; Hitler; Poland;
    Warsaw Uprising
Netherlands, 34
Niedzielski, Mieczysław. *See Żywiciel*
Niedźwiadek (Leopold Okulicki), gen-
    eral, 181–82
NKVD (Soviet National Committee
    for Internal Affairs), 32, 39, 42, 73,
    76, 145
Normandy, 122
Norway, 34, 43, 122
Nuremberg trials, 31, 35, 64, 101,
    115
Nurt. See Monter

Oberkommando der Wehrmacht (High
    Command of the German Armed
    Forces), 19, 31. *See also* Germany;
    Warsaw Uprising; *Wehrmacht*
Ochota, 8. *See also* Warsaw Uprising
Ognisty (Fajer, Lucjan), captain, 138
Okęcie, 51, 69, 106
Okulicki, Leopold. *See Niedźwiadek*
Oliwa (Kiwerski, Wojciech), major, 73–
    74
Orthodox, 58
Ostashkov, 145
Ożarów, 170

Palestine, 59, 65
Paris, 34, 52, 158
Paul, Allen, 146
Paulus, Friedrich, field marshal, 36
Pełczynski, Tadeusz. *See Grzegorz*
Pełka (Chyżynski, Mieczysław), major,
    132
Pentagon, 147
Pfeiffer, Edward. *See Radwan*
Piastów, 170
Piłsudski, Józef, marshal, 42–43
Poland, Poles, Polish: armed forces of,
    7, 8, 12–16, 20–22, 43, 144; army in
    the Soviet Union, 144–45; under
    British Command, 2, 3, 4, 25, 43–44,
    48, 68, 85, 94, 100, 108, 109, 122–23,
    160, 171, 177; and communism, 2,
    51, 76, 106–7, 111, 142, 143, 158,
    159, 171, 181–82; concentration

camps in, 36; conspiracy starts in,
    19–25; deportations of Poles, 33, 36–
    37, 75, 77, 110, 130, 144, 182;
    German occupation of, 22–24, 26, 30–
    37, 95; government-in-exile of, 25,
    39, 41–42, 48, 53, 56, 65, 67, 68, 72,
    76, 77, 103, 105, 107–8, 111, 122,
    143, 144, 181–82; and Great Britain,
    13, 24, 28, 44, 121, 122–23, 124, 134,
    178; Jews in, 10, 31, 33, 50, 55–66;
    in the 1939 campaign, 7, 8, 12–16,
    28, 85, 120; partisan units in, 45, 50,
    68, 70, 73–77, 76, 102, 108, 112, 180;
    partition of, 9, 29, 41; peasants in,
    107; Polish Red Cross, 145, 169; po-
    litical parties in, 24; *Rada Jedności*
    Narodowej (Council of National
    Unity), 159; in the RAF, 3, 44, 68,
    122, 124, 134; resistance in, 1, 2, 20–
    22, 41–47; revolts against Russia, 9,
    48, 85; scout movement in, 46; un-
    der Soviet occupation, 27, 29–30, 38–
    39, 160; and Soviet Union, 49, 50,
    67, 71, 76, 105–11, 158–59; war of
    1920, 9, 120, 143. *See also Armia Kra-*
    jowa; Great Britain; *Służba Zwycięs-*
    twu Polski; Soviet Union; Warsaw
    Uprising
Polesie, 74
Polish Historical Institute, 96
Polish People's Army. *See* Soviet Un-
    ion
Pomerania, 100
Poniatowski, King Stanisław August,
    9
Powiśle. *See* Warsaw Uprising
Poznań (Posen), 102, 112
Praga, 9, 10, 137–38, 140–41, 147. *See*
    also Warsaw Uprising
Prchal, Edward, 53
Prezes (Rzepecki, Jan), colonel, 84,
    126
Pripet Marshes, 30, 74
Prussia, 33, 43, 107, 120
Pruszków, 170
Przemysl, 32

Quisling, Vidkun Abraham, 35

Racławice, 85
Raczkiewicz, Władysław, president, 134
Raczyński, Edward, 123
Radosław (Mazurkiewicz, Jan), lieutenant colonel, 84, 87, 115, 125, 154, 162, 163, 182; in Czerniaków, 147, 148, 150–53, 155, 161
Radwan (Pfeiffer, Edward), lieutenant colonel, 80, 89
Rastenburg, 96, 99
Red Army, 39, 53, 67, 68, 158; in Poland, 38, 49, 69, 70, 71, 73–77, 108; and Warsaw, 4, 113, 150, 161, 167. *See also* Soviet Union
Red Star, 144
Reich, Third Reich (German State), 24, 28, 31, 32, 37, 44, 50, 57, 102. *See also* Germany
Reichstag (Parliament), 27
Reinefarth, Heinz, general, 102, 112, 115, 116, 125, 129, 133
Reinhardt, Georg Hans, general, 7, 8, 140
Rhineland, 28
Ribbentrop, Joachim von, foreign minister, 15, 29
Riga, treaty of, 144
Rode, Ernest, general, 95, 101, 177
Rohr, Ernest, general, 134, 148, 160, 165, 172
Rök, Marika, 99
Rokicki, Józef Waclaw. *See Karol*
Rokossovsky, Konstantin, marshal, 2, 98, 140, 141–42; as Soviet proconsul, 142, 183; and the Warsaw uprising, 81, 109, 110, 139, 140, 141, 142, 147, 152, 159, 166, 167, 180
Rola-Żymierski, Michał, general, 135
Romania, 13, 21, 22, 30, 41, 114
Rome, 158
Romer, Tadeusz, 108
Rommel, Erwin, 14, 119
Rómmel, Juliusz, 14, 15, 21
Roosevelt, Franklin D., president, 71, 107, 142, 146
Rowecki, Stefan, general, 11, 12, 22, 42. *See also Grot*

Royal Air force (RAF), 3, 53, 68, 73, 112, 122–24. *See also* Anglo-American Allies; Great Britain; London; Poland
Russia, Russians, 1, 28, 42, 48, 58, 70, 71, 72, 75, 77, 101, 143, 183; annexation designs of, 48; army of, 120; in German service, 94, 101, 102, 103, 106, 112, 114, 116, 122, 138, 171; and Poland, 142, 147; and the Warsaw Uprising, 139, 147, 165, 166, 180; in World War II, 147. *See also* Moscow; Poland; Soviet Union, Vlasov Army; Warsaw Uprising
Russian National Liberation Army (*RONA*), 101, 116
Rzepecki, Jan. *See Prezes*

Sachsenhausen, 52, 100
Sandomierz, 98
San River, 15, 29, 32, 41, 49, 70, 98
Scipio the Africanus, 99
Scotland, 3, 100
Scottish Command, 182
Sergyeyev, general, 74
Shirer, William R., 30, 50
Sikorski, Władysław, general, 25, 43, 48, 49, 53, 69, 107; death of, 53, 72; and Katyn, 146
Silesia, 13, 34, 37, 58, 100, 101
Skierniewice, 100, 113 177
Skroczyński, Albin. *See Łaszcz*
Slessor, John, air marshal, 124
Służba Zwycięstwu Polski (*SZP*–Polish Victory Service), 19, 22, 23, 41
Śmigły-Rydz, Edward, marshal, 8, 13, 22
Smolenski, 38, 50, 145, 146
Soból (Jankowski, Jan Stanisław), 5, 81
Sochaczew, 115
Sokołowski, Jan, 51. *See also Grot*
Solovyov, Vladimir, 143
Sosnkowski, Kazimierz, general, 4, 13, 25, 72; and the British government, 134; as commander-in-chief, 70, 71, 108, 123; on the Soviet Union, 4, 71, 140; on Warsaw Uprising, 4, 132, 134, 171

Sotirovic, Dragan. *See Draza*
South African, 124
Soviet Union, Soviet, USSR, 53, 73–77,
    142, 183; Asian republics of, 38;
    capture of Warsaw by, 181; German
    attack on, 35, 42, 47; liquidation of
    Polish officers by, 50, 142, 144–47
    (*see also Katyn*); and the 1944 offen-
    sive, 1–4, 85, 97–98, 102, 139, 140–
    41; occupation of Poland by, 15, 27,
    29–30, 38, 41, 68–70, 72, 76, 158–59;
    pact with Germany, of, 11, 15–30,
    48; and Poland, 47–49, 143–47, 159;
    and Polish Army under Soviet
    Command, 4, 71, 74–76, 107, 135,
    140–42, 147, 148, 151, 152–54, 158,
    160, 162, 180; and (Polish) Commit-
    tee of National Liberation, 4, 76,
    106, 147, 160; supplies to Poles by,
    139, 140, 147, 150, 158, 159, 167;
    and Union of Polish Patriots, 147;
    and Warsaw Uprising, 91, 102–3,
    105, 108, 110–11, 138–42, 142, 145,
    147–48, 152–53, 167–69, 172, 180. *See
    also* Poland; Russia; Stalin; Warsaw
    Uprising
Spain, 58, 101
SS (*Schutzstaffel*), 2, 31, 36, 51, 52, 73–
    75, 101, 179; and Warsaw ghetto,
    50, 56; in Warsaw Uprising, 79, 86,
    87, 93–95, 101, 102, 133, 154, 166
Staedke, Helmut, general, 100
Stahel, Reiner, general, 2, 86–88, 93,
    94, 96, 97, 103, 113, 115
Stalag XI A. *See* Altengrabow
Stalin, Joseph, 71, 141; death of, 183;
    and Poland, 30, 67, 71, 77, 111, 143,
    144, 146, 154, 182; and Warsaw Up-
    rising, 105–9, 138, 140–43
Stalingrad, 36, 37, 49, 56, 119, 142, 179
Starobielsk, 145
Starzyński, Stefan, 14, 20, 23
Steinberg, Baruch, major, 146
Stroop, Juergen, general, 50, 55, 56,
    62, 64
Sudetenland, 28
Suvorov, Viktor, 94, 142
Świt, 56

Szare Szeregi (Grey Ranks), 46, 125
Szczerba, lieutenant, 149
Szostak, Józef. *See Filip*
Szpilman, W., 12
Szternal, Kazimierz. *See Zryw*

TASS, 111, 159
Tatar, Stanisław. *See Erazm*
Tchernyakovsky, Ivan, general, 75
Tehran conference, 67, 71
Teutonic Knights, 58
Thermopylae, 181
Tito, Josip Broz, marshal, 158
Tokarzewski, Michał, general (also
    known as Karaszewicz-
    Tokarzewski). *See Doktor*
Treblinka, 57, 64
Trzaska (Krajewski, Henryk), lieuten-
    ant colonel, 74, 75
Tukhachevsky, Mikhail N., marshal,
    143
Tunguz (Zawislak, Józef), lieutenant
    colonel, 138

Ukraine, Ukrainian, 25, 29, 30, 38, 59,
    73, 143; in German service, 73, 95,
    122, 133, 171, 183; republic of, 72,
    76; Ukrainian Partisan Army (*UPA*),
    73
Union for Armed Struggle. See Zwią-
    zek Walki Zbrojnej–ZWZ
United Kingdom. *See* Great Britain
United States of America, Americans,
    9, 146, 158, 159, 160; Air Corps of,
    123; and flight to Warsaw, 123, 157–
    58, 166, 178
Ural Mountains, 145
Ursus, 170

Vasold, Manfred, 11
Vienna, Congress of, 9
Vistula River, 4, 5, 9, 10, 33, 35, 58,
    69, 84, 85, 97, 98; crossing of, 150,
    151, 152, 162, 167–69, 181; "mira-
    cle" of, 9; and Warsaw Uprising,
    89, 106, 108, 110, 111, 116, 119, 120,
    132, 138, 141, 150, 151, 154, 161,
    167, 172, 178

Vlasov, Andrei, general, 94, 95, 101
Vlasov Army, 94, 95, 100, 101, 112, 114, 125, 133, 138, 154, 167, 183
Volksdeutsche (ethnic Germans), 23, 33, 34, 95
Vormann, Nicolaus, general, 94, 100, 113, 115, 120–22, 131, 139

Wachnowski (Ziemski, Karol), colonel, 125, 130, 132, 161, 168–69
Wagner, Edouard, general, 31
Wałęsa, Lech, 183
Warsaw, 1, 28, 41, 73, 74, 76, 98; communists in, 111; description of, 9–10; destruction of, 1, 5, 99, 178–79; under German occupation, 20, 22–24, 46, 50, 70; ghetto in, 10, 50, 54–65; history of, 8–10; Jews in, 10, 58–59; Old Town of, 57; population of, 10, 95; siege in 1939, 7, 8, 12–16, 18, 42. *See also* Germany; Great Britain; Jews; Poland; Russia; Soviet Union; Warsaw Uprising
Warsaw Uprising, 65, 69, 76, 77, 79–83, 86, 95, 96–98, 102, 137–41, 161, 177, 179–81; capitulation of, 175–77; in city center, 80, 88–89, 102, 106, 116, 125, 137–38, 176; in Czerniaków, 138, 147–48, 149–55, 158, 161; German losses in, 179; German plans in, 95, 99–100, 101, 119; German prisoners in, 127, 132, 133, 165; in the ghetto, 65, 113, 125; in Marymont, 139, 167; mobilization for, 81–84; in Mokotów, 52, 87, 89, 106, 112, 116, 127, 131–32, 153, 161–66, 177; in Ochota, 116; in Old Town, 87, 96, 115, 116, 122, 125–27; plans for, 2–6; Polish losses in, 179; in Powiśle, 138, 147; and Praga, 2, 89, 137, 138, 140, 147, 151, 152, 153, 168, 169; in Saska Kępa, 139, 151; and sewers, 128–29, 131–32, 153–54, 163–64; supplies by air to, 90, 109, 112, 123–24, 138, 150, 157–58, 158; weapons in, 5, 84–85, 112; and the West, 158; in Wola, 81, 87, 100, 103, 106, 113–15, 126; in Żoliborz, 79, 81,

89–90, 106, 112, 116, 125, 130, 133, 139, 153, 161, 167–70. *See also* Germany; Great Britain; Russia; Soviet Union
Warta (Warthegau), 102
Wehrmacht (German armed forces), 8, 16, 56, 77, 140, 151; in Warsaw uprising, 84, 94, 112, 122, 125, 135, 165, 172, 176, 177. *See also* Germany; Poland; Warsaw Uprising
Weinzieher, Stefan, 22
Western Allies. *See* Anglo-American Allies
Westerplatte, 28
Weygand, Maxime, general, 9
Wilk (Krzyżanowski, Aleksander), lieutenant colonel, 75
Wilno (Vilnius), 72, 75
Włochy, 170
Woldenberg, prisoner-of-war camp, 148
World War I, 120
World War II, 72, 147. *See also* France; Germany; Great Britain; Poland; Soviet Union; United States of America; Warsaw Uprising

Yalta conference, 67
Yiddish, 59, 60

Zable, Arnold, 58
Zakopane, 32
Zawislak, Jozef. *See Tunguz*
ŻEGOTA (Polish Council of Aid to Jews), 62
Zelewski, Erich von dem Bach. *See* Bach
Ziemski, Karol. *See Wachnowski*
Zionism, Zionists, 59, 61
Znicz. *See Bór*
Zofia, 149
ŻOB (*Zydowska Organizacja Bojowa*– Jewish Fighting Organization), 50, 57, 61–65; founded, 61; in the Warsaw Uprising, 133, 169, 178
Żoliborz, 9, 65. *See also* Warsaw Uprising

Zryw (Szternal, Kazimierz), major, 164–65

Zuckerman, Yitzhak. *See Antek*

Związek Walki Zbrojnej (ZWZ–Union for Armed Struggle), 42–46

Zych (Borowiec, Andrew), 152

Zygielbojm, Szmul Artur, 65

Zyndram (Dobrowolski, Zygmunt), colonel, 171

Żywiciel (Niedzielski, Mieczysław), lieutenant colonel, 90, 130, 167–69

About the Author

ANDREW BOROWIEC took part in the 1944 Warsaw Uprising and after his liberation from a prisoner-of-war camp emigrated to the United States. A veteran foreign correspondent, he now writes for *The Washington Times*. He is the author of political studies on Yugoslavia, Greece, Turkey, Cyprus, and Tunisia, published by Praeger.